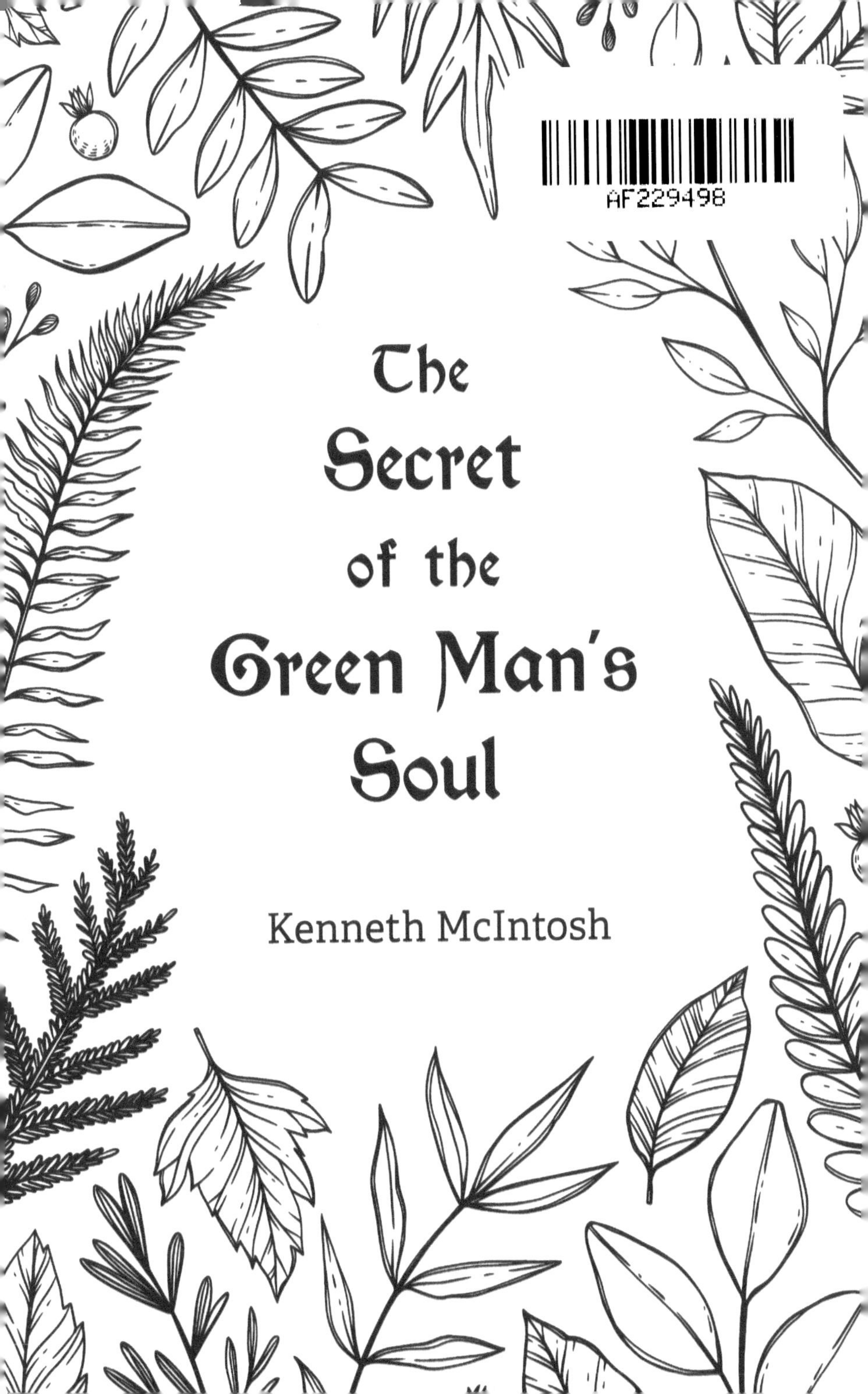

The Secret of the Green Man's Soul

Kenneth McIntosh

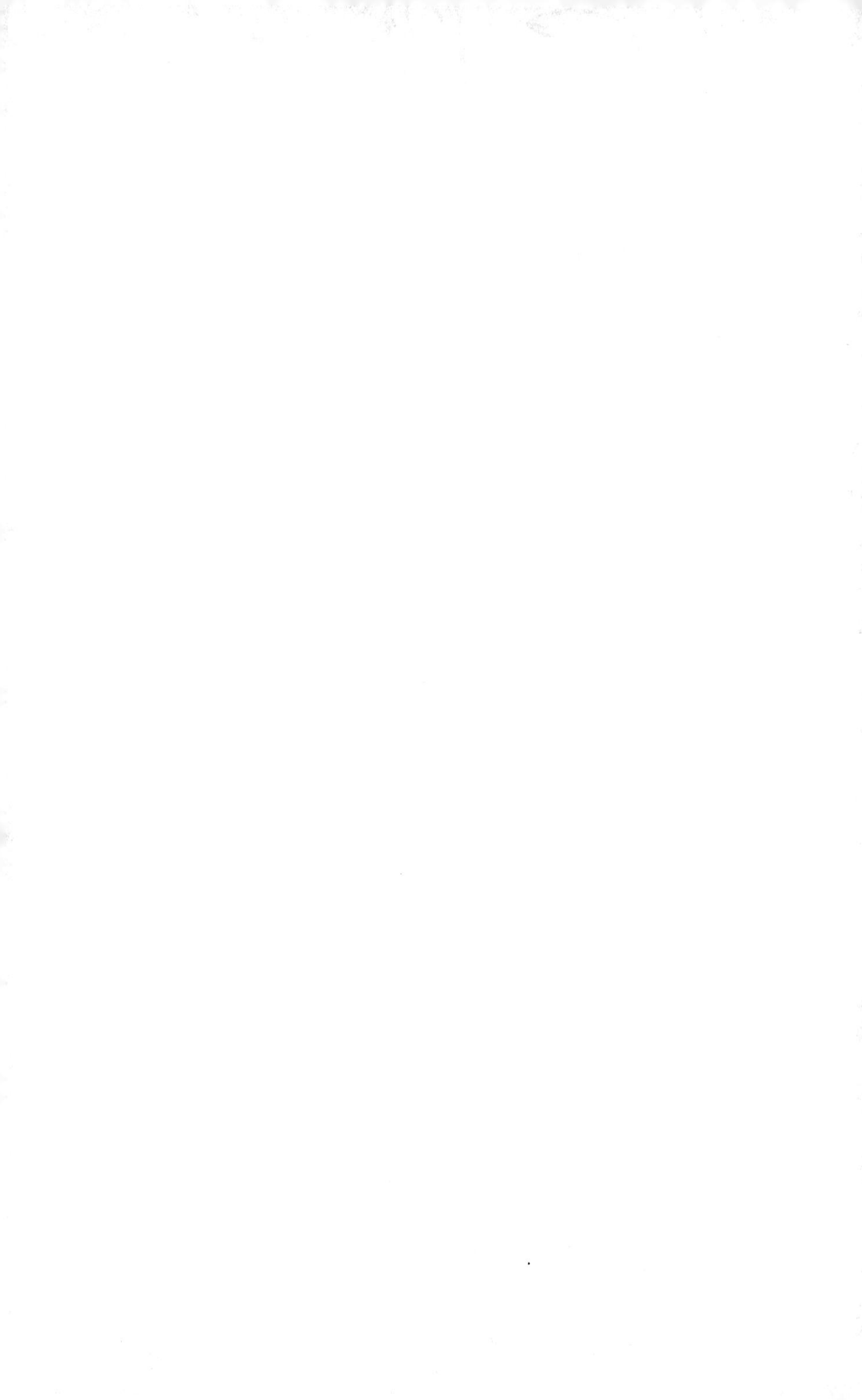

The Secret of the Green Man's Soul

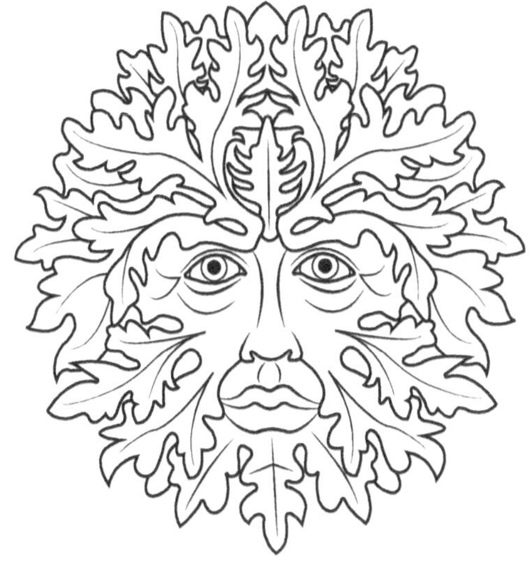

Kenneth McIntosh

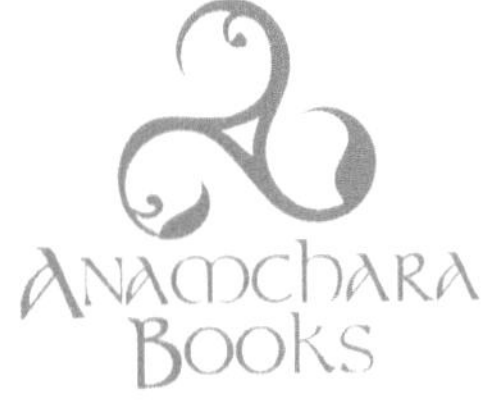

Anamchara Books

The Secret of the Green Man's Soul

Anamchara Books
Vestal, New York 13850
WWW.ANAMCHARABOOKS.COM

Design and illustrations by Micaela Grace.

paperback ISBN: 978-1-62524-898-5
eBook ISBN: 978-1-62524-899-2

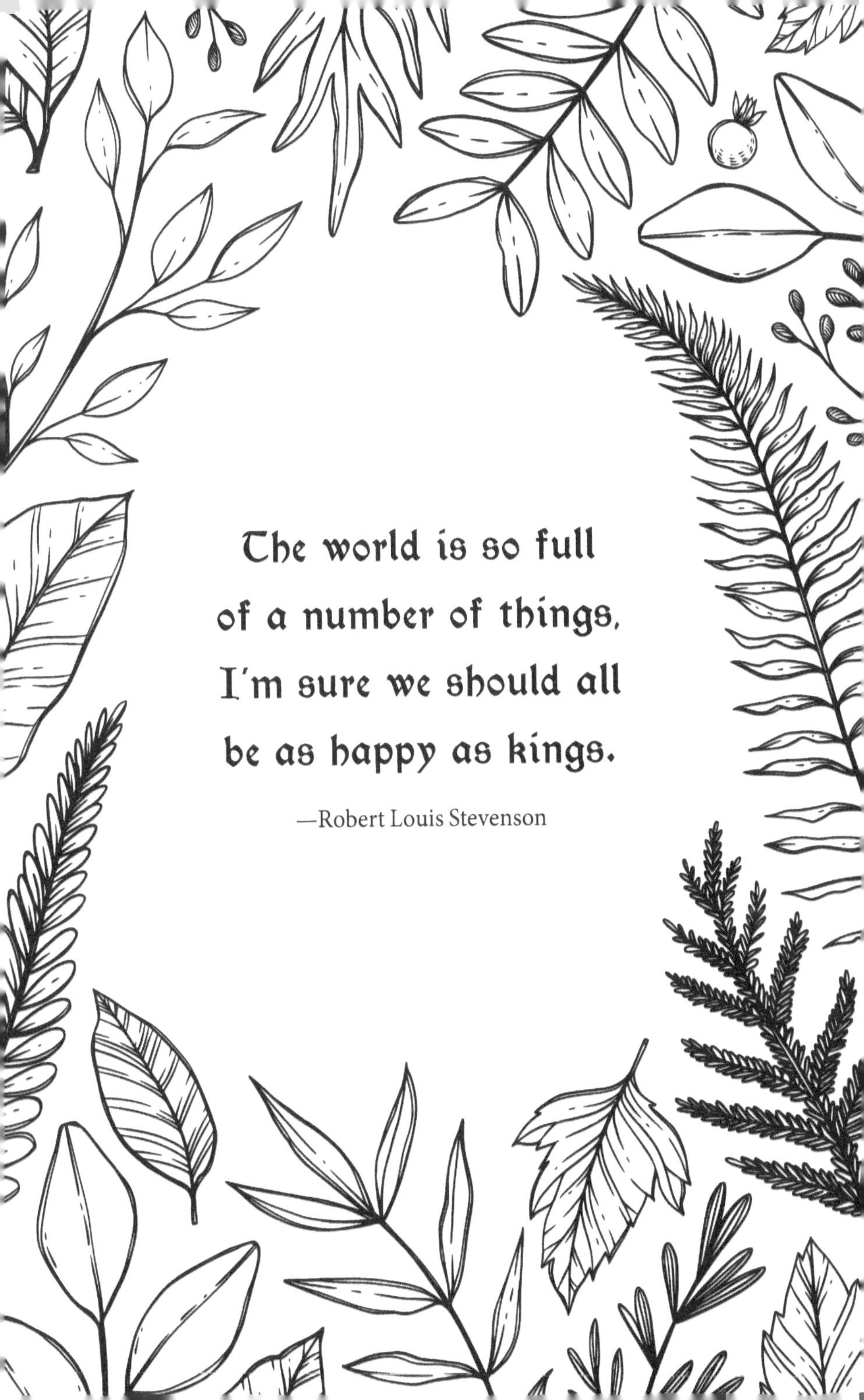
The world is so full
of a number of things,
I'm sure we should all
be as happy as kings.

—Robert Louis Stevenson

Contents

Author's Note

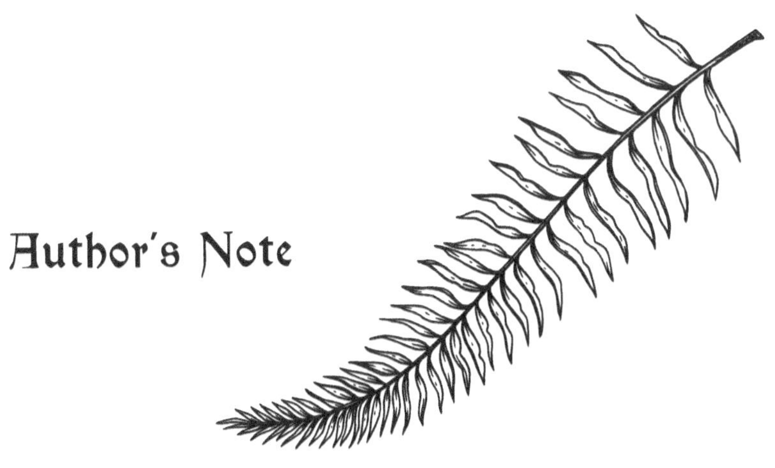

This is a story that involves many journeys—and no one travels completely alone. This book would not be possible were it not for the assistance of church volunteers and staff (guides, vergers, wardens, and rectors) whose names I regrettably neglected to write down. I wonder if they thought, "Not another tourist wanting to see the Green Man," but they acted cheerful and half the time I wouldn't have found him without their service.

This private obsession would not have then been shared with the public without a little more help from my friends. David Cole has added much to my journeys in England sharing his friendship, knowledge, and ideas. Other members of the Community of Aidan and Hilda in the UK have also helped my journeying. Jude McKenzie and Todd Barnell, both officers of the Northern Arizona Celtic Heritage Society, encouraged me to give a talk on the Green Man for the Flagstaff Highland Festival. Martha Shideler subsequently asked me to convert that talk into written form and published the resulting three-part article in issues of the *Independent Celt Newsletter*.

The original presentations first made their way into e-book form with the alchemical magic of Ellyn Sanna at Anamchara Books. She grew the original short article into first a short Kindle book, and now she has helped me to create an expanded print-format book, first a full-color version and now this black-and-white edition, improving it at every stage. More than that, her presence and friendship added much joy to visits at UK sites in this book.

Finally, my life companion Marsha makes all my travels delightful. I keep wondering if she is ever going to say, "Oh no, not another old church," but she has repeatedly risked becoming lost in the English countryside looking for obscure chapels, has fought for parking spaces near cathedrals in the cities, and peered into the corners with me to find the wonders of each medieval space.

With such companions in life, I am a wealthy man.

The Green Man is moving from the realms of dusty antiquarian pursuits into popular culture. There are more and more Green Man books published, websites, and Facebook sites. With so much information available, this book cannot claim to be definitive in knowledge or scope, yet I am hopeful that my experiences and musings may prove helpful even to those who are already well acquainted with the Green Man.

I invite you to come with me on my journeys as I came to know the soul of the Green Man.

— *Kenneth McIntosh*

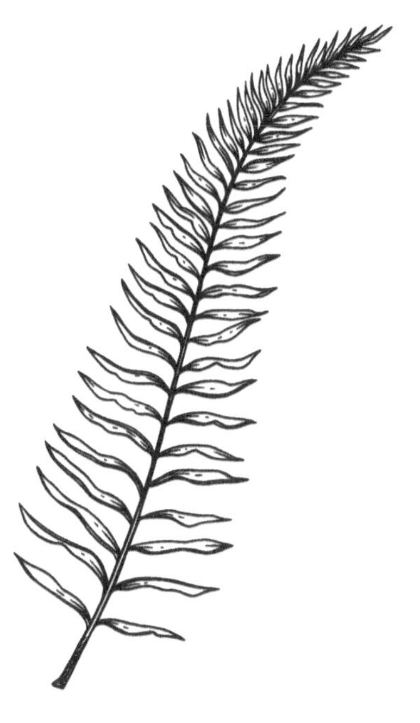

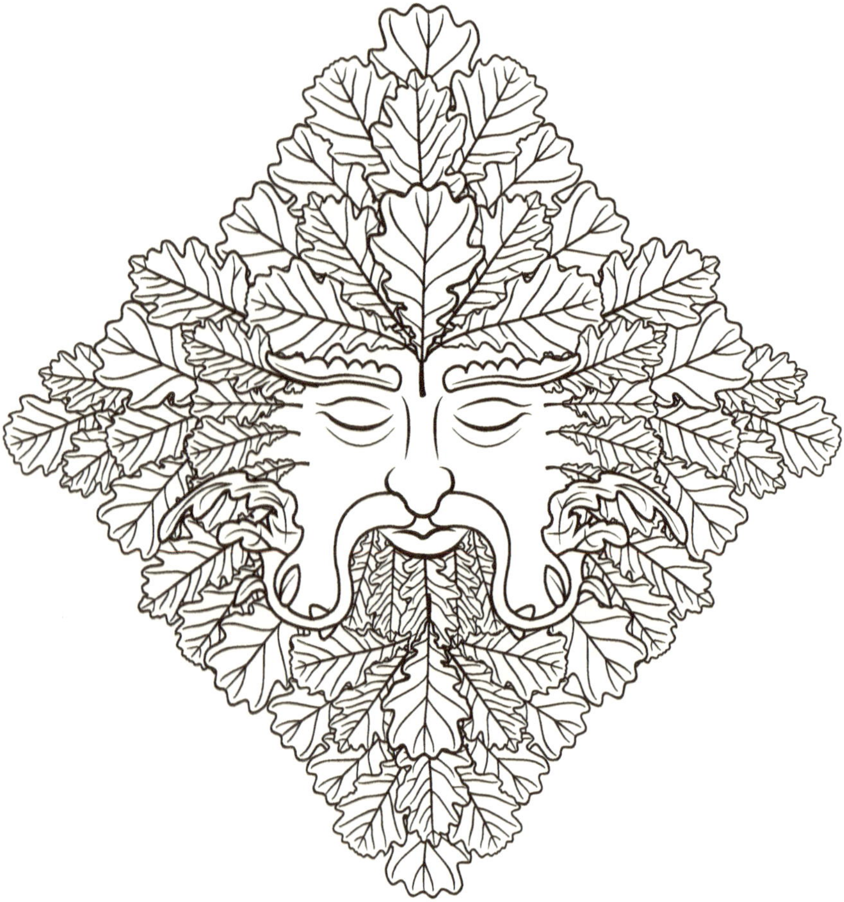

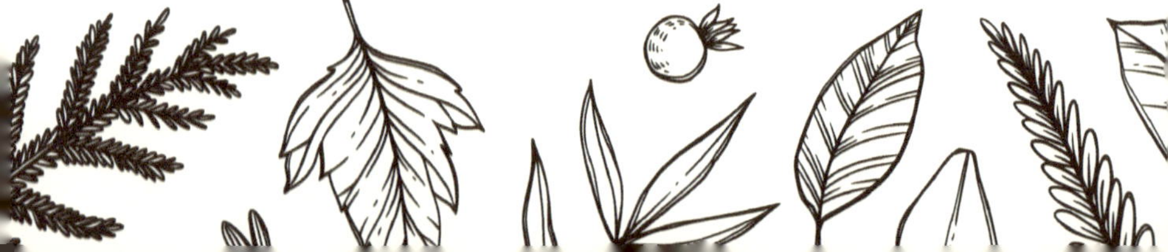

The original inspiration for this image is found under a thirteenth-century choir seat in Worcester Cathedral.

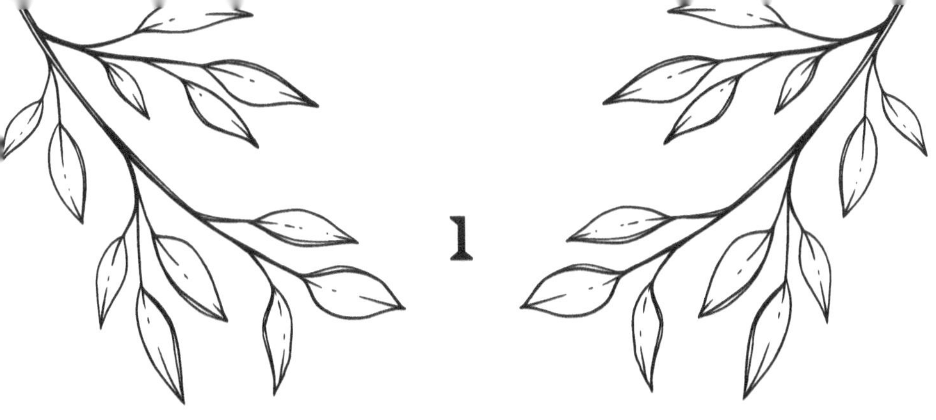

1

Ḣave You Seen
the Jack in the Green?

"**H**ave you seen the Jack in the Green?" asked the English Rock Band Jethro Tull in their 1977 album *Songs from the Wood.*

Yes, I have.

I have seen him in his better-known guise, the Green Man, carved in stone in medieval chapels and cathedrals. He danced beside me in a crowded street during an English May Fair and moved to the pulsing beat at a rave in Salt Lake City. He pops out at me from the pages of novels, and he's thrilled me on the theater screen. Yet I was almost fifty years old before I first sighted him.

A decade ago, my wife and I were on pilgrimage in what I call "my city" in Ireland. Like me, Kilkenny is named after Saint Kenneth (or Canice in Old Irish). A bust of Saint Canice stands in the city square, Saint Canice's holy well still gushes out water, and the massive Cathedral Church of St. Canice stands as an enduring monument to his memory.

I was like a kid in a candy store as a guide led us through the stone edifice, pointing out its peculiar delights. "And up there," she gestured upward with a flourish, "is our Green Man."

A young man's face, carved from stone, protruded from one of the arches high above us; he looked like he was singing happily, perhaps a member of the cathedral's medieval choir, mouth wide open belting out notes. But those weren't musical notes coming out of his mouth. They were leaves.

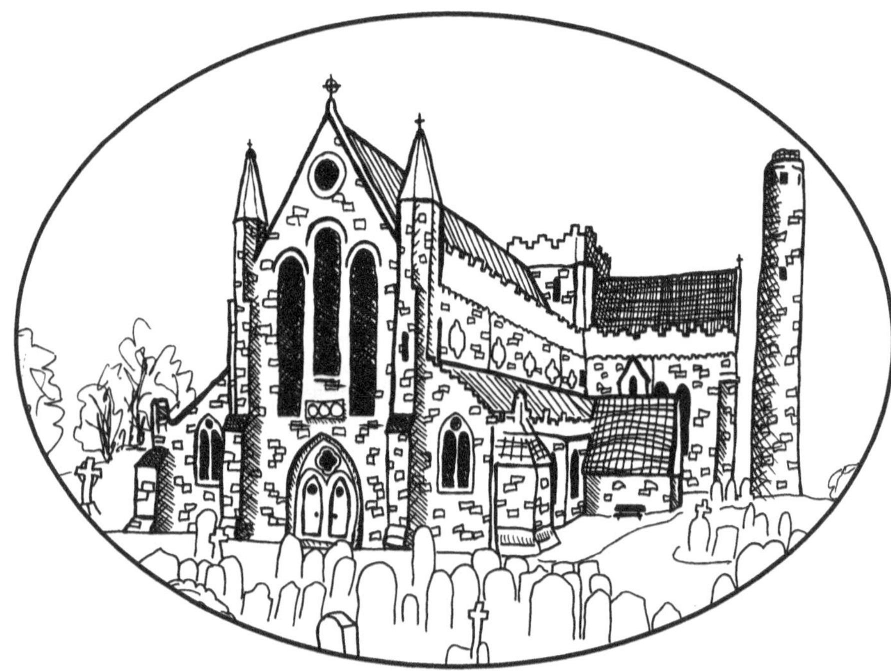

St. Canice's Cathedral in Kilkenny was built in the thirteenth century, but the round tower that stands beside it dates from the ninth century. An earlier wooden church stood on the same location, which has been the site of Christian worship since the sixth century.

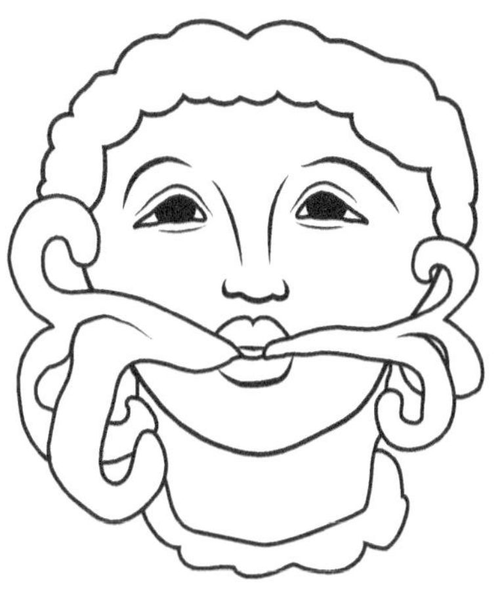

This is the stone face in St. Canice Cathedral that first drew me into my ongoing fascination with the Green Man.

As our guide explained the history of the Green Man to us (incorrectly, as I learned much later), we listened in fascination. Shortly after that, in another medieval church, we spotted another Green Man. And thus began our search for his foliated visage in numerous medieval churches throughout the British Isles.

Later, I learned about Jack in the Green, the Green Man's persona in folk dances and pageants of the Isles. That transformed him from a static work of art, bound by ancient confines of wood and stone, to a moving reality in today's world. I realized he had stepped out from the long-ago past and become a twenty-first-century cultural influence.

In whatever form he takes, whenever I see a Green Man, I'm drawn by his eyes. As the cliché puts it, eyes are windows into the soul, and I can't help but wonder: *What secrets lie hidden in the Green Man's soul?* His face is sometimes hard to read, obscured by acanthus leaves or painted dark green. Yet the eyes jump out from behind this leafy concealment, alert and wise. The stone faces are mute, and Jack in the Green dancing among the mummers does not sing. But the eyes say, *I have a hidden meaning. I was portrayed in a thousand different ways in the past, and I keep sprouting again and again down through the centuries. Don't you want to know who I am?*

Reproduction of the sketches from the notebook of Villard de Honnecourt. Villard's notebook is filled with architectural details, so his drawings of "faces with leaves" were likely details from stonework he had seen. Most scholars today believe his notebook served as a pattern book containing designs for manuscript illumination or metalwork.

The Green Man's core identity is indeed hidden, for in all the writing that survives from the Middle Ages, not a single document says, "You know those faces with the leaves that we carved in hundreds of churches? Well, those represent such-and-such." A notebook from 1230 by French artist Villard de Honnecourt does contain several faces that we would now call Green Men. The artist labeled his drawings simply "faces with leaves"—and told us nothing of the meaning of those faces or what they represented.

Other medieval images can be interpreted because the tales that convey their meaning have been preserved over the centuries. Portrayals of Bible stories, the saints, the Virgin Mary, and other religious portrayals are still symbols used in Christianity. Various occupation such as the baker, the blacksmith, the priest, and the fisherman can be readily identified. Mythological creatures such as dragons, mermaids, and unicorns correspond with stories preserved from medieval times until now. But where are stories that explain the leaf-sprouting face of the Green Man?

And he is clearly symbolic. All those Green Men didn't appear because one stone mason said, "I think I'll chisel some leaves coming out of this bloke's mouth," and then the design just caught on and became the rage. No, the Green Man has an instantly recognizable and strong sense of identity. He represented something important to medieval people.

As a symbol, even today, the Green Man is multivalent, and the same would have been true in the Middle Ages, when his face first became so popular. His image can be found across Europe—so even if we could know what an artist carving a Green Man in Giles Cathedral, in Edinburgh, Scotland, understood that image to mean, that could very well mean something quite different for, say, another mason carving a Green Man at the same time in Santiago, Spain. Furthermore, symbols are always being reinterpreted. That is part of the Green Man's continuing fascination.

For an example of how a single Green Man can produce a variety of interpretations, consider the drawing on the next page of a Green Man with grapes. This drawing is based on a fifteenth-century carving in Dunblane Cathedral in Scotland, but there are similar depictions in multiple locations, both ancient and modern. The grapevine growing from his mouth has a long and rich symbolism, leading to a variety of possible conjectures about this image.

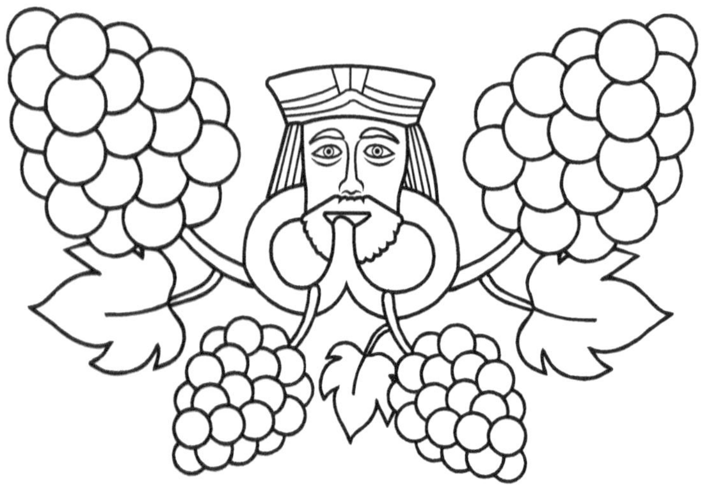

The Classical world connected grapevines with the god Dionysus (the Romans called him Bacchus), who was associated with rebirth after death. His return to life after being dismembered was symbolically represented by the grapevines, which must be pruned back sharply and become dormant in winter for them to bear fruit the following year.

Christianity has often been at pains to separate Christ from any parallels with Pagan gods, but Jesus himself may have been aware of the connection to the Greek god when he said, "I am the vine" (John 15:5) and compared the Realm of Heaven to a vineyard (Matthew 20:1). By claiming the symbolism of grapes for himself, Jesus connected himself not only to the Hebrew scriptures (where Israel is compared to a vine) but also to the Greek and Roman cultures that dominated his day. Jesus was in some sense a Green Man, bringing new life to both the spiritual and natural world.

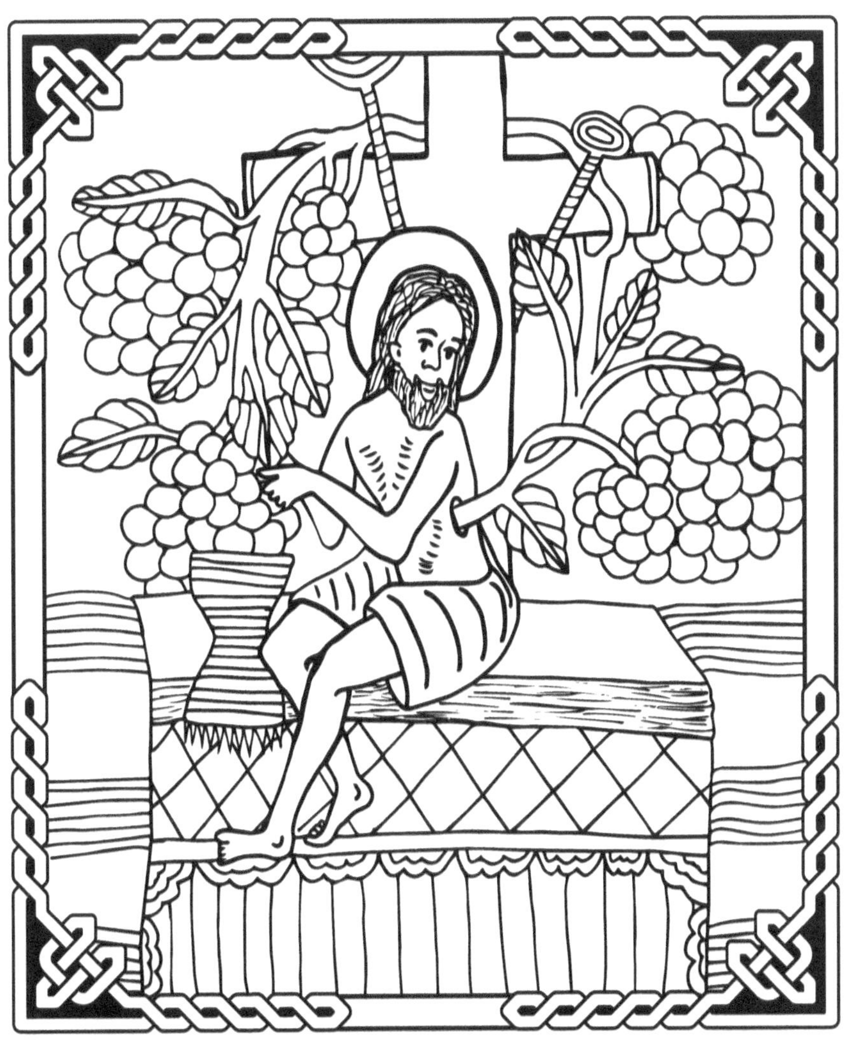

This reproduction of a medieval drawing portrays Jesus with a grapevine growing out from the wound in his side, graphically illustrating the concept that Jesus' death brings growing green life and burgeoning fruitfulness.

So we have rich and edifying symbolism. But wait! A church historian looks at these Green-Man-with-grapes portrayals and sees a moral warning. Medieval images often show the grapes coming out of his mouth, indicating that perhaps the Green Man had too much to drink and he's vomiting grapes. It's a warning against intoxication.

Is this Green Man a remembrance of ancient Bacchus, a symbol of Christ, or a plea for sobriety? Experts in art and history disagree. And that's a good thing to remember as you peruse this book. I'll quote people with ideas about the Green Man, and I'll tell you what I think of some interpretations. But who really knows? And that's part of the fascination of the Green Man, and why he's so much fun. In the end, you get to choose what the Green Man means for you.

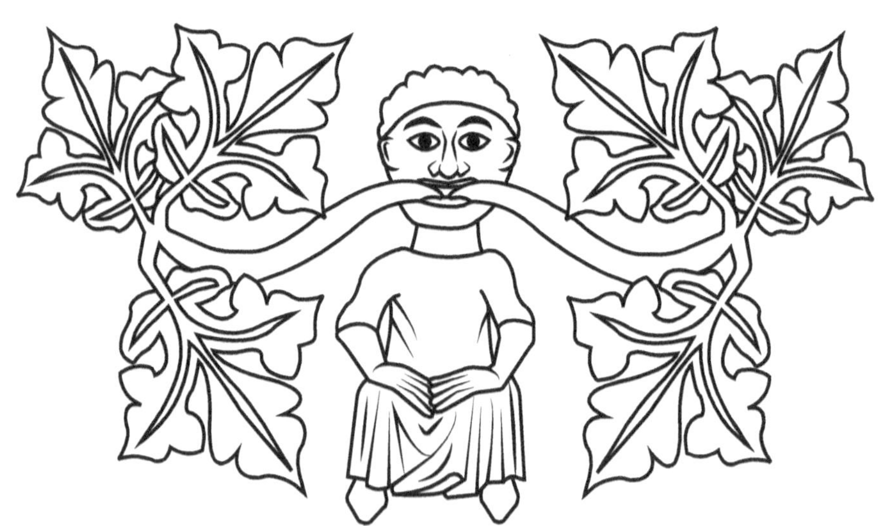

Green Man from Southwell Minster.

This book is an invitation to journey with me through the British Isles, staring into the Green Man's eyes. The tone is more whimsical than academic, because my Green Man travels have been largely serendipitous. I've looked for him wherever I happen to be, and then I've tried to learn more from research each time I see him.

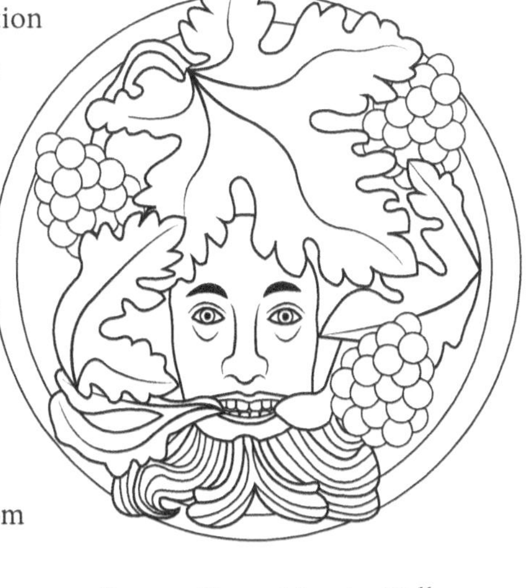

From a Green Man in Wells Cathedral in Somerset, England.

I don't promise to reveal all the Green Man's mysteries; Jack likes to hide in the Green, concealing his nature. But those piercing eyes invite us to look behind the leafy mask. They promise both meaning and mystery. So come, let's search for the secret of the Green Man's soul.

> The Green Man is the ancient
> guardian of nature. . . .
> He is life and rebirth.
> He is the end and the start,
> for what is the grave but a cradle?
> So listen for this noble guardian
> of Earth, listen. . . .
>
> —Angela Abraham

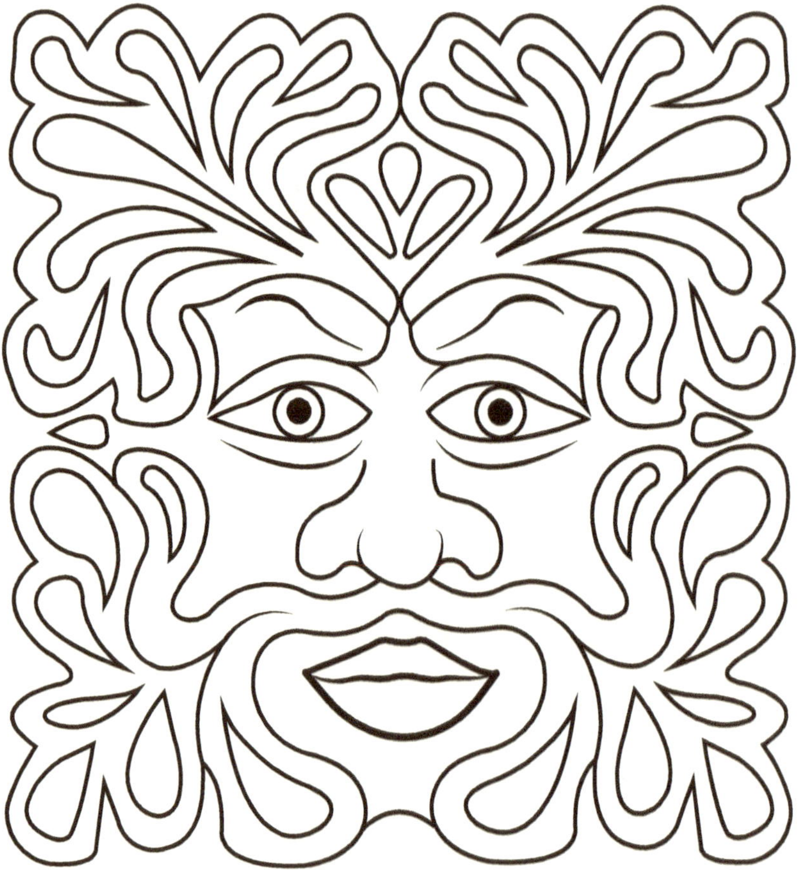

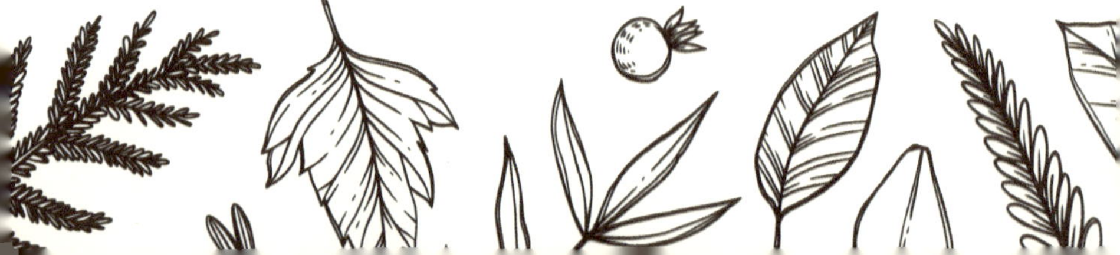

Based on a carving found in Sussex, England, this Green Man has acanthus leaves sprouting from his face. This is the most common plant to be found in medieval Green Men.

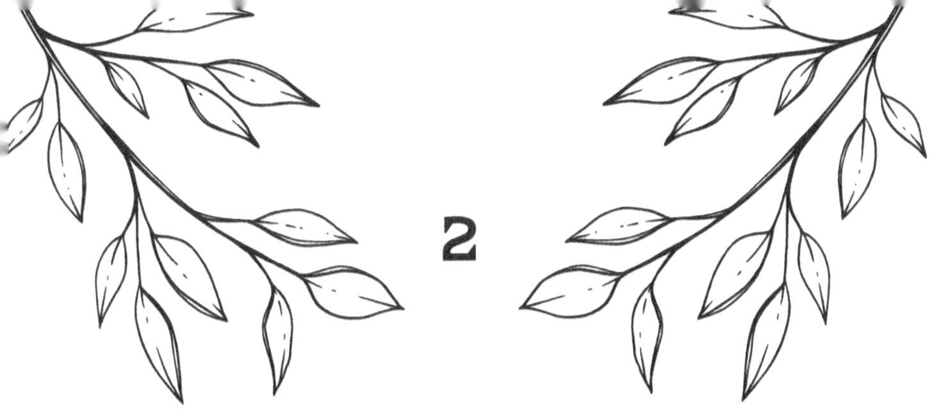

<h1 style="text-align:center">2</h1>

Leafy Faces in Medieval Spaces

During the Middle Ages, Green Men were created as architectural ornaments, especially in churches. They show up in more than two hundred churches in the British Isles, and there are more than a thousand examples. Art scholars refer to him as a "foliated head"—a face with obvious human features (eyes, nose, and mouth) and vegetation growing out from at least one orifice (most often the mouth but sometimes the nose, and less commonly the eyes and ears).

Because the Green Man is common to Celtic regions, he's sometimes assumed to be a Celtic symbol. However, he also appears in medieval churches and cathedrals throughout Europe, and variations on the Green Man theme can be found globally. My own travels and research have been in England, Ireland, Scotland, and Wales, so that is the primary scope of this book, but travelers in other parts of the world will have their own encounters with our leafy friend.

It can be a bit tricky trying to decide, "Is this a Green Man or not?" For example, laurel crowns may appear to be hair, or eyebrows in a carving may seem leaf-like. Solar beams or a lion's mane that surround a male bearded face can seem like foliage. I don't count such images as a Green Men, though. My rule is that when clearly identifiable leafy matter is coming right out of his face—that's a Green Man.

The foliage can be any kind of leaves, including ferns, plant leaves, or leaves from various species of trees— but acanthus leaves are the most common foliage seen on Green Men. These

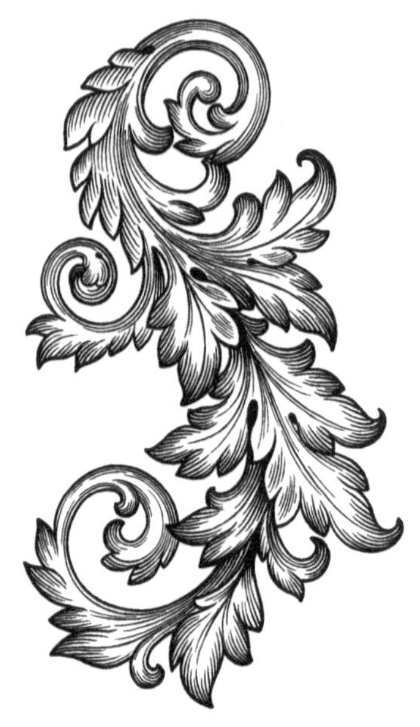

A typical stylized drawing of acanthus leaves used as a decorative element.

are often mistaken for oak leaves, a mistake I made myself until just recently. For centuries, however, the acanthus plant has been associated with life that endures beyond the grave. It was a common element in Greek cemetery carvings since before the time of Christ, and it has remained a popular decorative motif throughout Europe and North America. Its connection with Green Man images indicates this archetypal symbol speaks of the power of life to overcome death.

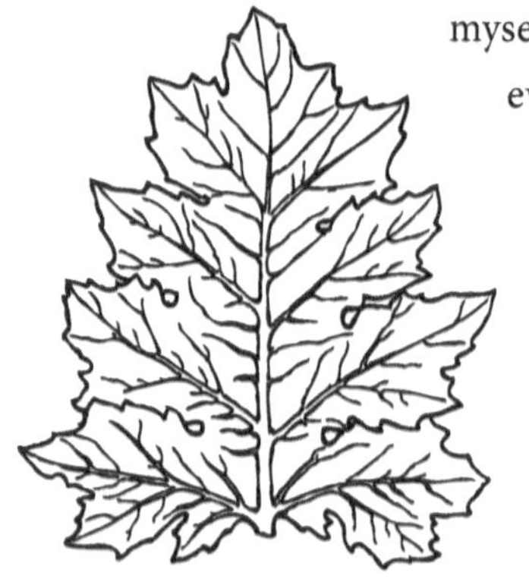

A more naturalistic drawing of an acanthus leaf.

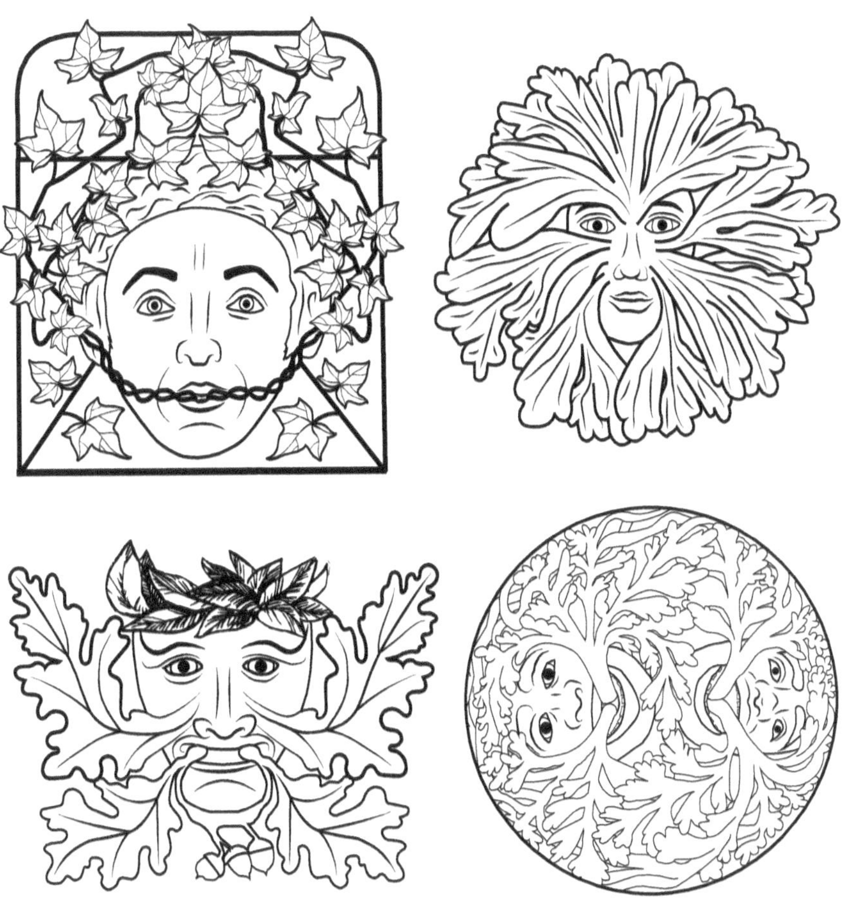

Although acanthus leaves are by far the most common Green Man foliage, these Green Men show the range of plant species that can be seen emerging from their faces. From left to right, top: a fifteenth-century German Green Man has ivy trailing from his lips; a fourteenth-century Green Man from the ceiling of Norwich Cathedral spews out staghorn ferns. From left to right, bottom: a French medieval Green Man carved beneath a choir seat has oak leaves and acorns issuing from his eyes and mouth; from the ceiling of Exeter Cathedral, these Green Men have a riot of wild carrot leaves spraying out from their throats.

The Green Man first appears in the British Isles around the time of the Norman Invasion, in the latter part of the eleventh century. This is a time when the Normans were seeking to recapture the glory of ancient Roman art, resulting in the Romanesque style of European architecture. Green Men made in this era do not represent distinct human faces. I found a good example of a particularly ancient Romanesque Green Man at Brecon Cathedral in Powys, Wales.

In 2016, my wife Marsha and I had spent a delightful day driving through the remote lush green hills of the Brecons. Come evening, we had worked up an appetite, and Brecon was the closest town large enough to offer a restaurant. We drove into town past the cathedral; when we decided to stop and investigate, we found that evensong was about to begin. (If you've never heard a Welsh choir and you ever take a trip to Wales, enjoy all the singing you can!) After the service, we shook hands with the clergy who happened to be standing beside a very large and ancient-looking baptismal font that—*aha!*—had four Green Men carved around its circumference, interleaved with symbols of the Gospels. I mentioned it, and one of the priests smiled.

"Ah yes, the Old Green Man," he said and proceeded to say that for a thousand years the children of the community have been christened with water from that vessel.

The cathedral's website states that the font dates from "1150 (but perhaps two hundred years before that)." If it does in fact date to 950, it is the earliest carved Green Man in a church in the Isles, but apparently its exact date cannot be proved.

Look at the face of a Green Man on that baptismal font and you'll see it is not a portrait of any particular individual; in fact, I can't tell if the face is that of a man or a beast. The leaves are highly stylized as well, matching the lovely Celtic knotwork above it, resembling art in the borders of manuscripts from the Early Middle Ages, such as the famous Book of Kells.

Green Men proliferate during the Gothic era of church architecture, between 1200 and the beginning of the Reformation in the sixteenth century. During this era, they become more three dimensional, the foliage carving becomes more naturalistic, and the faces are sometimes portraits of real people.

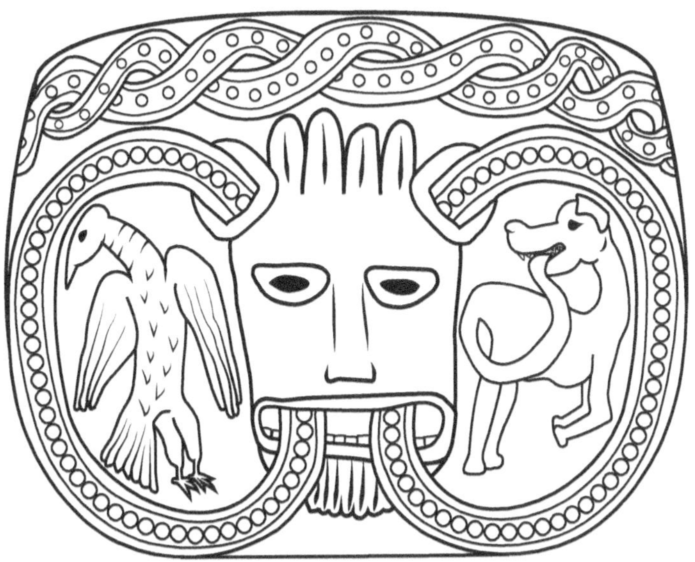

Babies are still baptized in the ancient font in Brecon Cathedral. Note the fantastical creatures enclosed within the vines.

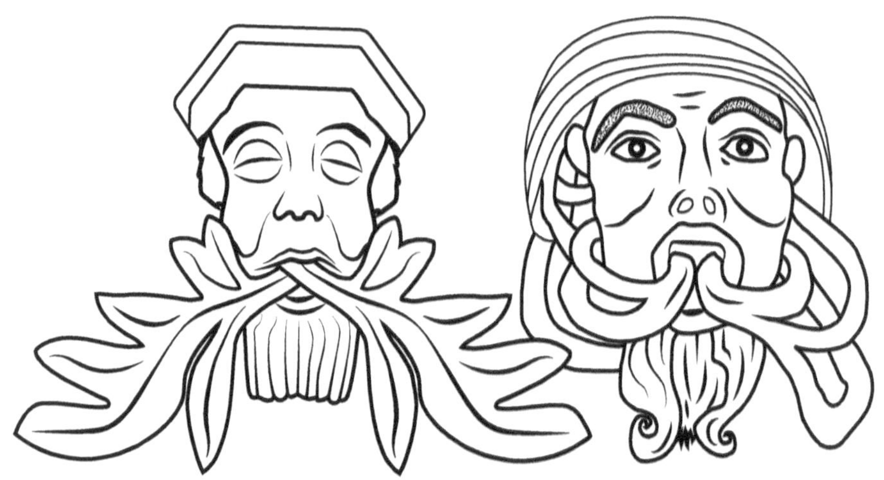

These two Green Gentleman on pillars at the Parish Church of Ottery St. Mary, Devon, England, portray actual individuals. Comparing these Green Men with that in Brecon Cathedral gives you a sense of the differences between Green Men carved before and after the Gothic period.

We spent a week in Devon in 2016 and had a day to explore, so we stopped at Ottery St. Mary Church. The whole building is exquisite, founded in 1337 for a college of monks. Samuel Taylor Coleridge, one of the great artistic and philosophical influences of the nineteenth century, grew up worshiping at this church. As we walked between the pews, our heads tilted back, we had a sense of openness and light, and we experienced a time of prayer and refreshment there.

If you look at the Green Men on the pillars of Ottery St. Mary's church, you are immediately struck by the realistic nature of their depiction. You can imagine what it would be like to meet them in person. One of the gentleman has his eyes closed, but the other one stares out from wide eyes beneath heavy brows. As I looked up at him, I felt like saying "Hey, what are you doing stuck up there?" I sensed an urgency in his stare, as if he were saying, *Come closer. I have important things to tell you.* (In fact, the Green Men at St. Mary Ottery Church did impart an important clue as to the Green Man's medieval identity, but I'll speak of that later in this book.)

Over the years, as we traveled around the UK, we learned that we might find a Green Man on either the interior or the exterior of a church. Most often he is carved out of stone, but he can also appear in the woodwork. Sometimes he is carved on the bottom of a misericord—a shelf-like seat found in medieval choir stalls.

This misericord shown on the next page, from Worcester Cathedral, links the Green Man with women's cleverness and strength. The story it portrays is an ancient folktale, "The Wise Daughter," which was recorded by the Brothers Grimm in Germany but is also known in England and in Norse countries; the story was even used in an episode of the TV series *Vikings*.

The tale goes like this: A peasant received some land as a gift from the king. When the peasant and his daughter plowed the field, they found a mortar and pestle made of gold. The daughter warned that if they gave the mortar to the king in return for his generosity, he would ask for the pestle as well; the father, however, gave the mortar to the king anyway, and just as the daughter had predicted, the king demanded the pestle and put the father in prison until he got it. When the king heard the father loudly lamenting the fact that he hadn't listened to his daughter's wise advice, the king summoned the daughter and gave her a challenge: to come to him neither naked nor clothed, neither walking nor riding a horse, neither on the road nor off it, with a gift that cannot be received. If she could prove her cleverness, he would marry her, and her father would be released.

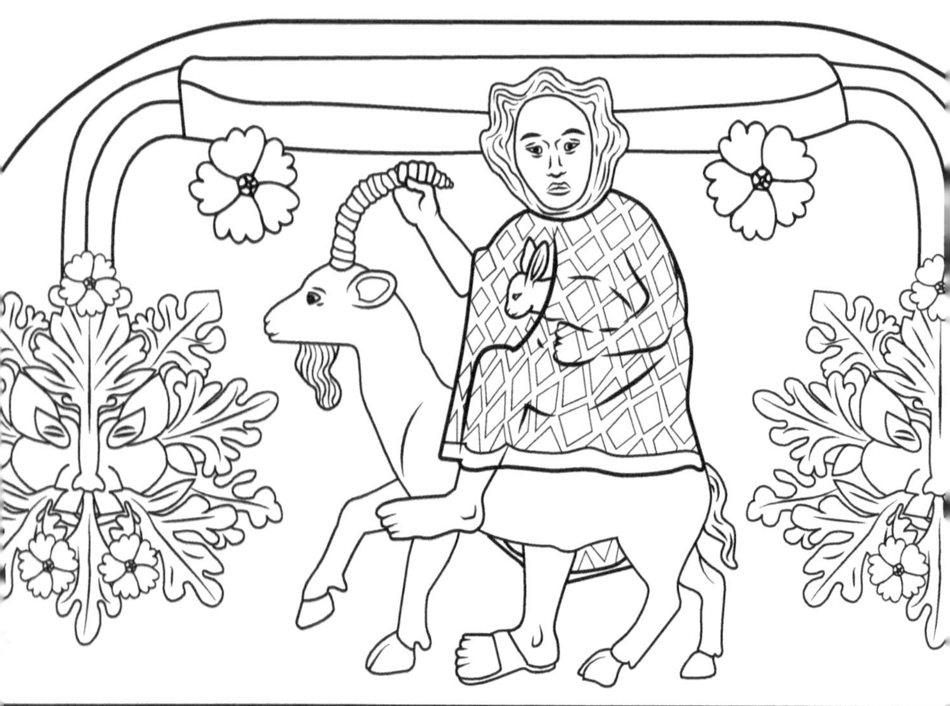

This thirteenth-century misericord in Worcester Cathedral portrays two Green Men on either side of a woman riding a goat. A misericord—sometimes called a "mercy seat"—was basically a ledge projecting from the underside of a hinged seat in a choir stall which, when the seat was turned up, gave support to someone standing. It allowed tired monastics the chance to take the weight off their feet.

The carving between the Green Men on the Worcester misericord shows the daughter's solution: she is wrapped in a fishing net, riding a goat with one foot on the ground, and holding a hare—she is clothed but not clothed, not walking but not riding a horse, and carrying a gift that cannot be received (since it would hop away). Perhaps the artist who carved these images connected the Wise Daughter with the Green Man because both are tricksters (one masculine, one feminine), archetypal characters that theologian Peter Rollins defines as "revolutionary figures that challenge the natural order. They poke holes in what everyone takes for granted and fight systems that oppress." Rollins points out that Jesus was also a trickster.

Green Men can also be found carved on the ends of wooden pews, many of which are in southern England, in Somerset and Cornwall. In 2014, when I walked into St. Nonna's Church in Altarnun, Cornwall, I wasn't expecting Green Men; I had heard merely that St. Nonna's was "a quaint old church." As we stepped through the doorway, my wife Marsha was immediately attracted to a display concerning the wedding scene for the *Doc Martin* TV show that had been filmed at the church—but our friend Ellyn and I were awed by the pew ends. There were seventy-nine of them, carved gloriously in bas relief, dating to just before the Reformation.

Pew #48 is described in the church's guide book as "Green Man above chalice guarded by dragons or perhaps a merman with sea serpents?" This is a fascinating image on multiple levels. The multivalent nature of symbols is on display, insofar as the historian writing up the guidebook wasn't sure if the image portrays a merman or a Green Man, dragons or sea serpents. The fact that this man, whatever he is, is coming out of a chalice—in a church—is fascinating, since there are numerous medieval portrayals like this portraying Christ emerging from a chalice. Theologians in this Gothic era emphasized the "real presence" of Christ transmitted via the communion cup, which means that this audacious image points to the Green Man as a Christ image. The "Cosmic Christ" in the New Testament was understood as "the soul of Nature," and the Green Man can likewise be understood as the intelligence or soul hidden within the natural world. Like Christ, the Green Man connects the realms of humankind and Nature. But what are those dragons/sea serpents doing drinking from the cup of Christ? Some images contain symbolism too deep to fathom. What I wouldn't give to go back in time and speak with the artist who carved this bench end!

Curiously, there are other bench ends in a Somerset church that share some themes with the Altarnun Green Man. One of these sixteenth-century carvings in the Church of the Holy Ghost in

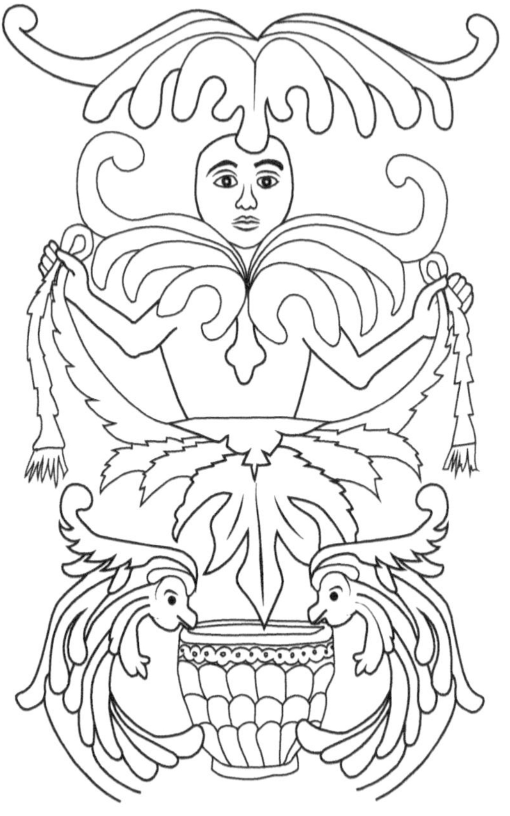

The pew end in St. Nonna's Church portraying a Green Man/merman emerging from a chalice. Symbolically, a Green Man and a merman were not so very different; one pointed to the vital Spirit within Nature on land, while the other signified something very similar within the sea.

Crowcombe, Somerset, has mermen shooting out from the Green Man's ears and grapevines from his mouth, while another one shows a two-tailed merman with foliage bursting from his lips and sea serpents from his ears. These Green Man images contain alchemical symbolism pointing toward the union of dualism: earth and water, body and soul, male and female. According to the alchemists, the mermaid (or siren) connects to the "Universal Mercury"—the all-pervading World Soul that calls out to us through Nature and all things. Combining the Green Man with mermaids created a further union of forest and sea, the entire natural world.

Oh-so-many Green Men! And each one points

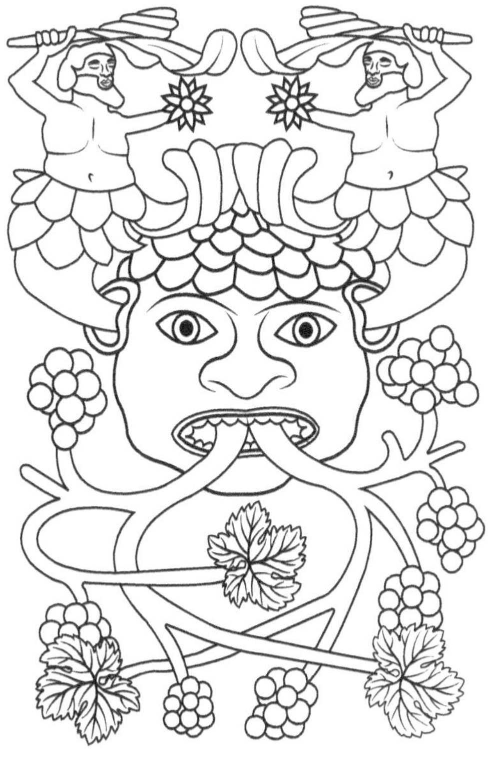

This drawing is taken from one of the Green-Men-plus-merman pew ends in the Church of the Holy Ghost in Crowcombe, Somerset.

to a mystery, a wild and lovely strangeness at the heart of our world. If we have often forgotten and overlooked the Green Man's message to us, perhaps we can be forgiven—given the fact that the Green Man has sometimes chosen to hide himself, as we'll see in the next chapter.

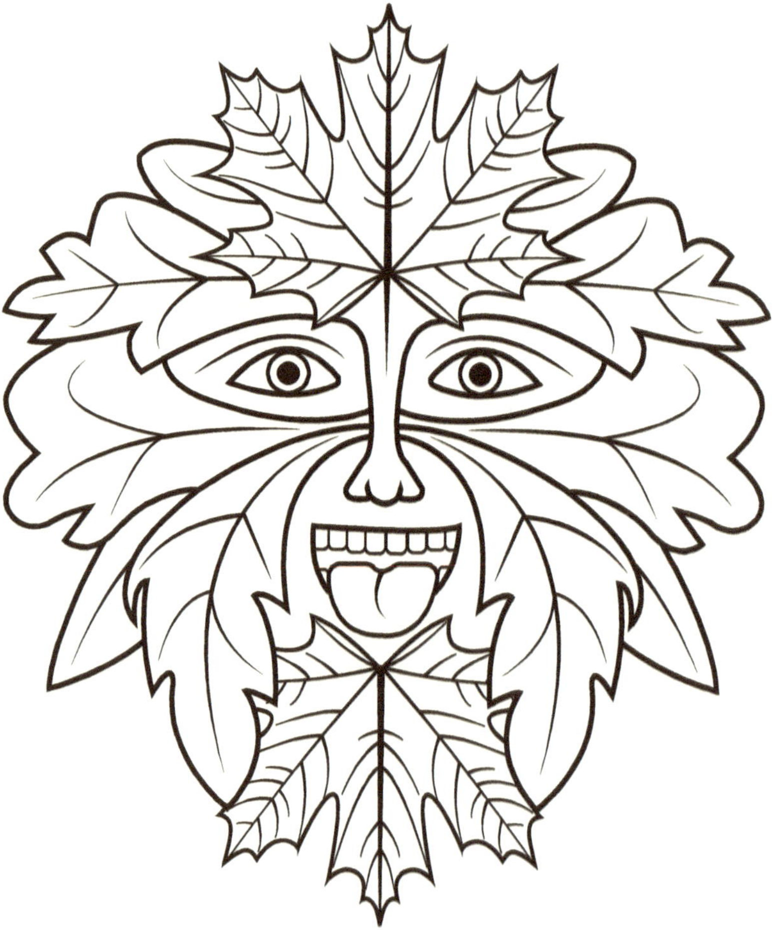

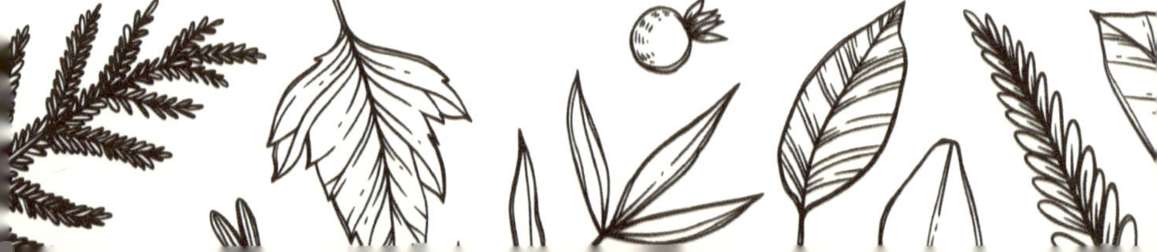

Taken from a pew carving in Winchester Cathedral. Note the protruding tongue.

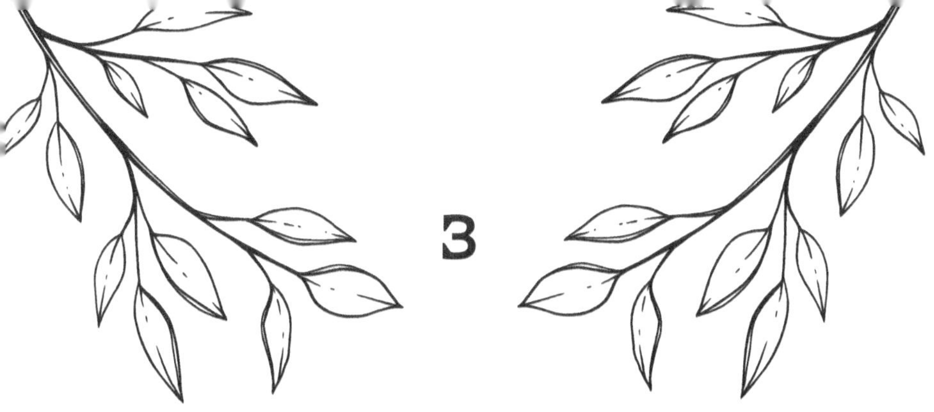

3

Green Man Hide-and-Seek

here in churches will you find a Green Man? You never really know. I've seen it alleged that the Green Man was placed in hidden places, as though he were an embarrassment. And it is true that sometimes he can be hard to spot. I suspect, however, that the Green Man hides out of sheer mischief rather than any sense of shame.

Before we visited Wells Cathedral in 2015, our friend David Cole (the author of several Anamchara books) had told me that a fine specimen of the Green Man was there—but I couldn't find it. I walked most of the day in the cathedral, just soaking in the grandeur and aesthetic perfection of the place, but I had no luck finding that foliated head.

That evening, I texted David. As it turns out, there are quite a few Green Men hidden here and there in Wells Cathedral, but the one David had in mind is not on public view; I would have to ask at the front desk of the cathedral. I was happy to return to the cathedral, where we spent another half day, and this time I did inquire at the visitors' entrance, where a volunteer directed me to track down the verger.

When I found the verger, he had an enormous iron keychain full of skeleton keys. He motioned me to follow, and we walked to an ancient-looking wooden door in the wall of the cathedral. That door was thick, rough-surfaced, and covered with darkened iron, like something out of a Harry Potter movie. After turning one of the skeleton keys in the lock, he pulled the door open on squeaky hinges, revealing a musty crypt in the wall. The verger pointed upward, and there—above the portal itself—was a detailed and puckish looking Green Man. He was hiding, but I didn't detect a trace of embarrassment in his expression.

Green Men also often hide their faces beneath misericords. As I mentioned in the previous chapter, misericords—or "mercy seats"—are shelf-like seats designed to aid tired members of a medieval choir by making it appear as though they were standing when in fact they had sat down to rest throughout the long service. Often times, images are carved on the bottom of the seat. In order to see the beauty hidden beneath the misericords, you must flip them up. Understandably, some churches are reluctant to have five-hundred-year-old bits of wood going up and down repeatedly on their aging hinges, so they are often unavailable for viewing. Some places of worship now display photos of the misericords so people can see their likenesses, while the actual carvings are preserved. But I have been lucky enough to see some of these.

You recall my enthusiasm for Welsh choirs; well, the singers are exceptional at St. David's Cathedral. The cathedral itself is impressive; its immensity dwarfs the tiny city around it. Inside, you can walk and walk, through chambers that ooze history from the time of its founding

Celtic saint through the Norman era and then the Gothic. The "new" ceiling was put up in the late Middle Ages.

And perhaps best of all, after an inspiring evensong choir service at St. David's Cathedral, a warden offered to flip up the misericords in the choir stalls so Marsha and I could see the carvings underneath. The misericords were each carved from a single piece of oak in the late fifteenth century. One of them was a powerful-looking Green Man.

Both the Wells Cathedral Green Man and the St. David's misericord carving are examples of why I appreciate the kindness and assistance of church staff, both paid and volunteer. Shy Green Men might not come out of hiding without the help of these men and women. But on a trip in 2014, I found the elusive Green Men at Hereford Cathedral all on my own.

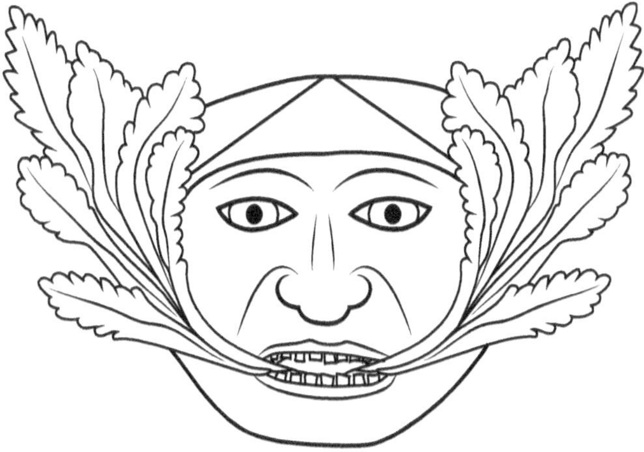

The muscular, grimacing face on a misericord in St. David's Cathedral is slightly reminiscent of the very ancient Green Men on the Brecon Cathedral baptistry in the previous chapter, though this visage is obviously more human and realistic.

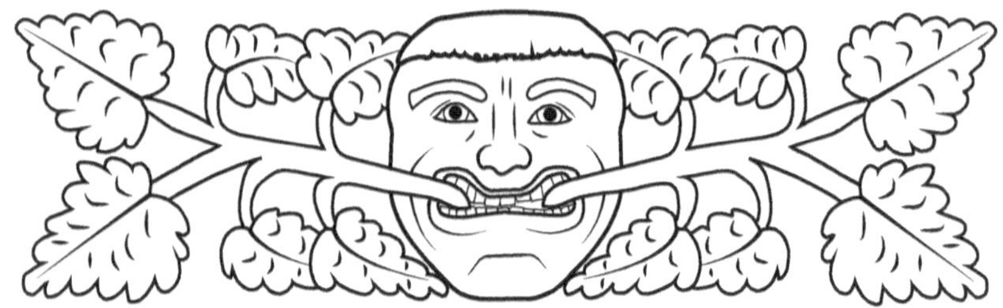

Like the Green Men I saw in other locations in Wales, this one in Hereford's Cathedral also has a broad warrior's face, with a grimacing mouth and clenched teeth.

As I exited the cathedral along the newly restored St. John's Walk, a passage that dates to the twelfth century and is a covered walkway between the main cathedral and the cloisters, I happened to glance upward—and spied the carvings up in the beams that support the roof. I believe these were designed to be somewhat hidden, despite the effort that went into them. They cover a range of symbolic and mythical subjects, and one beam portrays a naked nun. (I wonder if she was a reminder to the priests that they must stay vigilant in avoidance of lust? The famous saint Thomas de Cantelupe, enshrined in the cathedral, must have walked this corridor, and one of the evidences given for his sainthood is that he never kissed a woman, not even his own sister.) To my great excitement, on the first wooden beam of St. John's Walk, after exiting the cathedral proper, I spotted a Green Man in all his leafy glory.

St. John's Walk contains another Green Man, who was originally on a roof boss in the cathedral but fell from his perch long ago. Unlike many of his brothers, this little guy doesn't look angry or fearsome at all. In fact, of all the Green Men that I have seen, he wins the funny-face award.

The fact that many Green Men are sticking out their tongues has a variety of interpretations. Some authors say it shows the Green Man's wildness—or his sexuality and fertility. Other interpretations connect the gesture to what would have been the proper way to receive the Communion wafer. Perhaps it alludes to a verse in the Hebrew scriptures, Proverbs 15:4, which states, "A tongue that heals is a tree of life." Take your pick from all these meanings; there's room for them all!

In this chapter, I've been talking about the shy and elusive Green Man. Some writers in the past claimed that Green Men were typically placed in hard-to-see locations, covert symbols of unauthorized beliefs. From what you've read in this chapter, you might be nodding in agreement. Indeed, some Green Men seem to have been deliberately hidden—*but these wall-flower Green Men are the exception rather than the rule.*

This drawing is based on the Green Man from Hereford Cathedral, who must have been a reminder to the holy men of the church: "Don't be all vinegar-faced. Lighten up, guys!" The protruding tongue shows the Green Man's cheeky and irreverent trickster side.

After a decade of looking for him, I'd say the Green Man prefers to be bold and in your face rather than tucked away. I'll explain his boldness more in another chapter; for now, I offer just one example of how "out there" the Green Man can be.

In 2015, Marsha and I were traveling in Scotland with extended family and stayed at Dornoch Castle, which is right across the street from the cathedral. After dark, I stepped out for some fresh air, decided to stroll over toward the cathedral, and there was the Green Man. I'd have had to be blind to miss him! I spied him immediately, even in the darkness. He is on the exterior of the cathedral, on the right side of the massive front entrance, at eye level.

You know how churches have greeters out in front, ensuring that no one makes it into the sanctuary without a smile, a handshake, and a bulletin? Dornoch is one of a half-dozen churches where I refer to the Green Man as a "church greeter," because he's in the obvious position to meet anyone heading into the building.

But this Green Man isn't the friendliest of greeters. His pouchy eyes, flared nose, clenched teeth, and tusk-like vines coming out of his mouth make him look as threatening as a wild boar. This was also the decided impression of the other members of my party when they saw him the next day.

In cases like this, when the Green Man looks more frightening than friendly, I think he serves a clearly *apotropaic* purpose. In the ancient world, apotropaic magic was intended to turn away harm or evil influences, and this Green Man is a guardian, keeping something or someone out. Nowadays, churches are desperate for worshipers and will practically pay

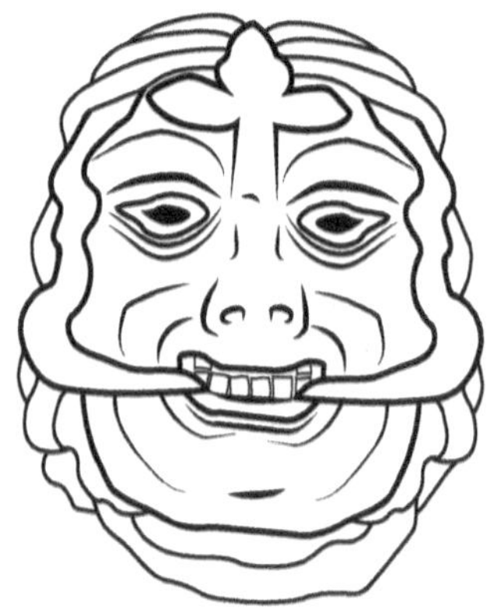

The Green Man who greeted me outside Dornoch Cathedral.

people to walk in their doors, but in the Middle Ages, churches were more concerned with keeping sin, pestilence, and evil spirits outside their sanctuaries. Fearsome Green Men may have been like the gargoyles who were also considered to be a means of warding off evil.

Or maybe this Green Man was intended as a warning to more tangible enemies? Bishop Gilbert de Moravia built Dornoch Cathedral in 1222. His predecessors had presided over their flock from Halkirk, but due to their brutal murder there, Gilbert chose to build Dornoch Cathedral at his own expense and moved the seat of his episcopacy to this safer location. The cathedral does look rather like a fortress. The Scottish church later recognized Gilbert as one of the noblest and wisest of their medieval leaders, and he was the last Scotsman given a place in the Calendar of Saints. Although we can't say for sure when the Dornoch Green Man was added to the cathedral, since the building has been damaged and rebuilt over the years, it's tempting to think that Bishop Gilbert could have placed that visage by the door as a stern warning to his human enemies.

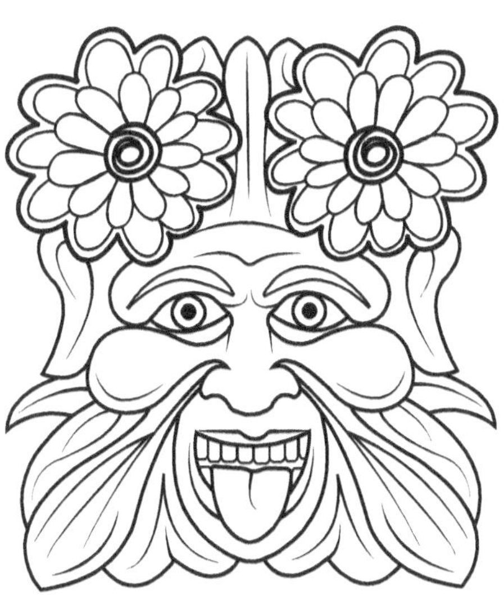

Based on a ceiling boss in Crowland Abbey in Lincolnshire, England.

Like Bishop Gilbert, the prelates of the medieval church were all male, and this relates to a commonly asked question: Why were there so many portrayals of Green *Men*? What about the women? Yes, clerics were male, but there are numerous medieval depictions of nuns, noble ladies, and peasant women. Medieval artists enjoyed portraying women. So why do we see—almost without exception—Green Men?

Well, that brings us to the next set of stops on our journey.

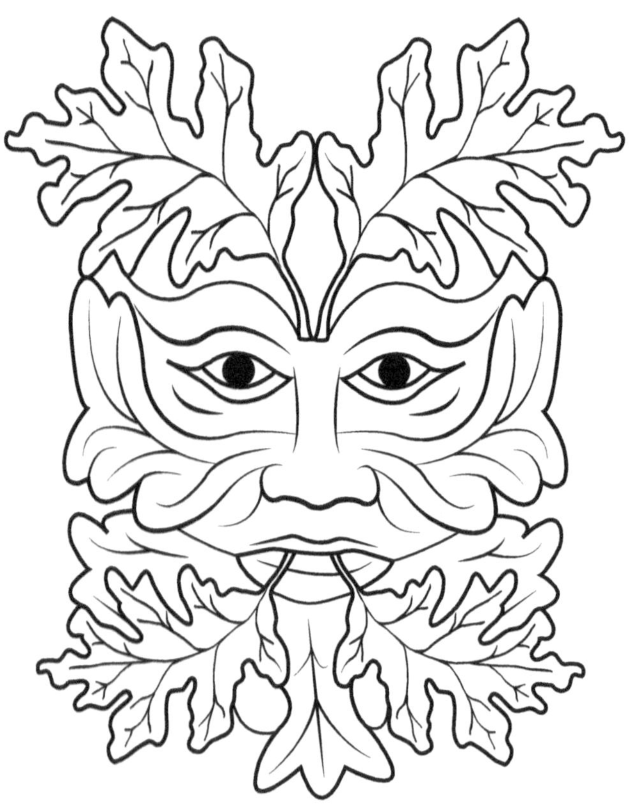

This Green Man's original is found under a thirteenth-century misericord.

He's something of a spy,
and if you have no need to know,
he's unlikely to tell you.
Still, one of his functions is to convince skeptics
of the existence of the marvelous,
to rescue those who are lost
in deserts of doubt and dryness.
So he's needed now more than ever,
and surely still moves among us,
playing his great game.

—Peter Lamborn Wilson

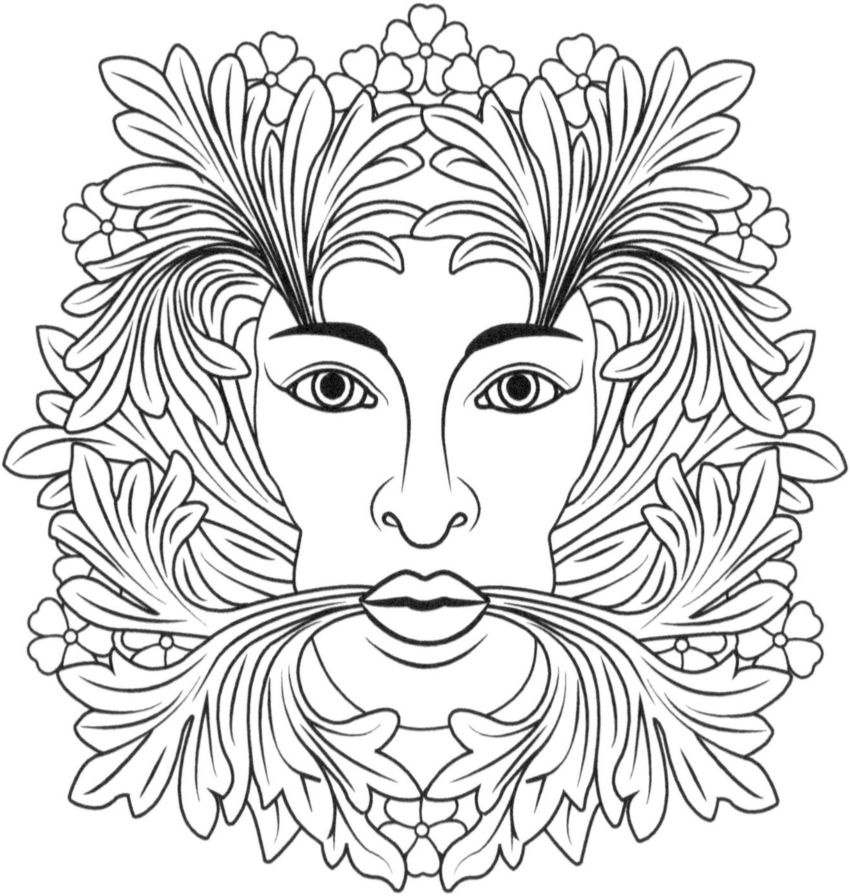

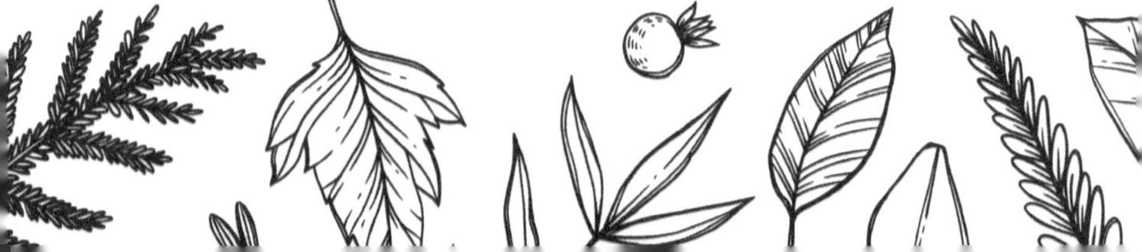

A modern portrayal of a Green Woman.

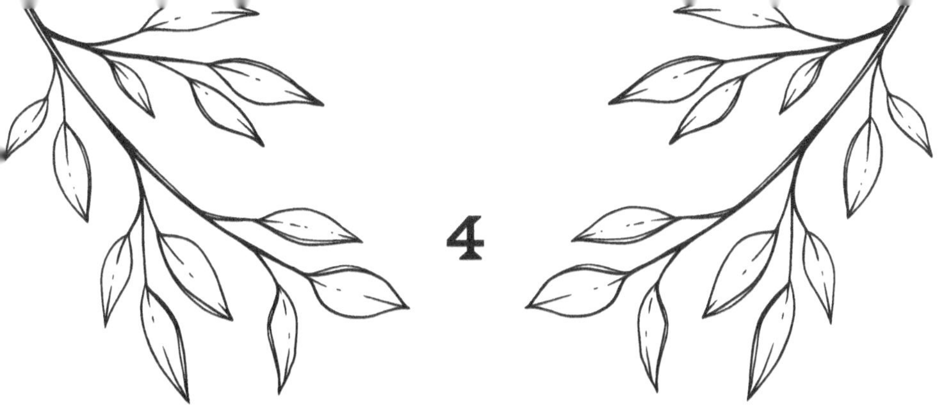

4

What About the Green Women?

I've spoken in a variety of venues about the Green Man: at Celtic festivals, churches, and in a pub. Whatever the venue, someone in the audience wants to know right out the gate, "What about a Green *Woman*?"

Today when women are making gains against harassment and stereotypes, and record numbers of women are achieving representation in governments worldwide, the absence of Green Women seems especially jarring. Is the Green Man a gendered idea, spawned by the patriarchy?

Feminine foliated heads in medieval churches are exceedingly rare, if they exist at all. I was excited, therefore, to encounter one in the Parish Church of St. Michael Archangel in Lyme Regis, Dorset, on a trip in 2014.

Marsha and I had gone to Lyme Regis because it was the home of Mary Anning, who is one of our heroes. A hundred years before any woman was allowed into the British Geologic Society, Mary unearthed fossils from the cliffs of Devon's Jurassic Coast. She discovered the ichthyosaurus and pterodactyl, and at a time when scientist didn't believe that any lifeforms had gone extinct on our planet (since the world was believed to be only 5,000 years old), Mary proved to a skeptical public that these prehistoric giants had come and gone from the Earth's stage a very long time ago. Self-taught, and poor her whole life, Mary Anning blazed a trail ahead of her male contemporaries in the Victorian scientific world. And she was a faithful member of the Lyme Regis Anglican church of St. Michael the Archangel, seeing no conflict between her scientific discoveries and her faith. There is a window and display honoring her in the nave of the church. So it seems fitting for Mary Anning's church to also have a Green Woman.

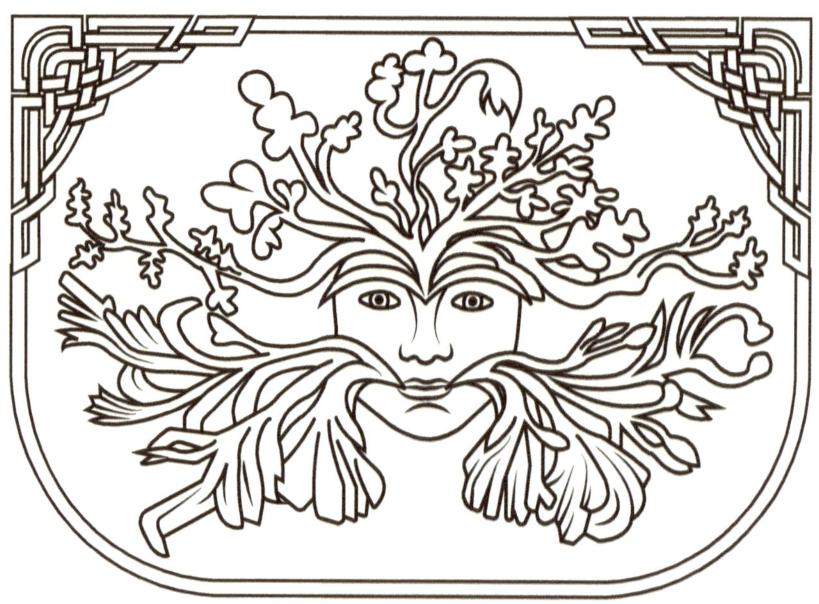

This drawing is based on the Green Woman in the church at Lyme Regis, where her face adorns the organ.

Initially, I was thrilled to discover this Green Woman, and in a church that is very old, dating back to the Saxon era. But after undergoing considerable effort to photograph this Green Lady, I discovered that she's rather young—in fact, created by a local artist in 2009. It's a nice addition to the Lyme Regis church, but I still had not seen a Green Woman from the Middle Ages.

More recently, I got excited again, thinking I'd found a genuine medieval Green Woman. I was in *ooh-aah!* mode in the Chapter House of Southwell Minster, which had been on my travel bucket list for some time. We finally made it there in 2018, and I was not disappointed. It's as grand as any cathedral, and the treasure of Southwell Minister is its Chapter House.

The Chapter House, where the canons of the minster met to rule over matters of church business, is one of the most impressive examples of Gothic stonework in the British Isles. Covered with delicate and lifelike leaves and branches, the walls are like a garden turned magically to stone. And there, amid the hawthorn and oak leaves, are eleven foliated faces.

Southwell Minster's Canon Nigel Coates explains the Green Man's symbolism thusly: "In medieval times meetings of the college of canons would include a chapter of scripture which would be read and meditated on. Like the psalmist they would delight in God's law. The Green Man becomes an image that illustrates what happens when someone meditates, chews over that word of God. It leads to a verdant and fruitful life producing leaves that do not wither."

As I walked slowly past the stone leaves, examining the faces in turn, I stopped in my tracks and stared at one face. I looked closer, considered carefully. The features did indeed appear feminine...

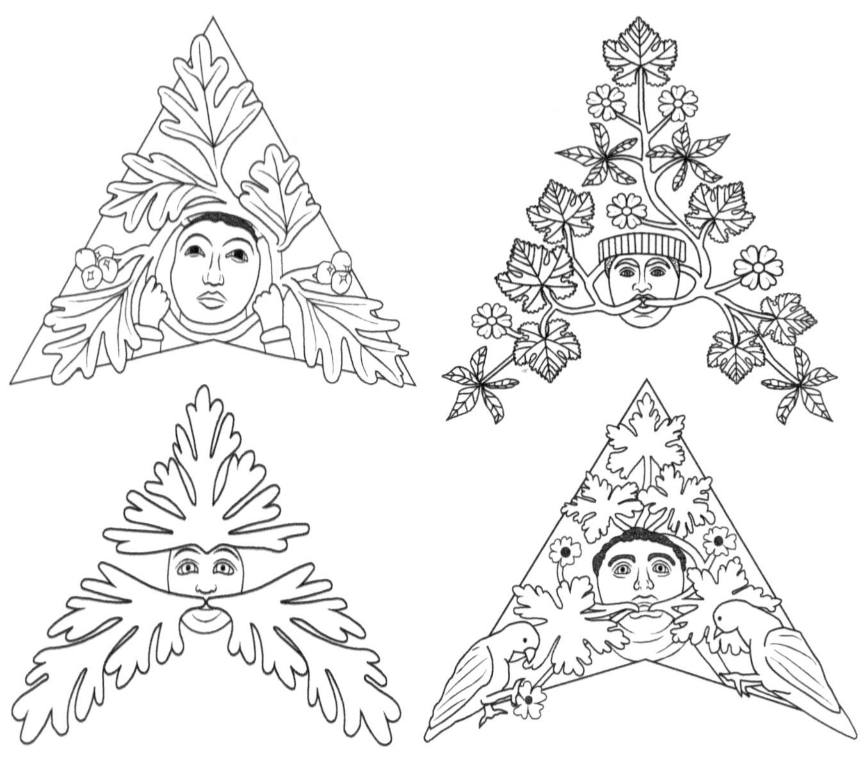

Four of the eleven Green Men in the Southwell Minster Charter House.

I exclaimed, "At last, here is a Green Woman!"

A knowedgeable Minster guide was standing nearby—I'd spoken with him earlier—and I said to him, "Wow! It's a Green Woman isn't it? I haven't seen one before."

He replied, "Well . . . erm . . . some people think so." He paused a moment and then said, "Wouldn't you like to see a carving that we all think looks like your president Trump?"

He led us to that, and we agreed it did look like the Mr. Trump.

Point taken: it's easy to see resemblances that were never intended by the images' carvers.

Later, I found out that Canon Coates says the image in the Chapter House could "possibly" be a woman. More reading on the Internet led to the fact that this carving has traditionally been known as "the Oak King." (Despite the fact that those are acanthus leaves, not oak leaves, framing the face.)

My sister (who gave me my own Green Woman plaque) looked at a close-up photo of the Southwell foliated face and said, "It's a gender nonbinary Green Person."

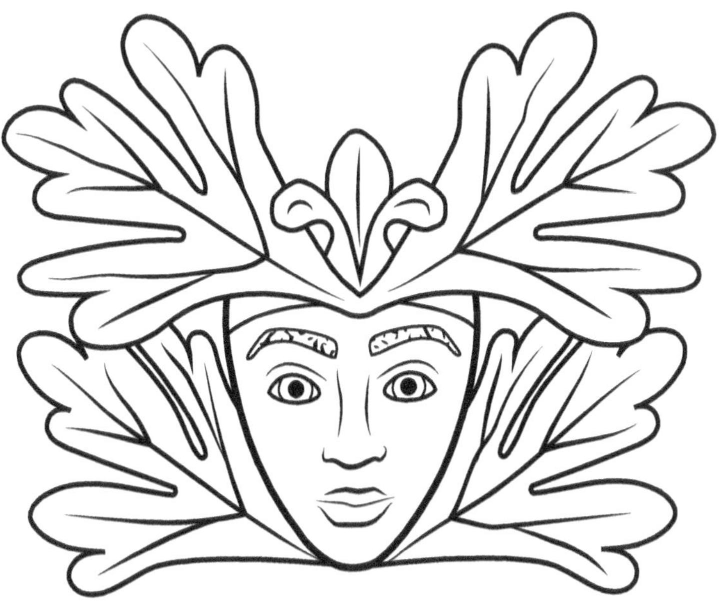

Is this a Green Man or a Green Woman? What do you think?

My sister may be onto something. Some folklorists surmise that the foliated head images in the Chapter House harken back to legends of the fairies who live hidden in the forests—and portrayals of these forest spirits tend to be androgynous, indicating both their youth and unearthly essence. Given its setting, this Green Person could well be Puck the Faerie (of Shakespeare fame).

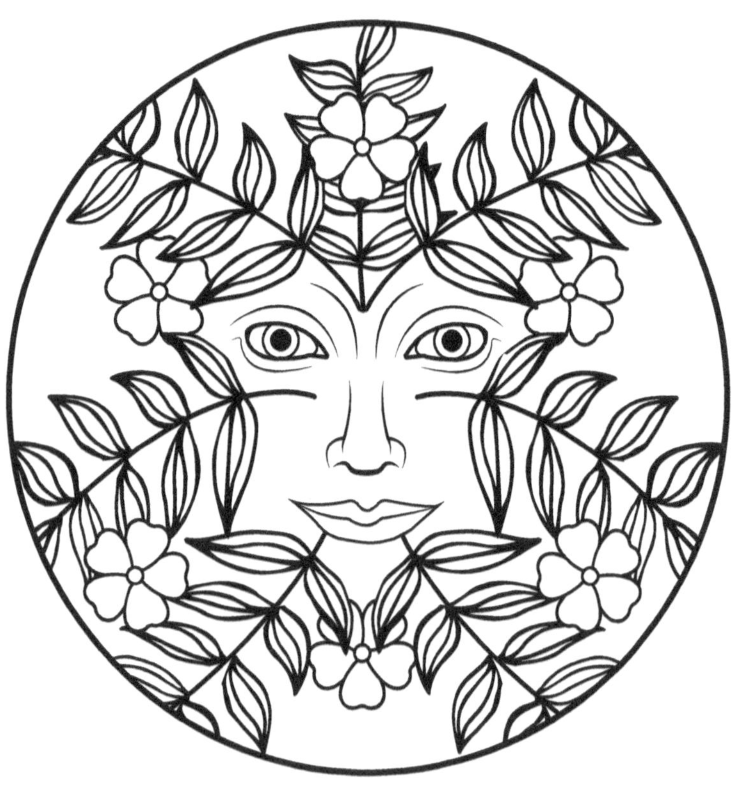

Male or female? It may be that in some ways, the Green Spirit transcends gender.

At any rate, now that I am well into my midlife, I have realized that there may be good reason to listen when people disagree with me—so I acknowledge that my Green Woman might be a Green Man. Or maybe Green Gender-Nonbinary.

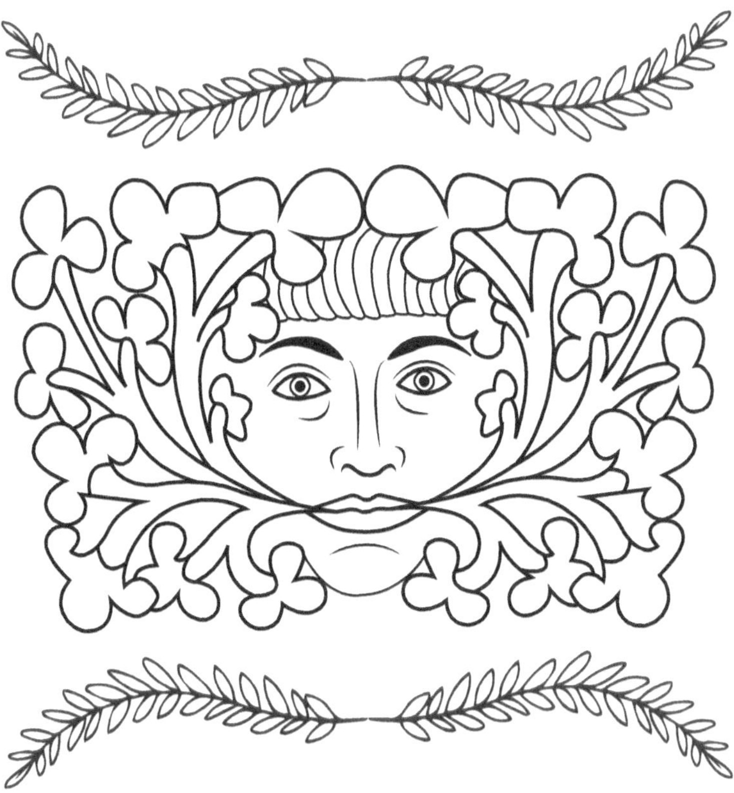

The original image, in St. Bavo's Cathedral in Ghent, Belgium, appears above the archway into the crypt, the burial chamber, linking the image with the verdant leafy life that springs from death. But is this face masculine gendered? Or could it be feminine? Or perhaps, we should refer to some of these foliated faces using the nongendered "they" pronoun!

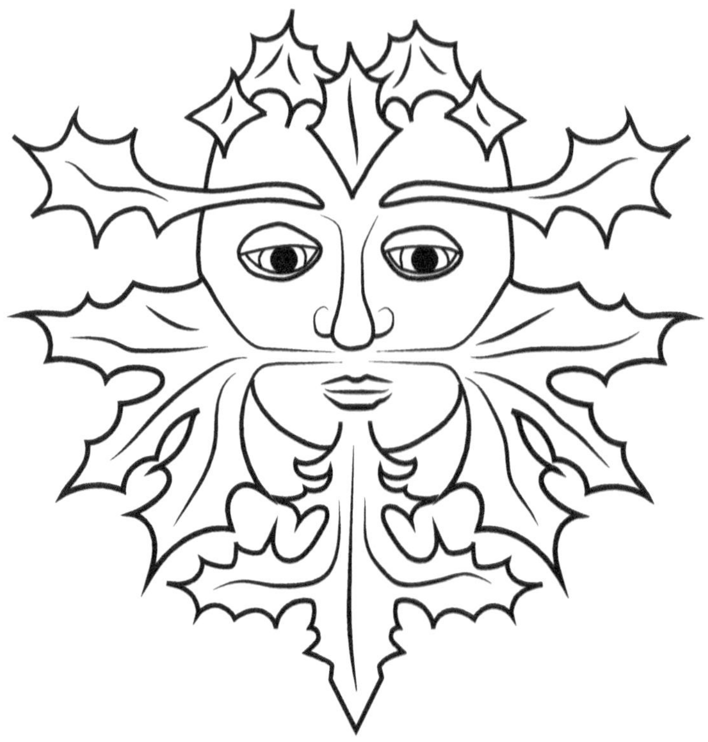

While it's true that most Green Men are clearly male, some appear more androgynous, as with this medieval misericord carving.

But all this brings us back to the original question: why the Green *Man*? There are thousands of medieval Green Man carvings, and almost all of them are clearly male. If we are to uncover the truth of the soul of the Green Man, we must realize that medieval artists *were portraying a story or an idea that required male gender.*

Before we get to that, though, we need to further consider the Green Man's habitat.

Mother of the forest,
the elusive one who wanders away,
. . . perfumed and fragrant,
offering varieties of food,
though she does not plow the land.

—Hymn to the Forest Goddess,
Rig Veda (~1500 BCE)

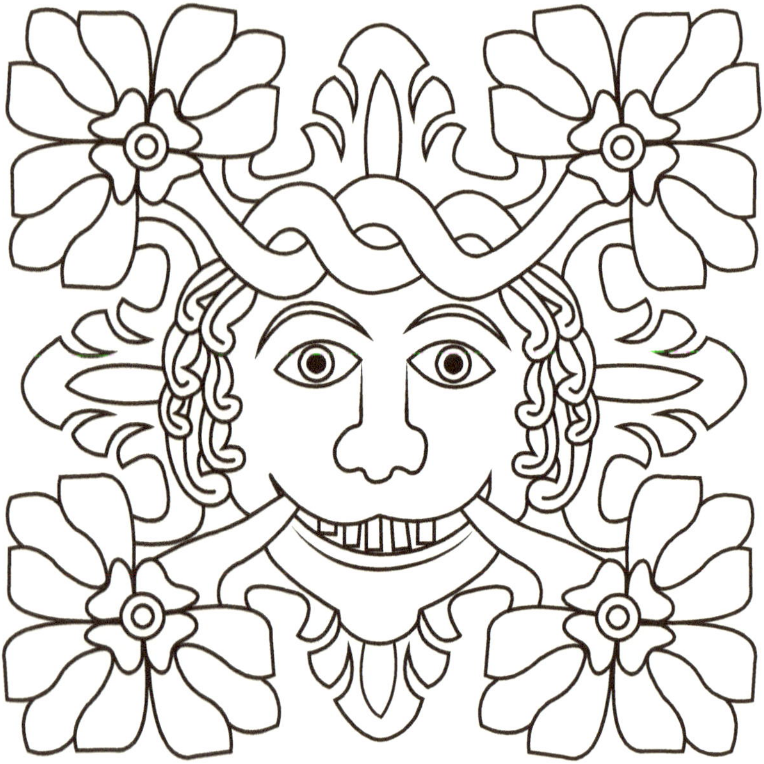

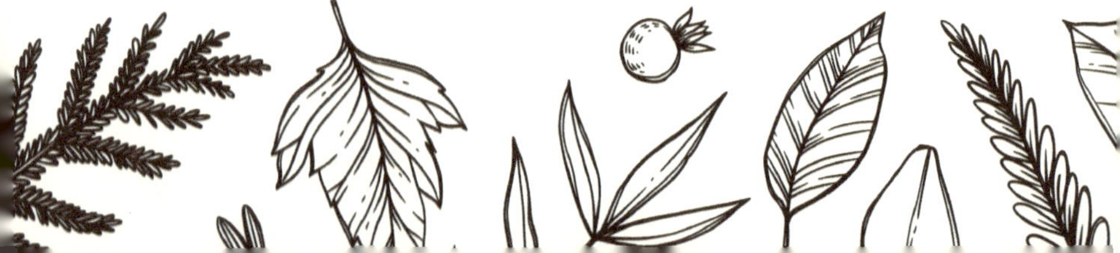

A happy little Green Man taken from the ceiling of the cloisters of Durham
Cathedral, where he and his seven brothers (all with very jolly expressions) serve
as bosses covering the joints in the wood. The cloisters were built at the beginning
of the fifteenth century, when the building was a monastery for Benedictine monks.
Other bosses in the ceiling portray an angel, a frog, coats of arms, and flowers and
leaves, indicating a vision of the world where the angelic hosts, the natural world,
the political world, and human beings are all joined and intertwined.

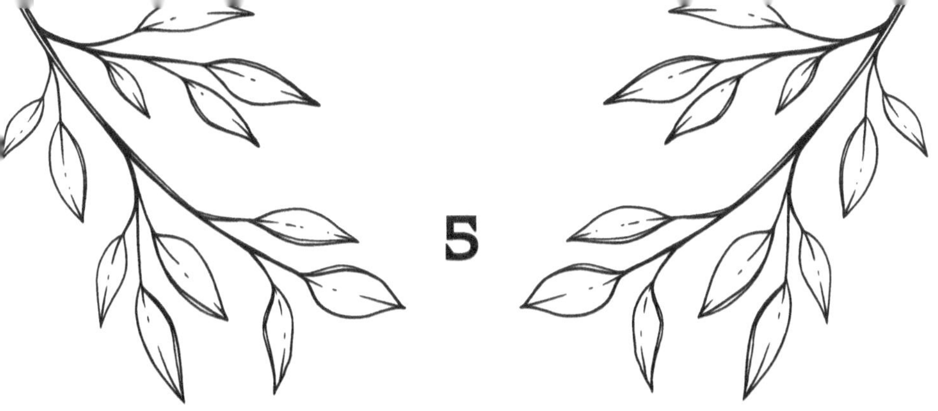

5

The Green Man's
Magical Medieval World

In 2011 Marsha and I had only a short time in Dublin and wanted to hit at least one old church. We learned we could make it to a service at Christ Church Cathedral, which has been a site of worship for over a thousand years. We got in just before the service began; afterward, the wardens promptly ushered us out, wanting to prepare the space for a soon-happening event. It wasn't an ideal way to explore a church, and we didn't see a Green Man.

We did, however, get a quick view of two neat details. One was the effigy tomb of the infamous Norman king Strongbow. In 1169, Strongbow and a thousand of his knights crossed over from England to fight for one Irish king against another. He then married the daughter of the king for whom he was fighting and took over a good part of Ireland, which led to more than seven hundred years of English rule over the Irish. It was a bit of an odd feeling seeing the fearsome warrior king lying in effigy next to the pews.

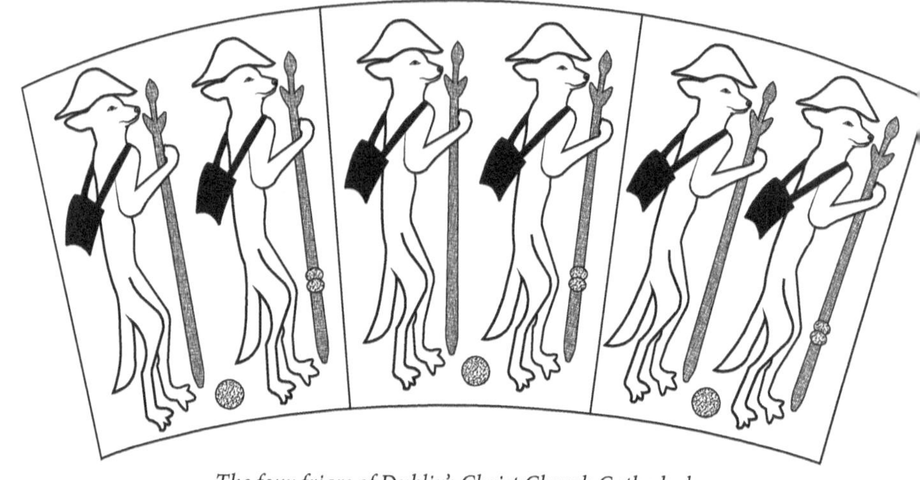

The foxy friars of Dublin's Christ Church Cathedral.

But the thing that sticks out for me from that brief time in Christ Church was the floor tiles depicting a procession of foxy friars. The tiles are replicas of originals that covered this floor in the Middle Ages, showing foxes, walking upright, wearing hats and backpacks, and carrying walking sticks, like medieval pilgrims. The story is that Christ Church became wealthy from the pilgrim trade, earning its keepers the appellation "foxy friars" for their skills at finagling tourists, a nickname that led to the tiles. Can you imagine any church nowadays putting pictures on their floor with animals dressed like the church staff? Or anything lampooning themselves? My takeaway was this: people in the Middle Ages had a good sense of humor and lively imagination.

Which brings us back to the Green Man. The medieval Green Man did not live alone; he dwelt beside other fantastic beings in a wonderfully strange, even outlandish, world, sharing an imaginal realm with creatures we now lump together as "mythical," including dragons, griffins, unicorns, angels, demons, pixies, ogres, and many more. Artists in the

Middle Ages delighted in portraying these fantastic creatures in paintings, illuminated manuscripts, tapestries, carvings on church walls, and on wooden furniture. They populated residences, pubs, and churches.

One such being was the Woodwose, the Wild Man of the Woods. Like the Green Man, he is an archetypal figure, having lived for thousands of years already in the folklore of the world before medieval masons thought to carve him. He harkens back to the hairy wild man Enkidu in the Gilgamesh Epic written in the Middle East before 600 BCE, and he lives on today in the popular image of Bigfoot. As the Green Man is the union of plant and human realms, the Wodewose is the union of animal and human realms. In quite a few images, Woodwoses and Green Men seem to merge, with hairy men sprouting leaves, indicating the marriage of humanity with all of Nature.

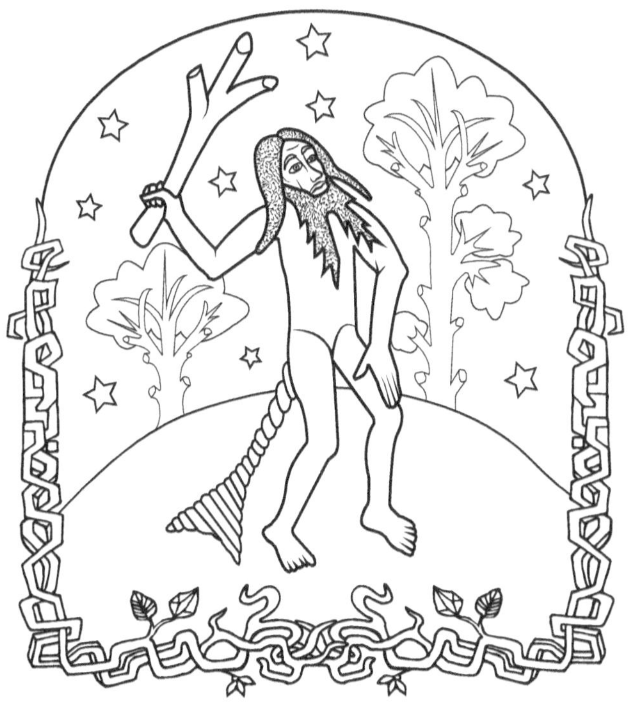

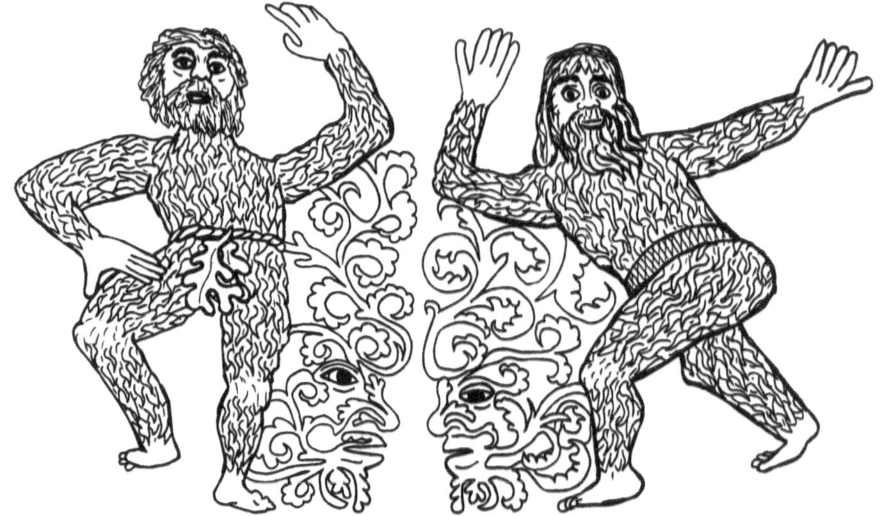

Wodewoses cavort beneath a sculpture of Christ's nativity, with Green Man faces in profile behind them in this carved stone frieze on the interior of Burgos Cathedral, Spain.

Unlike the Green Man, the Wodewose is always full bodied (possessing a torso and all four limbs) and can be either male or female. Male Wodewoses are often portrayed grabbing maidens, an expression of their animalistic, unrestrained virility. The male Wodewose is frequently portrayed in combat with dragons and wild beasts, though he is shy and avoids humans. Unlike the Green Man, we know the Wodewose's name and we understand more about his identity because people in the Middle Ages wrote down his stories, giving us a clear and simple match-up between legends and images.

But other medieval beings lack good explanation. One such figure is the Sheela Na Gig. The meaning of her name is disputed; Sheela Na Gig may mean "hag on her haunches." She is a female exhibitionist, spreading herself for all to see. Sheela appears in some of the same churches as the Green Man. The Church of St. Mary and St. David in Kilpeck, Herefordshire, England, for example, is famous both for its Green Men and its Sheela. Like the Green Man, Sheela first appears after the Norman Invasion, and like the Green Man, she is a distinct and easily identified artistic image; the medieval masons had a clear idea what Sheela symbolized.

And yet, like the Green Man, Sheela is a mystery. Anyone in twelfth-century England would see her image and know who she was and what she meant, but no one (that we know of) wrote that down. There's been plenty of conjecture. Is she a continuing memory of the Great Mother Goddess, an archetype dating back to the Stone Age? Is she an assurance that God will be with women when they go through childbirth? Is she Eve, who gave birth to original sin? Is she a symbol of the "new birth" found in church, the visual, symbolic portrayal of Jesus' statement that we must "be born again"? Or is she a warning that wanton women will entice men into lust? Historians and folklorists have suggested all these sometimes-opposing theories as to Sheela's identity.

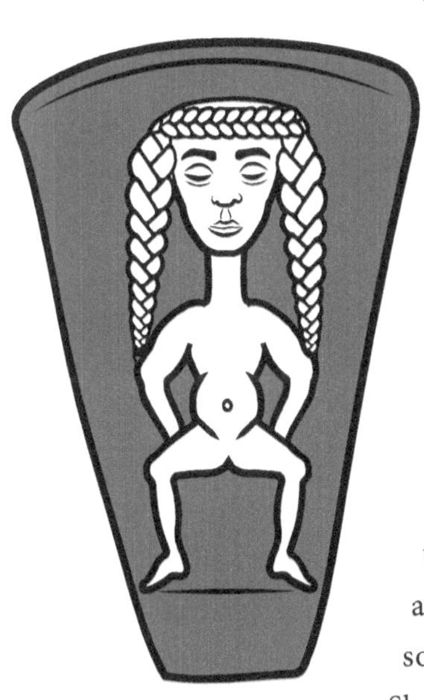

A Sheela from Rahara Church in Galway, Ireland.

Sheela's presence on more than sixty churches in the British Isles reminds us that medieval people easily juxtaposed things we would call "bawdy" with things we would term "holy." The ease with which medieval people mixed sacred and profane (or, rather, what we nowadays divide into "sacred" or "profane") can be seen especially in medieval choir stall carvings. Sharing the same space as tonsured monks singing the Lord's praises were depictions of domestic brawls, nubile mermaids, biblical stories, pigs playing bagpipes, people drinking, knights fighting dragons, and even a man with his pants pulled down mooning the viewer.

The Middle Ages can serve as a mirror to understand our own times, and they tell us that we "permissive" moderns may be more uncomfortable with earthy realities than our ancestors a thousand years ago. People in the Middle Ages held an affirming view of ordinary life and the physical world—including *everything* in the physical world. The great Oxford scholar, theologian, and novelist C.S. Lewis, in his book *On English Literature in the Sixteenth Century*, describes the medieval mind in this way:

> *High abstractions and rarified artifices jostled the earthiest particulars. . . . They talked more readily than we about large universals such as death, change, fortune, friendship, or salvation; but also about pigs, loaves, boots, and boats. The mind darted more easily to and fro between that mental heaven and earth: the cloud of middle generalizations, hanging between the two, was then much smaller. Hence, as it seems to us, both the naivety and the energy of their*

writing. . . . They talk something like angels and something like sailors and stable-boys.

One clue as to how people in the Middle Ages observed reality comes from bestiaries—books that included both real and allegorical creatures. These were medieval bestsellers. Between 200 CE and the thirteenth-century, writers and artists created more than a hundred different bestiaries. These included the African animals that were illustrated in the earliest Greek bestiary, as well as Northern fauna. From the perspective of folks living in the British Isles during the Middle Ages, the crocodile and the elephant were no less mysterious and amazing than the unicorn and the dragon. If readers had never seen an actual unicorn . . . well, most of them had never seen a lion or an ape, either. And each creature, whether familiar or otherworldly, had something important to say to the human heart and mind. The same creature often represented both Jesus and the devil, a paradoxical dichotomy that blurred dualistic black-and-white notions of good and evil. Each and every creature had some edifying symbolic meaning. The phoenix who rose from its ashes represented the resurrection of Christ. Bats navigate the dark because they have a God-given inner light that guides them through darkness.

And did you know rabbits ride on snails and have jousting events? There was a method to this madness; rabbits reminded medieval people that creatures that appear powerless can triumph over dominant forces in a society.

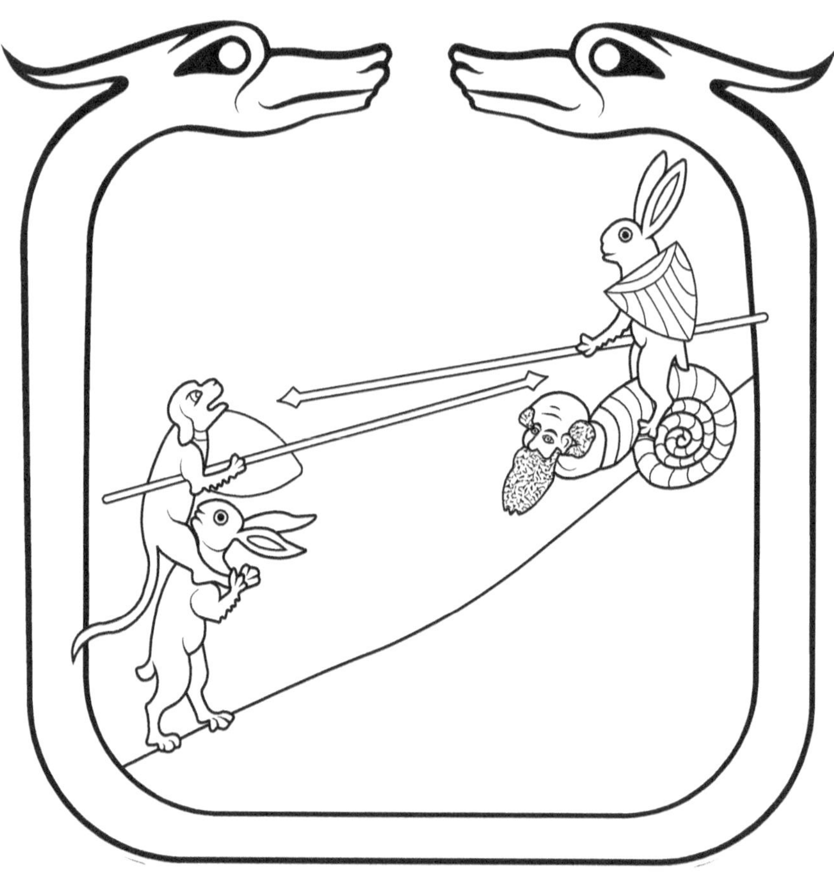

Rabbits and snails are the most harmless of animals, but we can imagine a topsy-turvy world where rabbits become warriors (and snails are their steeds). At first glance, this seems like a joke, but the reality is what Jesus shows us with his life: the victory of the less powerful over the dominant members of society, as well as the sheer joy and laughter of turning the world upside down. Warrior rabbits are a subversive symbol for all those who are downtrodden and weak in the eyes of the world.

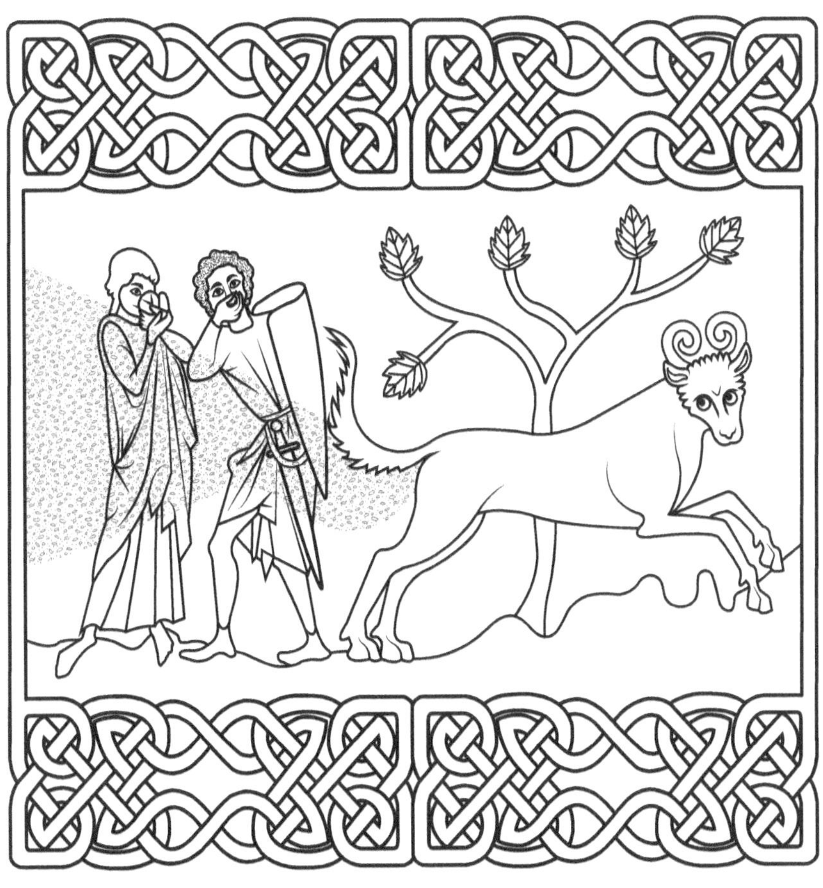

The bonnacon is a beast with a head like a bull, but with horns that curl in toward each other. Because these horns are useless for defense, the bonnacon has another weapon: when pursued, the beast expels its dung in a noxious gas that travels a great distance (as far as two acres), and burns anything it touches. In this way God provides for the bonnacon, says the medieval bestiary, for God despises not that which humans regard as useless or unworthy.

Wouldn't you like the bonnacon card for a fantasy role-playing game? In the medieval mind, even the bonnacon has its illustrative purpose, a reminder that God protects creatures that humans regard as useless or unlikable.

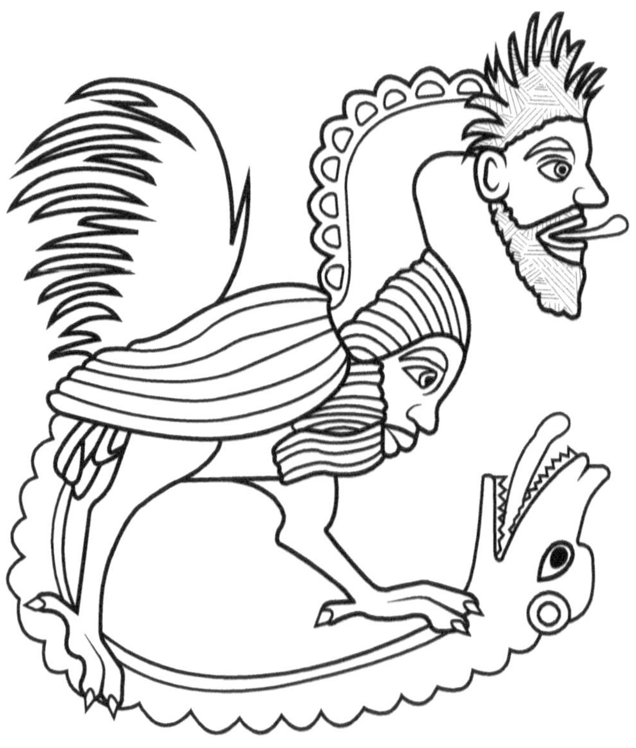

A depiction of a monstrosity from an illuminated Bible. According to the medieval worldview, monstrosities live at the Earth's edges, where they come in many shapes and forms. They defy human-made boundaries and encourage us to regard them with fear but also with wonder and curiosity, daring us to see in them the parts of our own selves that lie outside the norm, parts we may keep concealed, even from ourselves.

Bestiaries give us an important clue to the "why" of the bizarre medieval portrayals of the world. *Every aspect of the physical world taught a lesson.* Nature was "God's first book." In the psalmist's words, "The heavens are telling the glory of God; and the firmament proclaims his handiwork. Day to day pours forth speech, and night to night declares knowledge" (Psalm 19:1 NRSV). Since natural objects could proclaim God's truths, things like stars, trees, and even stones were imbued with sentience. This perspective, a legacy of older beliefs, was supported by Scripture like this one: "For you shall go out in joy and be led back in peace; the mountains and the hills before you shall burst into song, and all the trees of the field shall clap their hands" (Isaiah 55:12 NRSV).

The medieval world was therefore a magical and God-saturated place. Pigs and scullery maids, angels and demons, clouds, dragons, mice, and the service of Mass—all these things that seem oddly combined to our minds were unified in medieval thinking because they were all agents of God's self-revelation. In the Middle Ages, people refused to confine the Divine.

We may not be prone to decorating places of worship with such commonplace objects as people did eight hundred years ago, but we still see the sacred in Nature. The legendary Scottish-born naturalist John Muir said he'd rather be in the mountains thinking about God than in church wishing he were in the mountains—and that is also why I'm one of the facilitators for a local Forest Church gathering. Monthly, on a Saturday morning, a group meets at a trailhead or park and ventures into the wilds together to experience Spirit in the landscape, the trees, or the birds. We've gathered makings for wild teas, birdwatched with binoculars, trudged through snow, collected fall leaves into patterns, and improvised chants around a blazing bonfire at night. In all these ways we still experience that sense of the Holy that people long ago perceived in Nature.

And what about our animal friends? Are they not agents of God's grace? I've learned as much about God's kindness from our dogs and cats as I have from humans. I know a woman whose life was saved by her cat, which persistently ran back and forth yowling to summon help when the cat's owner was fallen and unconscious. This woman said her cat was in fact an angel, and who am I to argue? The folks who carved the Green Man in their churches and painted foxes on their floors shared this same sense of Divine presence in creatures.

And there are still places where holiness refuses to be pigeonholed. The Dalai Lama, regarded by millions of people as a model of enlightenment, can be seen on several YouTube videos laughing about inconvenient times to fart (that is, on airplanes, and while meditating with a group in silence). He even shifts his weight to share a bit of cheeky humor. As evidenced by their art, Europeans in the twelfth century would have appreciated his Holiness the Dalai Lama's earthy authenticity.

A bit later, in the fourteenth century, the famous mystic Julian of Norwich even saw Divine love and delight in the workings of our digestive system, including the rectum and anus. She wrote:

For God does not hold back from a single aspect of Creation, nor does the Divine One disdain to serve us in the simplest and most ordinary ways. Think how neatly our food is contained within our bodies, digested, and then is emptied out as needed, like a lovely drawstring purse that opens and closes. God is completely comfortable with all our bodies' activities; none of them offend the Divine Presence, for all our bodies' natural functions are Divine vehicles, filled with the love God bears us whose souls are made in the Divine likeness. (All Shall Be Well: A Modern-Language Version of the Revelation of Julian of Norwich, Anamchara Books)

The idea that the whole of reality is imbued with spiritual meaning can be termed sacramental. A sacrament, according to the website of U.S. Catholic bishops, has "a visible and invisible reality, a reality open to all the human senses but grasped in its God-given depths with the eyes of faith," and the specific sacraments defined by the Church include the Eucharist. The appearance of the Green Man in churches coincides with the timing of a new theological emphasis in the Western Christian tradition regarding the Eucharist: the real presence of Christ in the bread and wine. Pope Gregory VII (who was Supreme Pontiff from 1073 to 1085) decreed "the bread and wine placed upon the altar are, by the mystery of the sacred prayer and the words of the Redeemer, substantially changed into the true and life-giving flesh and blood of Jesus Christ our Lord." At the same time, tales of the Holy Grail captured the Western imagination, fueling the sense of Divine magic filling the world.

In medieval times, religion soaked into every nook and cranny of daily existence. Believing that bread and wine were the actual salvation-giving body and blood of Christ, it wasn't hard to imagine that cows, clouds, and troubadours were also imbued with holy nature.

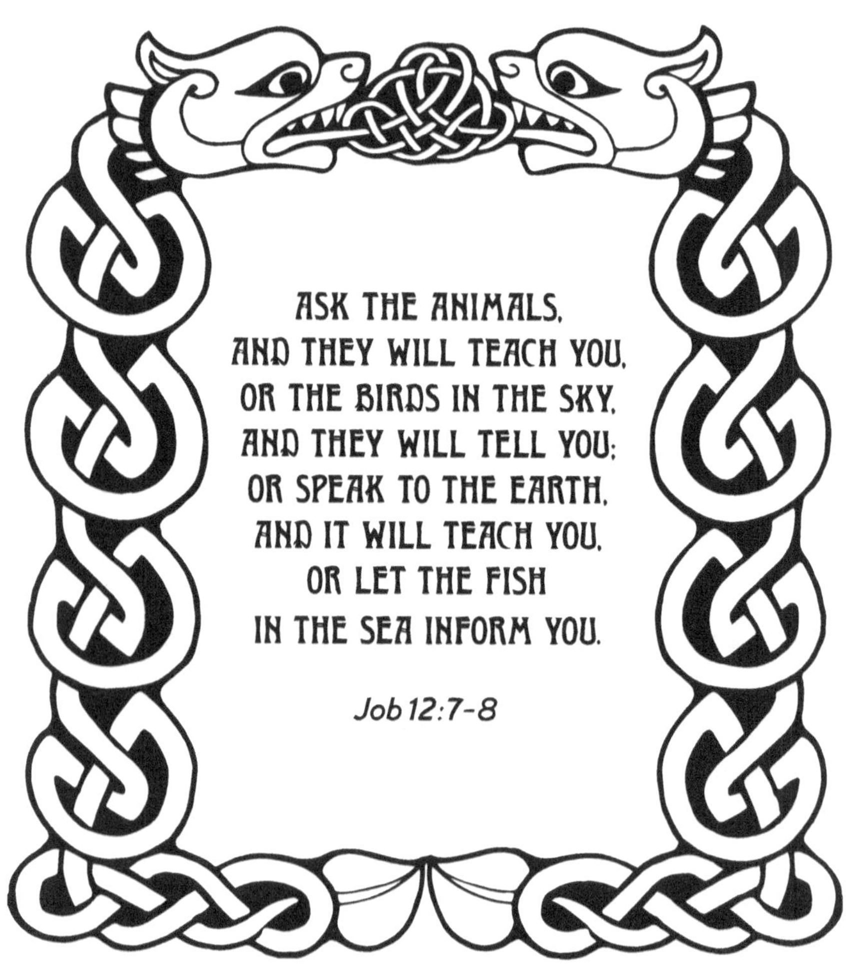
ASK THE ANIMALS,
AND THEY WILL TEACH YOU,
OR THE BIRDS IN THE SKY,
AND THEY WILL TELL YOU;
OR SPEAK TO THE EARTH,
AND IT WILL TEACH YOU,
OR LET THE FISH
IN THE SEA INFORM YOU.

Job 12:7-8

Hildegard of Bingen (1098–1179) added to this perception of the God-infused physical realm. Hildegard was a German abbess, writer, musical and theatric composer, philosopher, mystic, and polymath. A dominant theme in her writings is *veriditas*, which translates to "greenness." Hildegard did not invent the term—it had been used by other theologians since the fourth century—but she was part of its growing popularity in the twelfth century. Theologically, the term indicated the understanding that as God creates and sustains the Earth, so God creates "new life" through Christ in human hearts and then causes this life to flourish.

Veriditas—the greenness of Creation—points to God's presence in all things. This Divine inner essence allows both human and vegetative life to reproduce, grow, bring joy, and heal. One expression of Divine indwelling is the healing power of plants. Hildegard wrote, "O most honored Greening Force, You who roots in the Sun; You who lights up, in shining serenity, within a wheel that earthly excellence fails to comprehend. You are enfolded in the weaving of divine mysteries."

Veriditas and the sacramental worldview of the twelfth century help us understand the larger world of the medieval imagination where salvation and pigs and Green Men mingle.

And while Hildegard helps us understand the Green Man's appeal in the twelfth century, a more recent scholar revolutionized our modern understanding of the Green Man. Let's journey on now into the first half of the twentieth century. It's like *Downton Abbey* meets the Green Man.

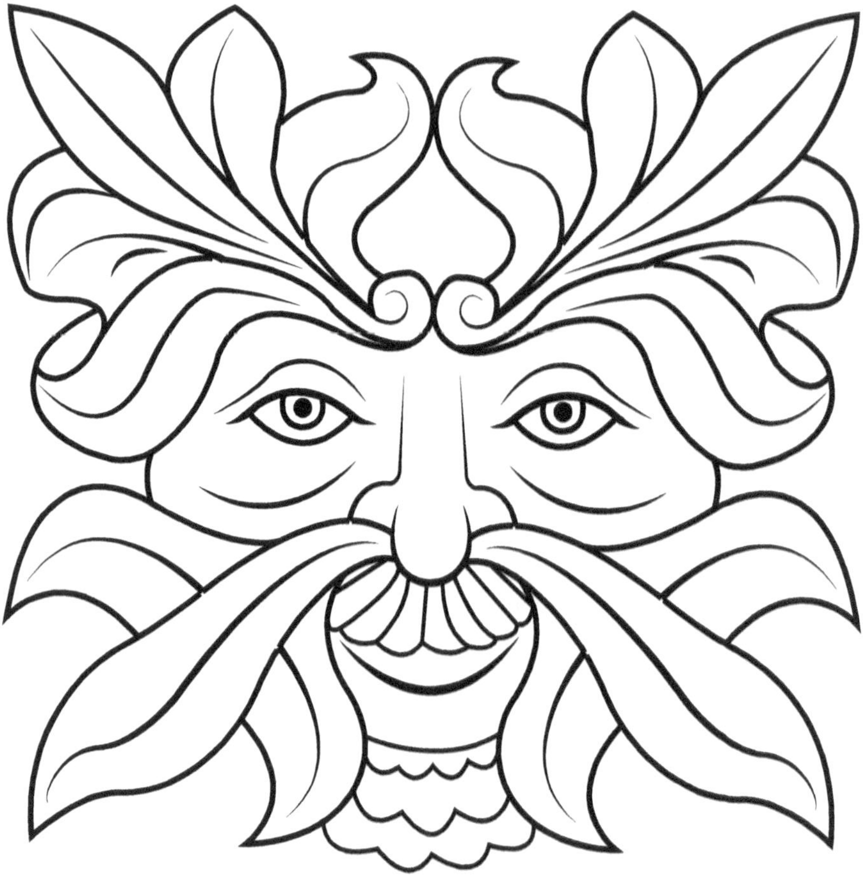

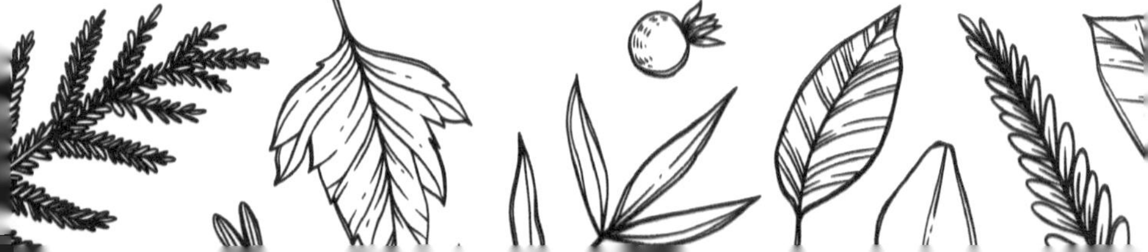

A rather dapper Green Man, sporting acanthus leaves, based on a twelfth-century image found in St. Mary de Crypt Church in Gloucester, England.

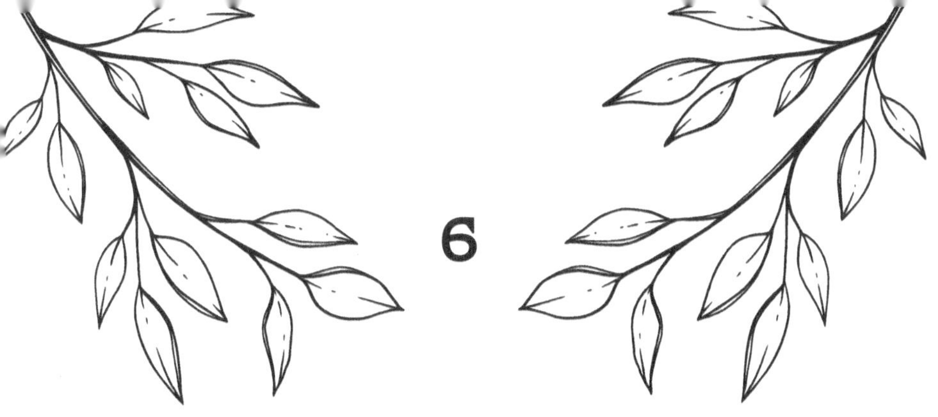

6

The Green Man Is
Introduced to Society

Sometimes when I'm staring at a Green Man in an old church, I wonder, *What sorts of people have stood here in the centuries past and looked at this same fellow? What were their impressions?* Oh, to have a time machine!

I like to imagine an especially important encounter between a Green Man and Lady Julia Somerset, Duchess of Raglan, that occurred somewhere around 1931. The particular Green Man in question lives in the Church of St. Jerome Llangwm, a Norman era church in Pembrokeshire, Wales. He resides on an arch in the chancel (the part of a church where the priest serves communion). His meeting with a young folklorist changed Green Man history.

I only know Lady Julia from a couple of portrait photos at the National Portrait Gallery and a few brief descriptions. I imagine her as someone like Lady Mary Crawley, the eldest daughter of an aristocratic (and fictional) family on the Masterpiece Theater television series *Downton Abbey*. Both Lady Julia and Lady Mary are fashionable, elegant, and self-assured; they take advantage of the greater opportunities afforded to their gender following the end of the first world war.

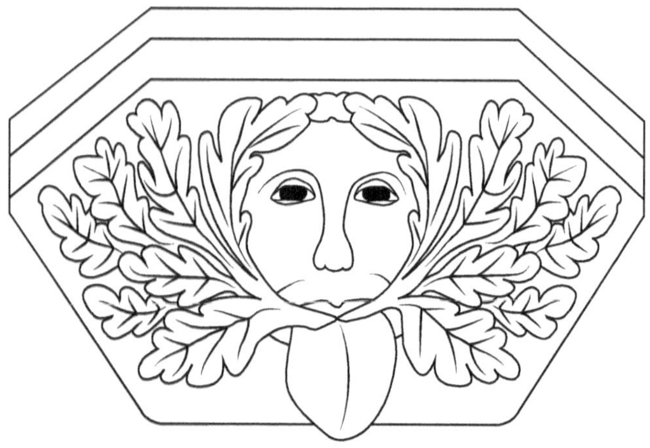

This Green Man may be the one who impressed Lady Julia in the early twentieth century. He also has two brothers in the same church.

When she meets the Green Man, Lady Somerset is in her thirties and is married to Fitzroy Somerset Fourth Baron of Raglan. Both Raglans are members of the Folklore Society. Their ideas are influenced by other folklorists, including James Frazier and Jessie Weston. Frazier's *The Golden Bough: A Study in Comparative Religion* suggests that today's Western religions stem from ancient belief in a harvest god who marries the Goddess, and who dies and rises again, representing the seasonal cycles. Weston's *From Ritual to Romance: An Account of the Holy Grail from Ancient Ritual to Christian Symbol* extends Frazer's thinking to the Arthurian Grail legends. Both books continue to hold enormous influence in popular thinking about mythology and religion today, especially in the burgeoning revival of ancient Earth-based religions. Books on the Grail, from *The Mists of Avalon* to *The Da Vinci Code*, follow ideas in Weston's book.

All of this shapes the fertile ground in Lady Julia's imagination when the vicar of Llangwm church directs her attention to the Green Man. She is fascinated! She writes later, "It seemed to me certain that it was a man and not a spirit, and moreover that *it was a "Green Man." So I named it*" (italics mine). But she wasn't the first to use that name.

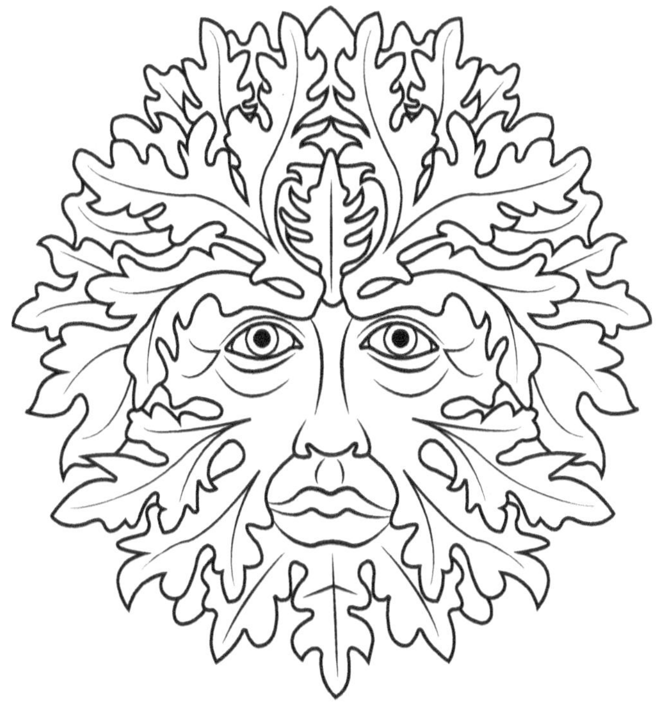

This Green Man, based on a modern-day wall plaque, is immediately recognizable to us as a "Green Man"—but without Lady Julia's article, we might have given him a different name. In fact, the Green Man might never have gained his place in our imagination without Lady Julia.

Although Lady Julia is often credited with coming up with the name "Green Man," the name had actually been around for a long time, since the seventeenth century or earlier. Always before, though, it had been used to refer to Jack in the Green (who we'll discuss more in chapter 9). But as high-society Brits became fascinated with folklore, they made the connection between Jack and the foliated heads in churches. Before Lady Julia's article was ever published, another antiquities scholar, C. J. P. Cave, had written:

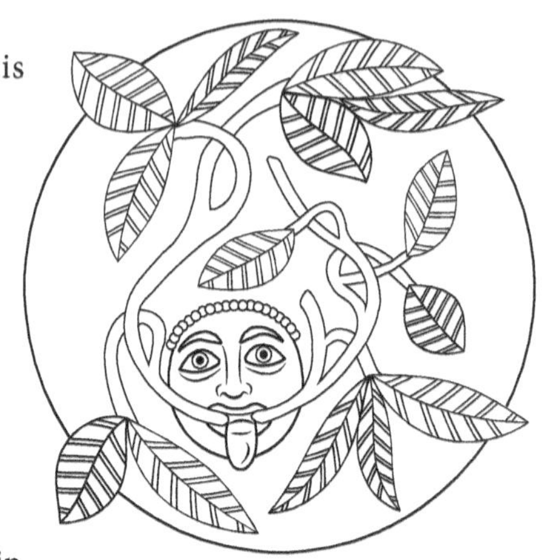

What is the soul of the Green Man? If you ask Lady Julia, he is a pre-Christian fertility god, who has gone undercover to infiltrate Christian churches in the Middle Ages.

One of the commonest of roof boss figures remains unexplored. This is the head with foliage coming from the mouth. It is found from Norman to the very end of Gothic times. It occurs in sculpture and in manuscripts. In the latter, it might be taken for the illuminator's fancy for drawing strange forms, but the definiteness of the motif and its wide diffusion make it likely that it had some meaning. Often the figures are impossible to distinguish from the foliage bosses around without field glasses, and sometimes only a photograph will reveal eyes peering out between foliage like a Jack in the green. . . . And may we not see this likeness a clue to the origin of the figure? One certainly goes back to pre-Christian times, may not the other? May not the leafy faces be what Sir James Fraser calls representatives of the tree spirit?

A few years later, Lady Julia reached a similar conclusion: "The fact is that unofficial paganism subsisted side by side with the official religion, and this explains the presence of the Green Man." According to this theory, our friend is the fertility god of ancient times, "the figure variously known as the Green Man, Jack-in-the-Green, Robin Hood, the King of May, and the Garland" and "Attis and Odin."

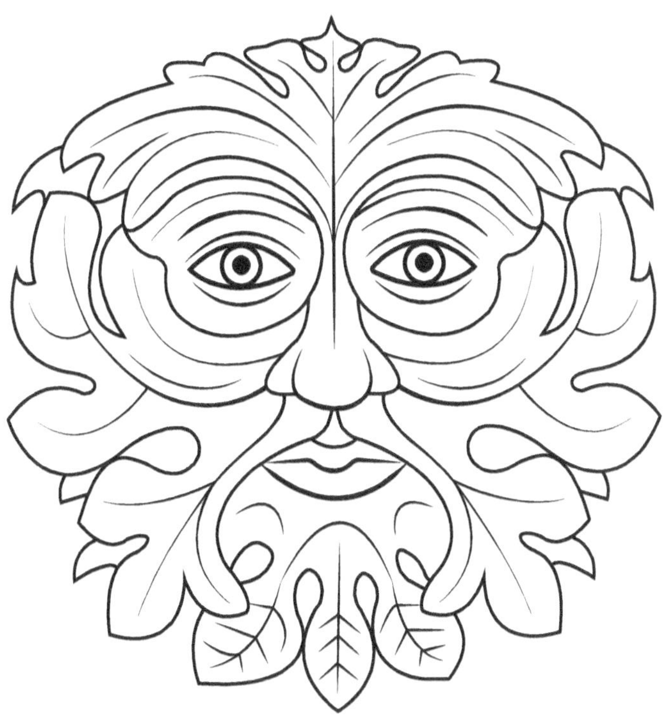

This Green Man is inspired by a doorknocker in Derbyshire, England.

The Duchess of Raglan was an outstanding scholar of her time, as were many of the other folklorists of her day, but theories about history are constantly challenged, and her belief that the Green Man portrays officially forbidden Pagan deities is now out of favor among historians. Alex Woodcock, an archaeologist with a PhD, an authority on Romanesque architecture, and a stonemason, writes in his *Beakheads* blog that Lady Raglan's identification of the Green Man as an undercover Pagan deity succeeded:

> *due in part to the prevailing opinion, during the middle decades of the twentieth century, of the medieval period as largely pagan. According to this understanding the bulk of the people had remained true to their pagan roots, despite centuries of Christianity, the church allowing their imagery into its buildings as a means to pacify and ultimately convert them. Such an understanding was dismantled in the 1970s and '80s as detailed historical surveys were undertaken and published, which revealed medieval Christianity to be far more complex and nuanced than had previously been understood. But nonetheless, the idea of the Green Man as a pagan totem persisted and is by far the most popular interpretation today.*

Still, we owe a huge debt to Lady Julia and her fellow folklore scholars—and their ideas make me wonder: What *were* the Green Man's roots? It's time to take a look at the Green Man's family tree.

Some people might look at any given Foliate Head
and feel it is a demon or a tortured soul.
Others might look at the same face and see . . .
a person green with viriditas;
a sympathetic and powerful entity
willing to intercede with God;
in short, a folk saint.
Thinking of the Green Man as a folk saint . . .
allows us to understand how a
figure rooted in paganism,
which once appeared on pagan temples,
could become, for medieval
Christians, a focal point.

—Stephen Winick

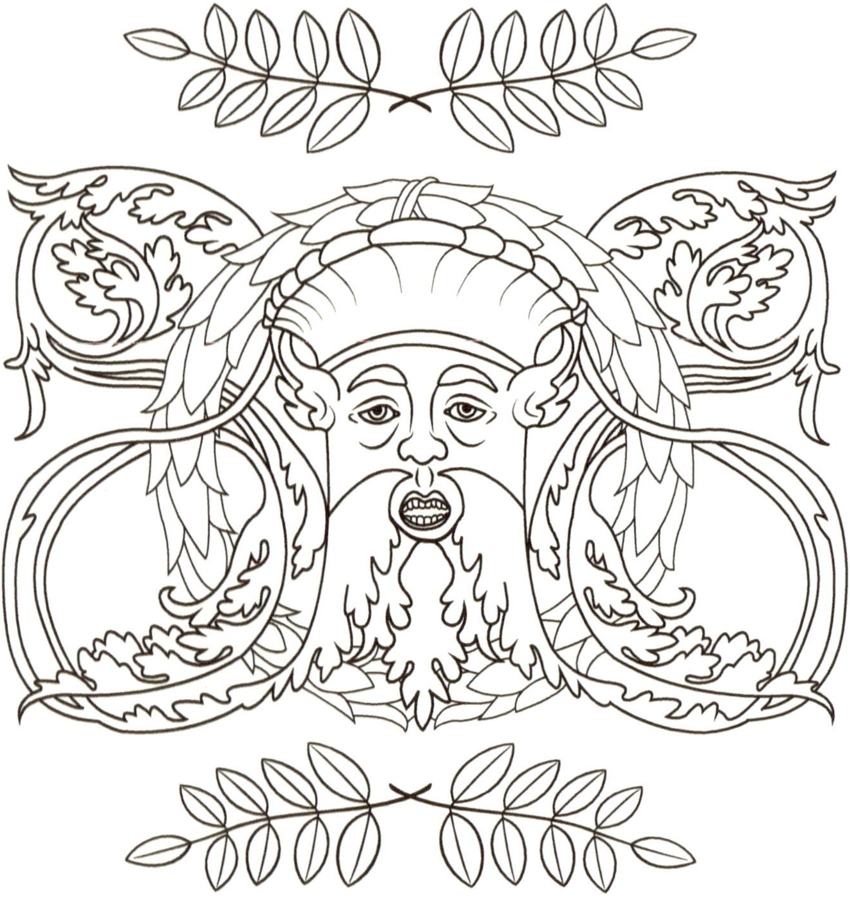

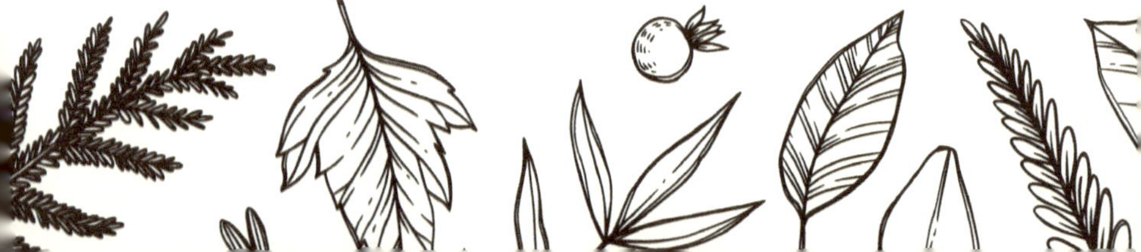

This Green Man was originally drawn by Hans Sebald Beham, a German print-maker who lived from 1500 to 1550.

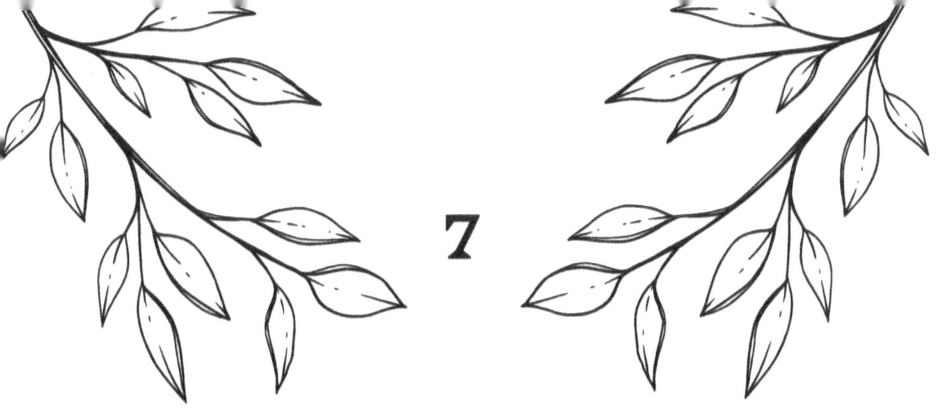

7

The Family Tree

Since Lady Raglan's day, there's been much written about the ancient roots of the Green Man's family tree, tracing his descent from ancient Nature deities and images from the Classical world. I look at pictures of these pre-medieval "Green Men," and I look at the faces in Gothic sanctuaries and wonder, "Was that really your great-great-great grandfather?"

When researching roots and relations, one must be cautious. Just because people look like they're related, doesn't make it so. In the town where I used to live there was a man who looked just like me, and we shared a friendship and common social circles. He was a teacher at a local school, and I worked for a time with the students in that school's creative writing course. One day I stepped into his classroom as he was about to step out and I agreed to watch the class for a few minutes; students were busy and didn't notice the exchange. A minute later one of his students walked up to the desk and started talking—he was look- ing right into my face, just a few feet away—going on and assuming I was his regular teacher. That's how close the resemblance was. People referred to us as "twins," though there was no blood relation between us, a reminder that resemblance doesn't prove family identity.

And if you've done much genealogy work you know how easily you can get off on the wrong branch researching the family tree. Let's say you are a Jones from Wales. You come upon a record of Ann and John Jones who had a daughter, Emily, in 1902. And you know that your great-grandmother was Emily Jones, born in Wales, in 1902. It's tempting to mark down another generation on the family tree, assuming Ann and John are the next generation going back in time. But, wait! Although this seems like an obvious connection, there were a surprising number of Jones from Wales, and there can be several Emilys born the same year. After more research, you discover a photocopy of your Emily Jones's baptismal record and you see that her parents were Richard and Evi—not Anne and John. Oops! This sort of mistake is common when people try to trace their family tree.

Likewise, we must be careful connecting dots in the Green Man's lineage. There are two easily made mistakes. First is the assumption that one artistic creation must be the inspiration for another. It's possible for artists to create similar motifs without any influence or knowledge of a previous artist's work; this has happened repeatedly throughout history.

Even if one image influences the artistic form of another, it's possible that the meaning of images has changed over time. A craftsman in the Romanesque era of the Middle Ages may copy the shape of a foliated head from ancient Roman times but have no idea what that image meant to a craftsman a thousand years earlier. The medieval artist would ascribe an entirely different name and symbolic meaning to that image, having no knowledge of the name and symbolism ascribed by the Roman era artist.

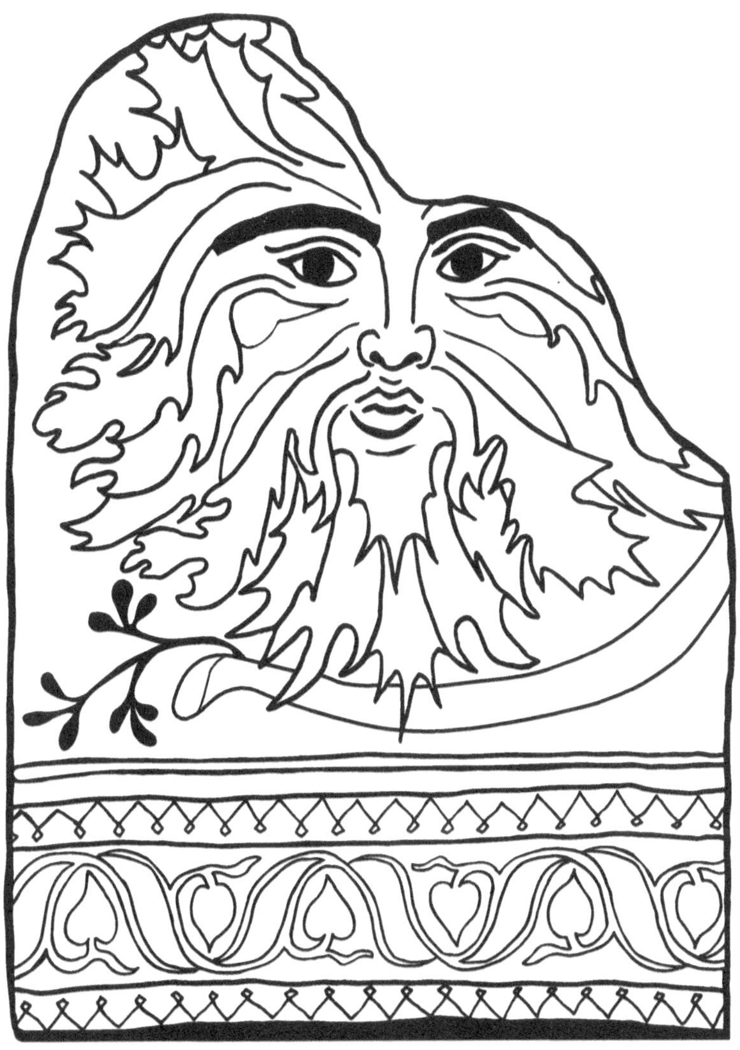

This floor mosaic (on display in the Istanbul Museum) from the late Roman era shows a foliated head that looks suspiciously like a Green Man—and yet its symbolism was likely quite different from that intended by Western Europeans several centuries later.

With that in mind, let's look at images that are similar to the later Green Man. As well as the ancient Middle Eastern figure Humbaba, there are also later Middle Eastern Green Men that have a strong visual resemblance to the medieval foliated heads.

We can also find family resemblance to the Green Man in sources geographically closer to his later medieval home, in the ancient art of the Celtic people. The Pfalzfeld pillar, from the fifth century BCE, for example, shows a head with shapes emerging from it that may be leaves. Whatever the exact meaning may have been, it's likely that the carving indicates the veneration of ancient Celtic peoples for disembodied heads.

Disembodied heads held great power within ancient Celtic thought. According to the Welsh myth cycle *The Mabinogion*, when the warrior-hero Bran was mortally wounded, he asked his fellows to cut his head off, telling them to take the head with them and it would continue to dispense wisdom. They did so, and the head fulfilled its promise. Eventually, the head was buried in London, where

This carving from Hatra, Iraq, may depict the ancient Mesopotamian folk figure Humbaba, Lord of the Cedar Woods. It does resemble the foliated heads that Norman stonemasons carved on medieval churches, but there may be no direct historical link between them.

it protected Britain from invaders. The tradition of Bran's head continues to today, as ravens are kept at the tower of London and many tourists hear the story that if the Tower of London ravens are lost or fly away, the Crown will fall and Britain with it. Bran in the old Celtic tongues means "raven," and the ravens are a remembrance of Bran's head protecting the Isle.

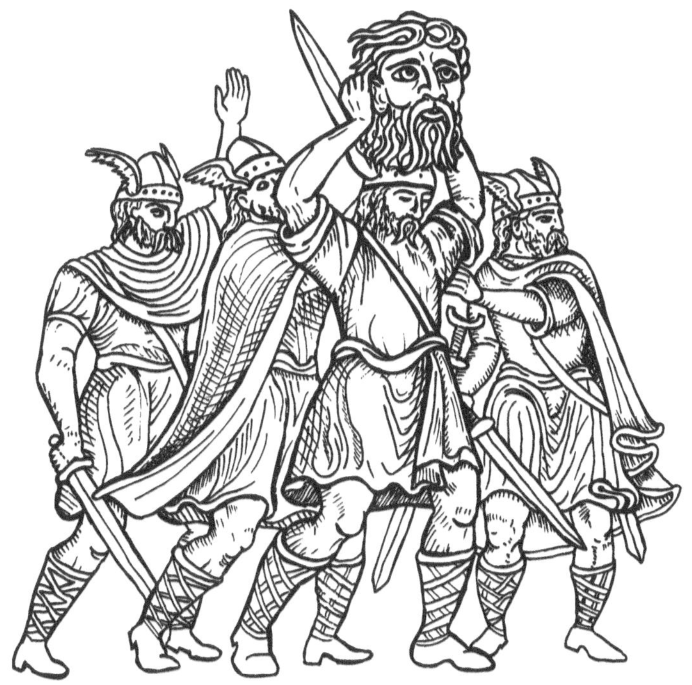

The Grail myth also holds resonances of the Celtic cult of the severed head. Originally, the Grail was not a chalice but a platter, and in one Welsh version of the story, the Grail holds a severed head, reminiscent of Bran's head. It is tempting to see echoes of the Celtic head cult in the Green Man's appeal through medieval times, though such a connection is merely speculative.

In the centuries before and after Christ, "all roads led to Rome." From the time of Julius Caesar up until the collapse of the Roman Empire, Latin governance, customs, and art dominated the Western world, and for a thousand years after the fall of Rome, European culture attempted to re-create Roman standards. So, when looking at any icon of the Middle Ages—such as the Green Man—it would make sense to look for Roman roots in the family tree. And there are in fact Roman images that bear a strong resemblance to the Green Man.

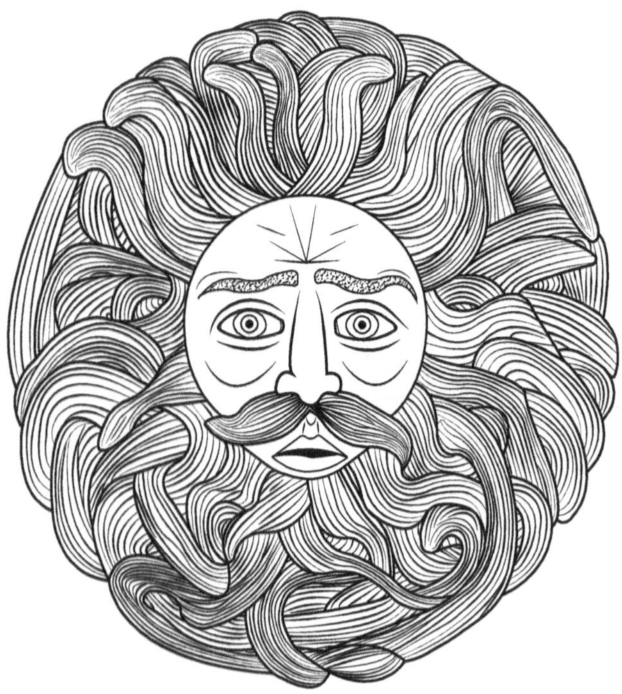

This image, based on a carving from the ancient hot baths in Bath, England, is often cited as a Roman-era Green Man. It's also a good example of how ambiguous the meaning of art can be, since the figure's beard and hair have been explained variously as serpents, sunbeams, seaweed, or foliage.

The tendrils of the Green Man's family tree extend from the ancient Hellenistic world through the Byzantine era. The Byzantine era links the time between ancient Rome and the Middle Ages; this was when the Roman Empire had moved from the banks of the Tiber to the city of Constantinople (named after the Roman Emperor Constantine, responsible for the conversion of the Roman Empire to Christianity). Constantinople was also known as Byzantium, and today is Istanbul, Turkey. Could the foliated heads found from this era have helped to shape the Green Man we know and love?

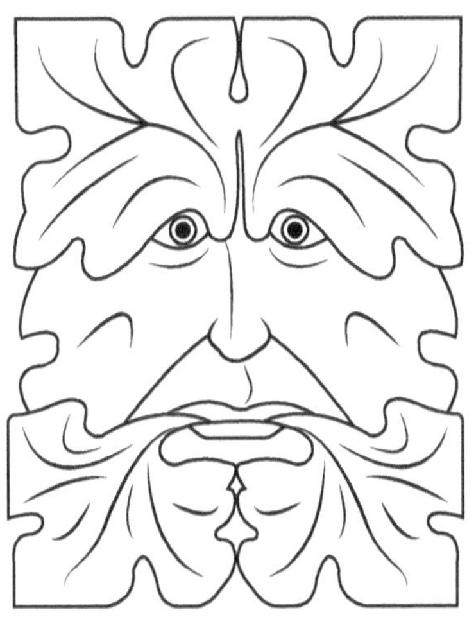

This acanthus-sprouting head is based on a carving that dates back to the first century. It was originally found in Rome and is now in the Musée de Vésone, Périgueux, Dordogne, France. The image has been identified as Pan, the god of Nature who connects the Divine with the natural world. There are numerous examples of these "leaf faces" from the Classical world. They appear to be leaves pressed into the contours of human visage—not so much vegetable-human hybrids, as vegetation mimicking human form.

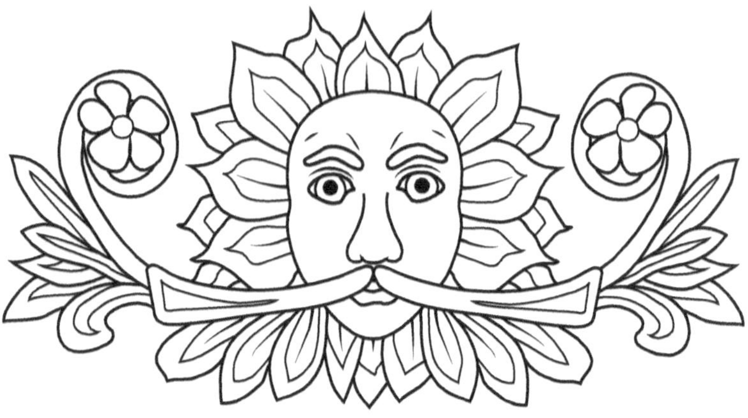

A Green Man from the Byzantine era is on the Tomb of St. Abre (4th–5th century CE) now in the Church of St. Hilaire-le-Grand at Poitiers, France. If this Green Man was secretly inserted into the interior of a Norman church, no one would think it out of place; it's a perfect example of a foliated face. It's also very unusual during this time frame—only a few examples of Green Men from this historical period have been identified.

As we continue to climb up the Green Man's (speculative) family tree, we find ourselves in the Early Middle Ages. The greatest art form of this period was illuminated sacred texts. As the Latin alphabet and reverence for the Bible spread into newly Christianized lands, ancient Celtic and Gemanic designs combined with the artistic heritage of Greece and Rome, flowering in extraordinary works of paint, gilding, and ink on velum (parchments made from animal skins).

Today, tourists wait in line to see the Book of Kells in Trinity Library and reproductions of the artwork abound. I love to get lost in a book with full-size glossy pages reproduced from the Book of Kells or the equally amazing Lindisfarne Gospels. The designs seem almost infinitely complex and interwoven: motifs from Middle Eastern carpets, Roman mosaics, Neolithic temples, and Byzantine churches join in a wildly flowing and brightly colored dance. And the Green Man—or his cousins—does emerge from some of the pages of these Early Middle Ages tomes.

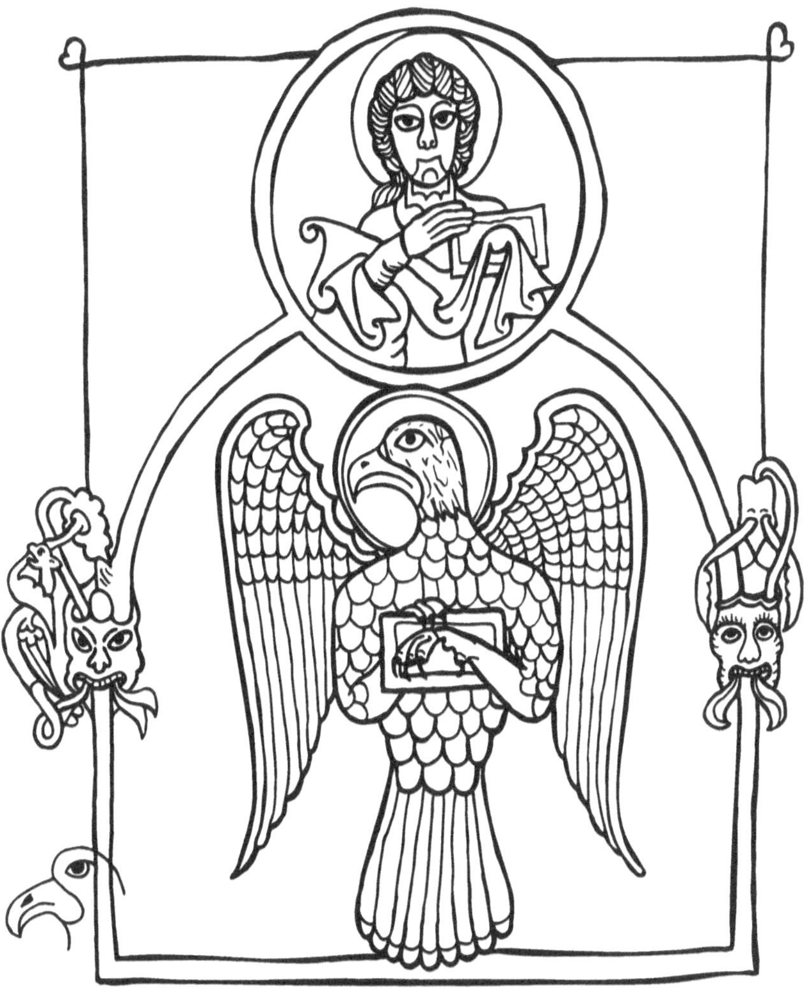

These two Green Men flank the eagle, the symbol of John's Gospel, in the Book of Cerne, a ninth-century Anglo-Saxon prayer book, whose pages include Celtic, Anglo-Saxon, and Mediterranean influences.

Here, I feel confident that we have a link in the Green Man's family tree. These Green Men that appear in the Book of Cerne and Codex Egberti are similar to the Green Men on the baptismal font in Brecon Cathedral—perhaps carved at the same time as the Codex Egberti was manufactured—and they also bear a resemblance to the Green Men at Kilpeck (which we'll visit in the next chapter). These Green Men appear in the context of Christian faith, and there is artistic continuity from the Byzantine period into the later Middle Ages.

It's likely that some of the Green Men who appear so commonly in Norman churches during the Middle Ages are in fact artistic reproductions of images produced in the ancient Roman world. But remember a point made in the beginning of this chapter: *Even if one image influences the artistic form of another, it's possible that the meaning of images has changed over time.* I very much doubt that a stone mason in the eleventh-century, seeing a Roman mosaic with a foliated head,

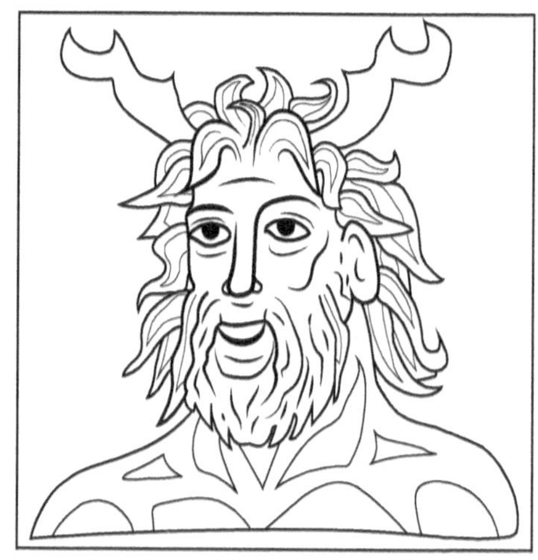

This drawing of a second-century Roman mosaic portrays a man with vegetation coming from his head—but it's more likely he's a sea god (with seaweed hair rather than leaves and crab claws for horns) and not a Green Man. Still, these ancient images all point to a unity between humanity and Nature, an understanding based on the foundational sense that a deep and magical Mystery is at play in reality.

would think, "I'll just carve a Roman river god into the chancel of this church." He may have been inspired by the art and moved to create his interpretation of that leafy visage, but he wouldn't necessarily know the words and stories that went with that artistic inspiration. He'd more likely think about the foliated face in terms of stories and symbols prevalent in his own time.

So we may have found the inspiration for the *artistic form* of the Green Man, but we haven't yet gotten to the root of *meaning* in the medieval Green Man. For this, we will have to investigate further.

Beloved Pan,
and all ye other gods who haunt this place,
give me beauty in the inward soul;
and may my outward and inward self
be at one.

—Plato

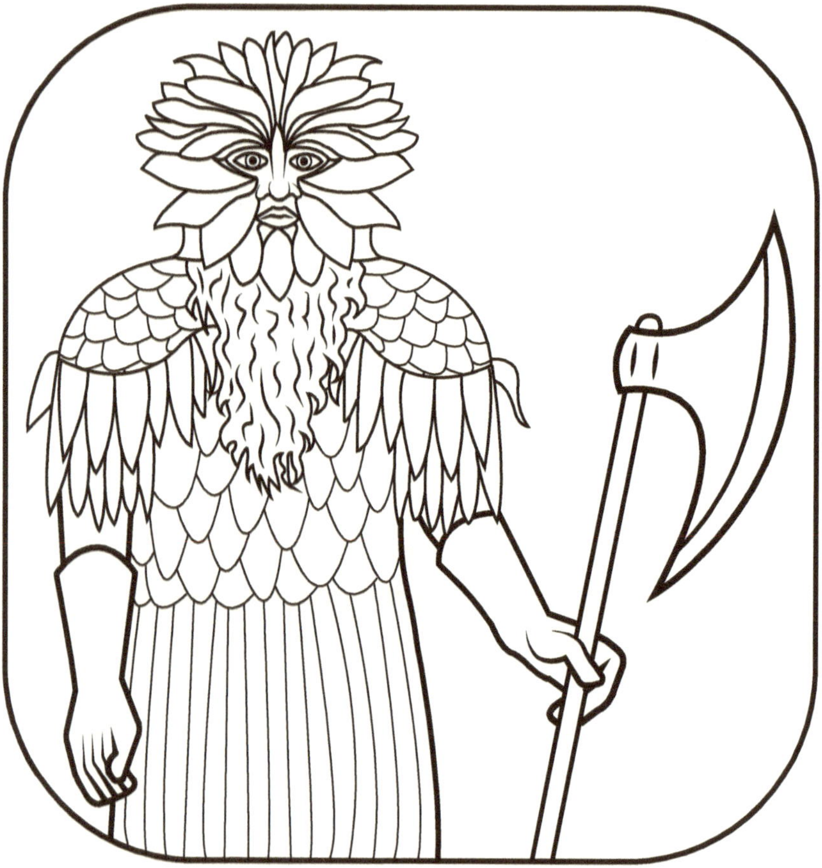

The Green Man's story has on occasion merged with the legend of the Green Knight.

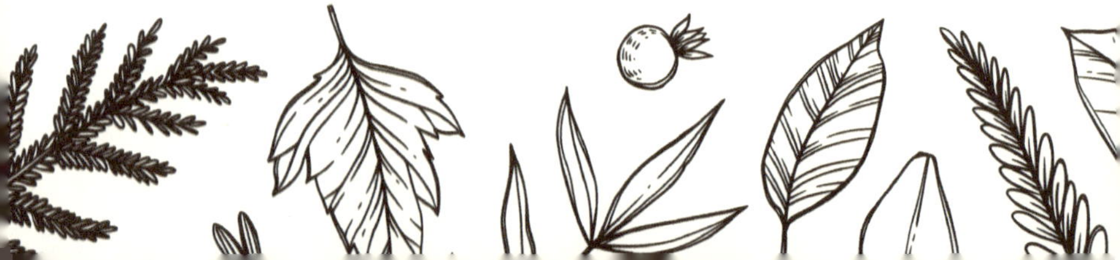

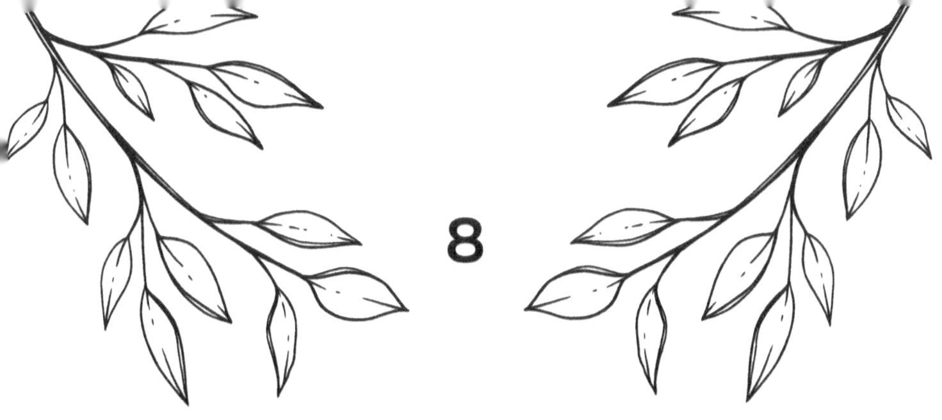

8

The Green Man in King Arthur's Court

Do you have any odd relatives in your family? You know, the ones who make gatherings so much more interesting, and then provide occasion for more talk after they are gone? The Green Knight, a character from Arthurian legend, may be the Green Man's crazy relative—at least some medievalists think so. But he's as fearsome as he is amusing.

Speaking of weird relatives, some family members might think that's—*ahem*—me. If so, I blame my parents for encouraging me to read and letting me follow my own interests. In elementary school, I got into Arthurian mythology and it hooked me. It also played no small role in the strange interests I still pursue in adulthood.

Have you ever seen something that seemed both strange *and* familiar? That would be the definition of an oxymoron, but that's what I found as a boy reading the legends of the Round Table. Characters had such outlandish ideas, the names were unfamiliar, and events happened randomly. Knights ride into dark tangled forests just on a whim, where they meet hermits and strange women and shape-shifting beings. They are given riddles or dares. Sometimes the stories end but give no explanation for events, either for the reader or for the characters in the stories. Although these tales were odd, reading them as a child, I felt like I belonged in these stories. They were easy to imagine and, having glimpsed the imaginary realms of Camelot and Albion, I wanted to enter in and stay.

I asked my father why I felt both captivated and mystified by Arthurian legends and he said to me, "Kenneth, these are the stories of our people from long ago. *They tell us who we are.*" In the years since then I've earned a degree in English, then an advanced degree in religion and have taught in college about ideas like "archetypes" and "the hero's journey." And in all that time, the best definition of *myth* is the explanation my father gave me so long ago. Myths are the stories "that tell us who we are."

That explains how a story can be both strange and familiar. Celtic and medieval legends seem strange because they occur in a world so distant from our own, in time, culture, and language; yet they speak to us in our soul (*psyche* is the Greek word for soul). They communicate to our subconscious and ancestral memories, and hence wield great power.

One such tale is that of the Green Man's purported family member, the Green Knight. He is as bizarre as any character in the strange Arthurian realm, literally bigger than life, an enigma even to the other characters in the medieval tale.

He is already old before he appears in the tale of *Sir Gawain and the Green Knight,* written in the late Middle Ages. A pre-Christian Irish tale of the hero Cuchullain tells of a shape-shifting mage named Cu Roi, which follows a similar plot as the later medieval tale. Although the collections of tales about Arthur and his companions were written during the Norman era and afterward, the characters, plots, and devices in these tales often harken from the mists of the deep Celtic past.

The tale of the Green Knight proceeds thusly: A strange and terrible being rides into Arthur's court amid the Round Table Yuletide feast; he is a giant. "And all garbed in glittering green this giant and his gear. In his one hand he held a holly branch, that is greatest in green when groves are bare, and an axe in his other, one huge, monstrous." He issues a challenge to exchange blows—which Sir Gawain accepts. When Gawain cuts off the Green Knight's head, the green giant picks up his severed head, puts it back in place, and tells Gawain to meet him in a year hence so that the Green Knight can deliver his blow to Gawain's neck.

Spring and summer come and go; then, after All Hallows' Day, Gawain, "for good known, and, as purified gold, void of every villainy, with virtues adorned," embarks to meet the Green Knight and fulfill his half of the bargain. Gawain wanders through tangled woods, combats dragon, wolf, and Wodewose, sleeps in the rain and on the frosted ground, praying to Mary all along the way.

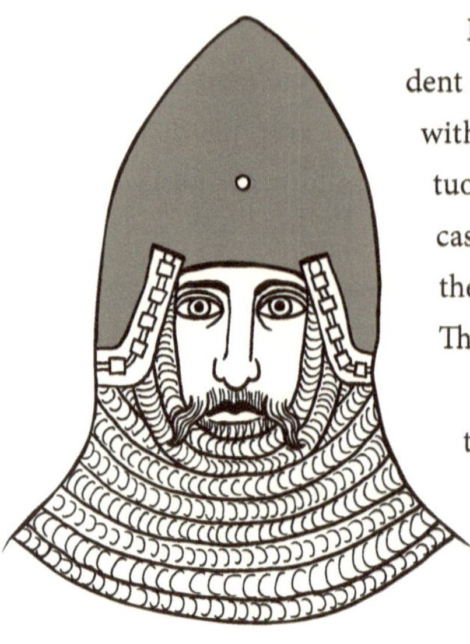

Chain mail like this was designed to protect the neck from blows. Nevertheless, heads were lost in battle, and decapitated heads play a significant role in ancient symbolism, both in the Celtic world and also in India and the Near East. In the 13th century, the great Sufi poet Rumi wrote, "When you see in your pathway a severed head, which is rolling towards your land, ask of it, ask of it, the secrets of the heart: for from it you will learn the hidden mystery of the Divine."

Eventually he arrives at a resplendent castle where the porter greets him with hospitality, and he feasts sumptuously in a rich hall. The lord of the castle is most gracious, and the lady of the castle is breathtakingly beautiful. There is also an old hag in the castle.

The lord tells Sir Gawain that the Green Knight's chapel is nearby. He invites Gawain to stay and rest before his encounter with the Green Knight, also inviting Gawain to a game: they will part during each day, and at day's end, they will exchange whatever they happen to obtain during the day. Gawain agrees to this.

Each day, the lord of the castle goes hunting and harvests his prey, and each day, the beautiful lady presses herself on Gawain. He is tempted to sin, but the Virgin Mary protects Gawain as reward for his prayers. On the first day, the lady of the castle kisses him, and Gawain passes that on to her husband in the evening. The second day, she gives him a brace of kisses, which he also passes on. Then on the third day, the lady gives him three kisses and a magical green woven belt, which she promises will protect him. Gawain in turn passes the three kisses to his host, but he does not mention the magical garland.

On New Year's morning, Gawain and his hosts sadly part, and he makes his way to the Chapel of the Green Knight, which is overgrown with vegetation, dark and ill boding. The Green Knight greets Gawain and congratulates his integrity in keeping their appointment. Gawain prepares himself for the Green Knight's axe: "Strike but the one stroke, and I shall stand still and offer no hindrance, come work as you like, I swear."

The first two axe blows, the Green Knight pulls short of Gawain's neck, and on the third strike, he only cuts Gawain slightly. Then, the Green Knight reveals that he is the lord of the Castle who has been Gawain's host. He withheld the first two blows because Gawain was completely honest on the first two days of their daily exchange, and the slight cut is because Gawain was honest about the kiss but not the green belt. The Green Knight embraces Gawain and invites him back to the castle for revels. Gawain then returns to Arthur's court and tells his story; Arthur decrees that the Knights of the Round Table shall each wear a green sash as memento of this amazing adventure.

It's typical of Arthurian myth, both strange and compelling. There's obviously a lot going on beneath the surface of this tale. Medieval scholar John Speirs, building on the work of both Weston and Frazer as Lady Raglan had before him, wrote:

> *The Green Knight whose head is chopped off at his own request and who is yet as miraculously or magically alive as ever, bears an unmistakable relation to the Green Man—the Jack in the Green or the Wild Man of the village festivals of England and Europe. He is in fact no other than a recrudescence in poetry of the Green Man. . . . He is the descendent of*

the Vegetation or Nature god of almost universal and imme-morial tradition whose death and resurrection mythologizes the annual death and re-birth of nature.

C.S. Lewis wrote that the Green Knight is a living "coincidence of opposites"—"half giant, yet wholly a 'lovely' knight'; full of demo-niac energy, yet in his own house, as jolly as a Dickensian Christmas host; now exhibiting a ferocity so gleeful that it is almost genial, and now a geniality so outrageous that it borders on the ferocious; half boy or buffoon in his shouts and laughter and jumpings; yet at the end . . . with the tranquil superiority of an angelic being."

The tale of the Green Knight came to my mind when I was visiting the Parish Church of St. Mary and St. David in Kilpeck, Herefordshire, which shares that same strange and compelling, myth-infused char-acter. The Welsh border region in its entirety is a liminal place—an in-between landscape where modernity and history, fact and legend, English and Celtic, hill and village all intersect. Since Roman times, differing cul-tures, with their passions, hatreds, and tales, have mated and killed, merged and contested there.

This unusual full-bodied Green Man, based on a carving from a choir stall in Winchester Cathedral, bears a sword and a shield, indi-cating that his creator might have seen some connection between the Green Man and the Green Knight.

It was a lovely spring day as Marsha and I drove up to the Kilpeck Church. I'd long wished to see this rural marvel of Romanesque art and was not disappointed. The church was built beside the local Norman castle, but now that keep is reduced to a picturesque ruin atop a grassy motte and bailey; when we were there, a flock of sheep grazed beneath the fallen ramparts. The land was already sacred before these buildings were erected: the castle and church were built near springs, ancient yews, and on a ley line.

The church is an artistic tour-de-force, with the doorway, arches, windows, and eaves ornately carved with intertwining and fantastical images. It is representative of the Hereford School of architecture, which incorporates Celtic, Saxon, Viking, and French motifs. The church is dedicated to the Virgin Mary and St. David of Wales, reflecting the Welsh-Norman character of the Marches. It's a wild menagerie and pastiche of early-medieval life, with magical creatures like manticores and ouroboroses and a head disgorging serpents, along with people making music and dancing, a dog and a hare, and an iconic Sheela. It seems as if the lord of the adjacent castle wanted his chapel to contain as much embellishment as that contained in nearby Hereford Cathedral.

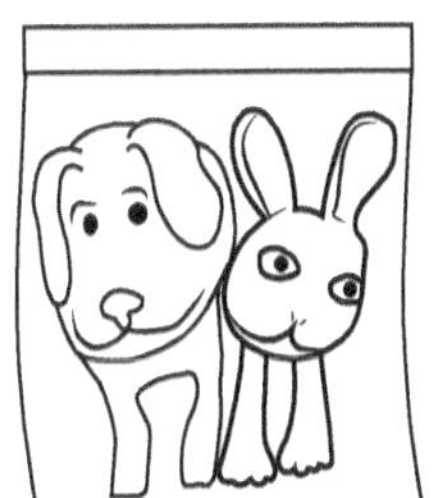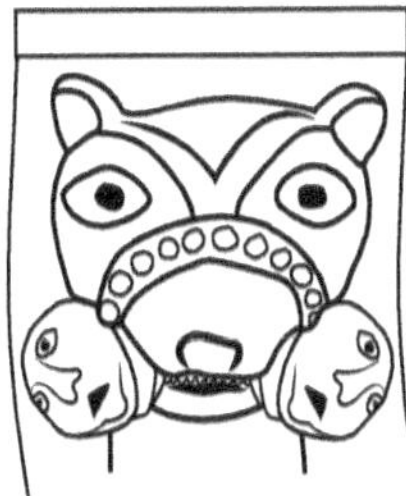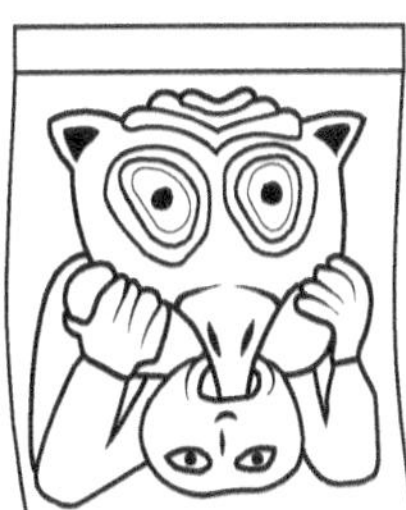

Some of the Kilpeck Church carvings: (from left to right), a dog and a hare, a bear eating sinners, and a birdman. The style of many of the carvings seems like modern-day cartoon illustrations.

The prevalence of Nature motifs brings the outdoors into the church—or vice versa, while the surreal style of the figures creates a "thin place" suspended between mundane reality and legend. The exterior of the church seems situated in the faerie realm, whereas the inside is a peaceful and enfolding Christian space, dominated by Christ's apostles. As I walked slowly around the church and then inside, I could easily imagine the Norman lords and ladies and knights of the castle, along with Welsh peasants of the land, who lived in a world of strange powers, of Nature and magic intermingled. Entering the church, they passed from the realm of powers, both military and supernatural, to observe the renewing power of the Eucharist.

And there are Green Men. The most notable is the "greeter" on the column to the right of the doorway. He's hardly a friendly, welcoming greeter, and I hesitate to say "Green *Man*" insofar as this figure is something more-than-human. He is more of a mask, or a spirit, a being from another realm radiating fearsome power.

Otherworldly and imposing, this Green Man shares the spirit of the Green Knight. And yet, I'm not sure they are the same. The Green Knight and this outlandish foliated head share connections with the natural and magical realms—but did the medieval storyteller intend a connection with the same Green Man we see in churches? It's hard to tell. In the first written account, the Green Knight is described as:

> *Well garbed was this giant geared in green, and the hair of his head like his horse's mane. Fair fanned-out flax enfolds his shoulders; a beard big as a bush over his breast hangs.*

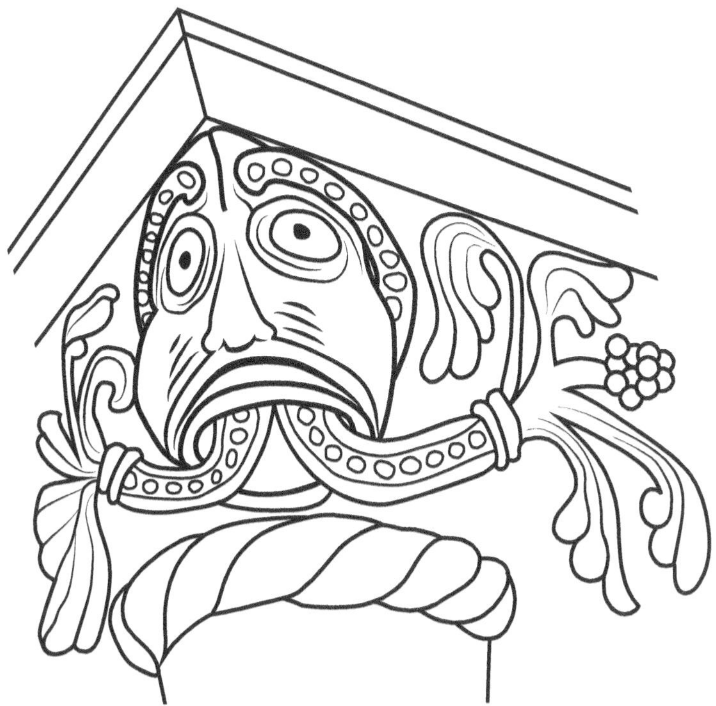

The foliage that erupts from the mouth of the Kilpeck Church's doorway Green Man appears to be rope or beadwork and extends into leaves and a cluster of grapes.

The references to "flax" and "bush" are vegetative, but there's no mention of leaves or tendrils from his mouth or nose or ears. So—is the Green Knight a Green Man? Some scholars point to medieval references to the Knight as a "Green Man"—but I leave the reader to decide. For now, let's turn our attention to another tradition that may bear some relation to our foliated friend.

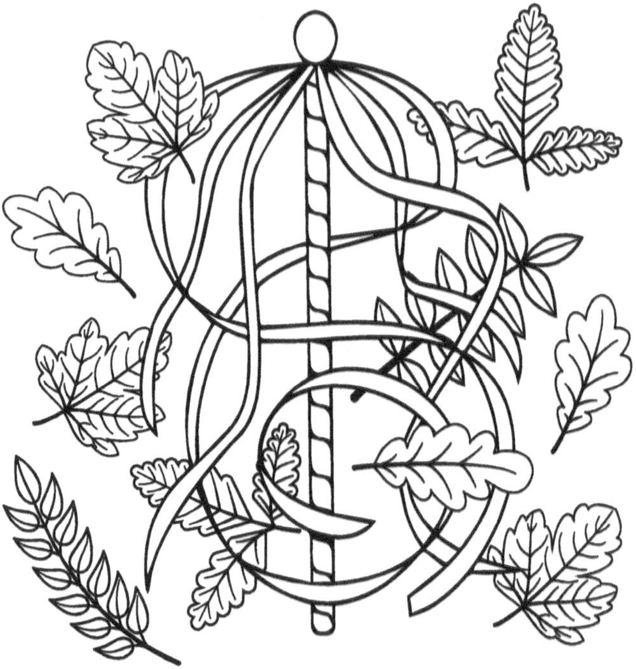

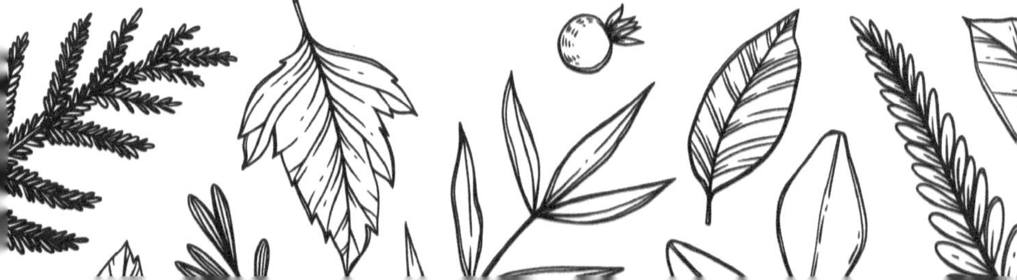

The symbolism of the maypole has been continuously debated by folklorists for centuries, but no definitive answer has been found. Some scholars have suggested that maypoles are symbols of the sacred World Tree from Germanic Pagan beliefs, and other scholars have seen phallic symbolism in them. Most historians today, however, believe that maypoles originated during Christianity, in the fourteenth century. The anthropologist Mircea Eliade theorized that the maypoles were simply a part of the general rejoicing at the return of summer and the growth of new vegetation, with their shape allowing for garlands and greenery to be hung from them.

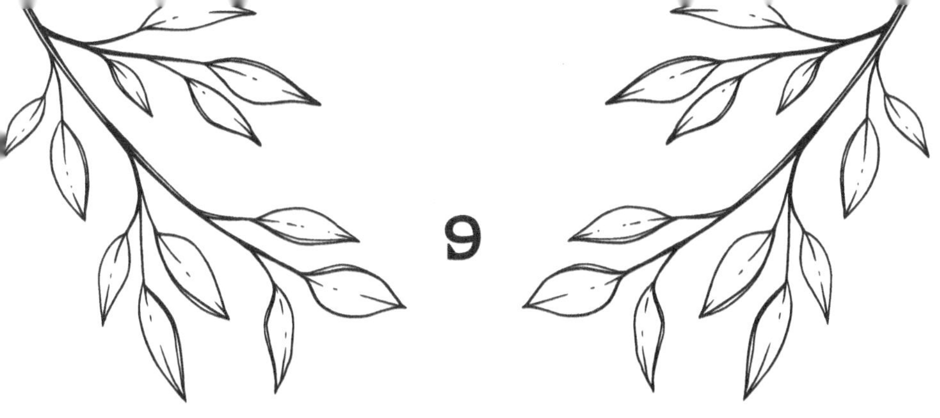

9

Jack and the Maypole

How many calendar dates in your life can you remember, years later? "On that day I was at such-and-such" or "I was with so-and-so." You doubtless recall dates like the birth of a child, a wedding, the funeral of a loved one, or perhaps significant birthdays. I'll always remember where I was on May 1, 2016.

My wife Marsha, our friend and editor Ellyn, and I were staying in a rambling medieval house in Devon, England, where we were vaca-working on writing business. I was excited to be in Southern England as Beltane approached. (May Day, formerly known by its Celtic name Beltane, was one of the Celts' chief festivals, marking the beginning of summer.) I had done my research, and there were two events I wanted to attend.

May Day morning, we started out at the magical hour of 3:30 a.m. and drove over an hour between hedge rows through unlit roads, arriving in the chilly pre-dawn at Haytoor Rocks in Dartmoor. Dartmoor is one of the strangest, most haunting environments in England, both barren and lovely. Its desolate moors and dramatic rock escarpments seem like a Mars-scape at times, and Wistman Wood with its moss-covered dwarf oaks is the perfect enchanted forest. No wonder Arthur Conan Doyle placed his story "The Hound of the Baskervilles" in Dartmoor.

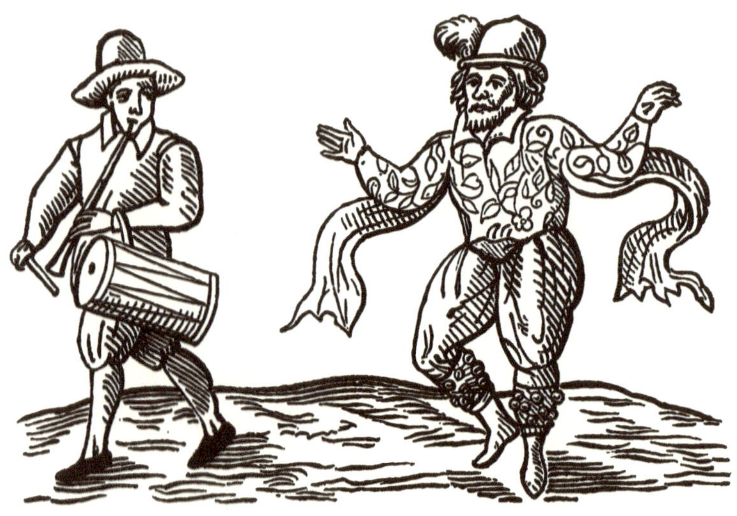

The earliest written mention of Morris dances is from the mid-15th century. This medieval illustration of a Morris dance indicates that many of today's elements were present then: drums, flying scarves, and jingling bells on the dancers' legs.

Beneath the craggy granite outcropping at Haytoor Rocks we gathered with a small crowd of folks to celebrate the Beltane dawn with Morris dances. The place is so isolated that the dances were done right in the middle of the road—and not a car came by to interrupt. There were three dance troupes there, with their attendant musicians. Onlookers were friends or family of the dancers. Part of the excitement of being there was the sense that this was not a performance—at least not performance for a human audience. I experienced the dances as *ritual*, enacted for the land, the rising sun, the ancestors.

No one is certain where we get the expression "Morris dance." Some suggest the word derives from the medieval word "Moorish" (Muslim), but that is by no means certain. We know these dances are older than the Reformation, because Protestants protested them—but how far back in history are their origins? Julia Somerset and other folklorists point to the Morris dance tradition as a survival of pre-Christian rites having to do with both fertility and the resurrection of new life out of death. Some Morris dancers hold up deer's antlers

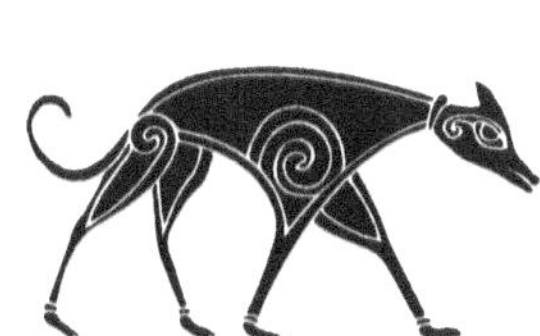

Humans with antlers are portrayed in several ancient images, indicating the merging of human and animal. The tradition of Morris dancers brandishing deer antlers may hearken back to this imagery.

as they dance—why? No one remembers, but customs like that seem to give credence to an origin in the ancient Nature religion.

One of the troupes on this May Day morning was the Beltane Border Morris group. They performed in blackface— perhaps recalling the prominence of chimney sweeps in May Day celebrations of the eighteenth and nineteenth centuries—and wore long shredded strips of black fabric. Their dance was combative; rows of dancers whirled and charged one another, screaming what can only be described as battle cries, and clashing hardwood sticks so roughly that chips flew. It was dance, sport, and melee in one. Those folklorists who are inclined to see ancient fertility rituals in the dance will point to this as ritual combat between the forces of winter and of summertime, performed on Beltane as summer engages in climactic and victorious battle against cruel and resistant winter.

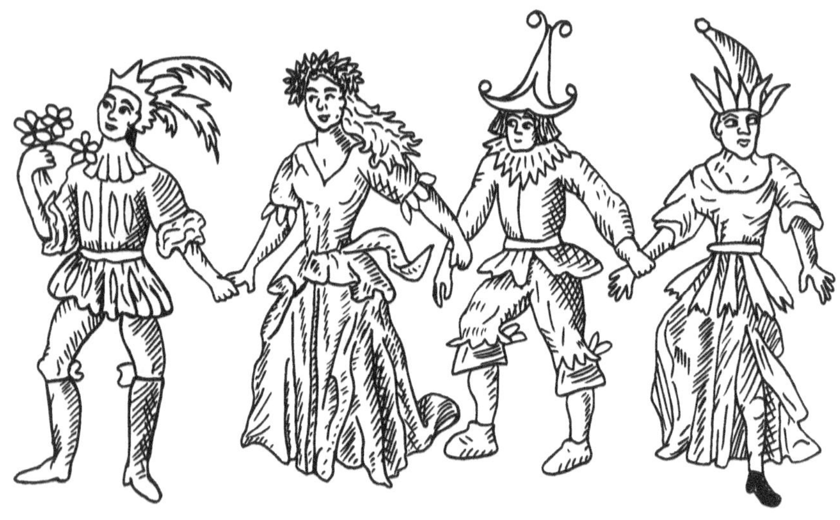

Mummers were another form of medieval entertainment that often merged or overlapped with Morris dancing. Mumming involved elaborate costumes, exaggeratedly comic performances, and allegorical plays.

And as another Morris troupe danced, a vegetative figure strode into their midst—our friend Jack in the Green! He was wearing a camouflage ghillie suit, designed for soldiers and hunters, and a leaf-face mask patterned after the classic foliated heads in churches, and he carried an unmistakably phallic staff. He served as a human maypole, standing amid the dancers whose movements swirled round about him. While his outfit was modernized, this Jack in the Green was rooted in countless leafy ancestors who have appeared on May Day mornings in centuries past, an icon of summer greenery once again filling the land.

After the dance troupes finished their choreographed rituals, the rest of us were invited to join the revelries. A dancer handed us hardwood sticks, and they showed us how to dance in opposing circles, whacking our sticks against one another. We entered into the dance, gingerly batting with the staffs, gleeful as we joined the ancient rite.

And then, when the dawn had driven darkness off the moors and crags, the crowd dispersed. The roadside that was filled with accordion music, the clash of sticks, and loud shouts, was lonely and silent again. Marsha, Ellyn, and I drove north to Glastonbury for our second Beltane celebration of the day.

We arrived before festivities began and relaxed in a warm coffee shop with papier-maché dragons in the window display. I ordered a coffee with whisky, just the thing to restore warmth internally. Then we explored the streets of this medieval town, with its crystal shops, bookshops, and a store called The Green Man and the Goddess.

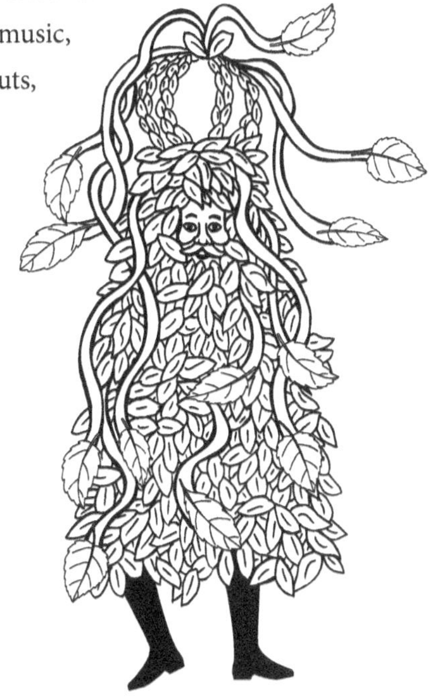

The 19th-century Jack in the Green looked much more like a walking tree than the Jack I saw on Dartmoor—but like his modern-day brother, this Jack also functioned as a human maypole.

Glastonbury is a myth magnet—a town that has attracted the legends of the Goddess, Merlin, Saint Patrick, Saint Brigid, and King Arthur all into one place. To disparagers, it is woo-woo-ville, where competing reincarnations of King Arthur stand on crates while young people beat drums by the Market Cross. Yet it has always been a place of myth, both Pagan and Christian. The Chalice Well with its lovely grounds and ancient yews can claim continuity with the same springs venerated as holy before Rome's legions entered its environs. The Tor may be a pre-Christian ritual site, the navel of ancient Avalon, and the Abbey—while perhaps not actually founded by Joseph of Arimathea, as was claimed by its medieval bishops—was built atop one of Britain's most ancient churches. A sign on the Abbey Grounds marks the spot where the graves of Arthur and Guinevere were allegedly unearthed in the Middle Ages, an attempt to put to death rumors that the once-and-future-king would rise to lead a Welsh rebellion against Norman overlords. The George and Pilgrims Inn, still serving travelers in the midst of the town, has done so since the time when Chaucer wrote *Canterbury Tales*.

Crowds began to gather . . . and gather and gather. Soon the quaint medieval streets were crammed full of modern celebrants, shoulder-to-shoulder. Glastonbury's Beltane festival is not a reenactment of May Days past but a contemporary celebration of annual renewal. Two human-filled life-sized dragons (if "life-sized" can rightly apply to fantasy beasts), like the dragons in Chinese New Year's, danced through the streets. There were dramas (though I could not fight through the crowds to get the gist of them). And there were Green Men. Lots of Green Men.

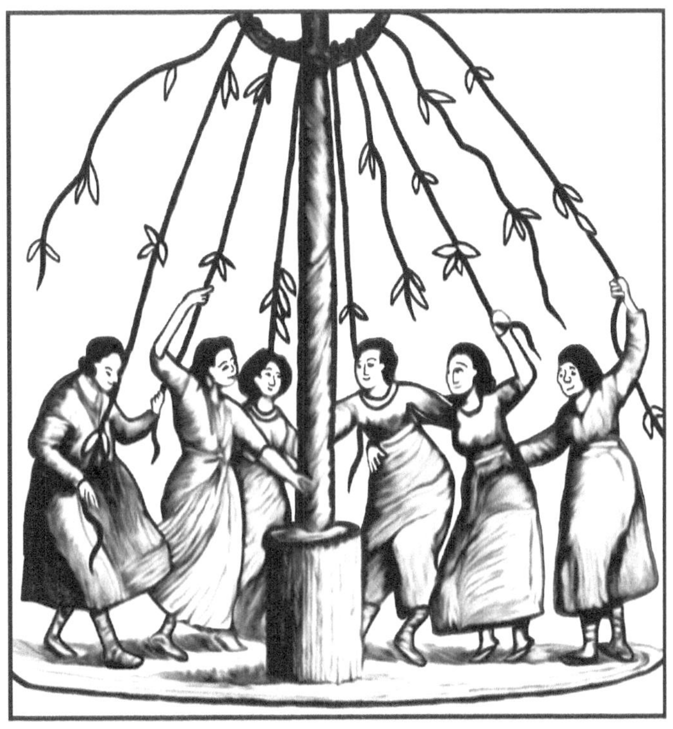

Maypole dances were one way medieval people celebrated the link between the seasons and the community; they saw themselves as part of a long chain of living things that included the Earth and the Heavens, humankind and Nature, forming a never-ending dance of connection.

The Green Men carried the maypole—a sizable trunk—into the town square, then up a long hill to the field where it was erected and festooned. A May Queen and May King were "married." The May King was costumed as the Green Man.

Clearly, the Green Man is a ubiquitous symbol of this modern continuation of the ancient Beltane rites. Renewal of the old

Celtic Nature religions has emphasized the importance of the Green Man as a symbol of Beltane, and modern dancers dressed as Jack in the Green design their outfits to resemble the medieval foliated faces. This reinforces Lady Raglan's assumption that leaf-faces-in-churches and Jack-in-the-Green May-Day dancers are one and the same.

But … Jack in the Green in preceding centuries didn't look like these modern Green Men. When I see pictures of a traditional Jack in the Green, I'm reminded of Monty Python's *Holy Grail* and the knights who say "Neek," when they command King Arthur, "Bring us … a shrubbery!" A historical May Day Jack in the Green, enclosed in a series of hoops covered with leaves, looks like walking shrubbery—or a Christmas tree with a pair of feet and eyes poking through the green (see the image on page 105).

The earliest documentation of a May Day Jack in the Green is 1770, and throughout the past two and a half centuries, Jack in the Green has been linked with the guilds of chimney sweeps, appearing on May Day with a troupe of men and women sweeps, their faces blackened denoting their trade, engaging in bawdy song and gesture and asking for donations from passers-by.

With the more refined sensitivities of the Victorian and Edwardian ages, Jack in the Green began to disappear from May Day festivities, but the burgeoning growth of Nature religions in the twenty-first century has resulted in a multitude of Jacks in the Green dancing on May Day throughout England. (For those interested in a more thorough write-up of Jack in the Green and folklore traditions, I recommend *The Green Man in Britain* by Fran & Geoff Doel.)

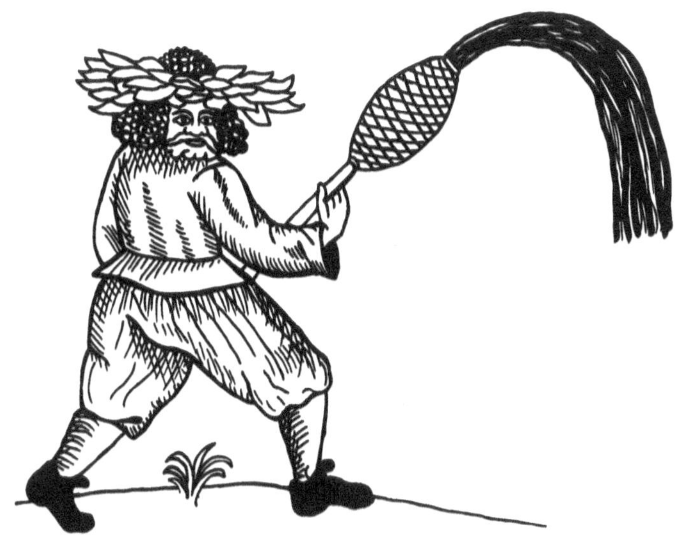

This early seventeenth-century fellow looks more like the leafy faces in churches, as opposed to the walking Christmas tree that was also Jack in the Green. This medieval portrayal of Jack shows him in his role as "sweeper" or "whiffler," swaying a container of snapping fireworks to make room in the streets for the Morris dancers who followed him. A description written in 1686 refers to "twenty Savages or Green Men, with Squibs and Fire-works, to sweep the Streets, and keep off the Crowd."

When we try to understand his message, Jack in the Green presents the same difficulty that we encounter with the leaf faces in churches: a lack of explanation in historical texts. The revelries of the peasantry didn't receive a great deal of attention in the writings of the Middle Ages, and when folkloric rituals do appear in old texts, knowledge by the reader is assumed rather than explained. Adding to the difficulty in understanding, it is hard to discern which elements in Morris dances and May Day rituals are ancient customs that have been passed on mouth-to-mouth, and which are modern interpretations.

The appellation "Green Man" coupled with staged events pre-dates the eighteenth-century documentation of Jack in the Green. The script for a play titled *Historie of Promos and Cassandra*, published in 1578, includes the entry of two men "appareled lyke greene men at the mayor's feast with clubs of fireworks." We can make the likely guess that these characters looked like the illustration of a Green Man with a firework club published five decades later (shown on page 109).

As I stood in the cold dawn of that Beltane morning, watching the Morris dancers and their friend Jack in the Green, I felt a palpable sense of continuity with the ancient past. I realize that when I taught comparative religions in college—where all statements had to be made with the precision of academia—my intuitions about Jack would not have flown far. And yet, while some folklorists today are inclined to reject the beliefs of Lady Raglan and her peers regarding the pre-Christian origins of Morris dances and Jack in the Green, I wonder.

Unlike the carved foliated faces, Jack appears in festivities that were performed outside of churches, and were not connected with explicitly Christian rites. The dour Reformers of the sixteenth and seventeenth centuries apparently had no objection to the foliated visages in their places of worship—but they did rail heartily against May Day celebrations. And Jack in the Green, clad in deciduous leaves, appeared for centuries precisely on the first day of summer (according to the ancient Celtic seasonal reckoning). Can all that be coincidence?

Doesn't Jack, in all his leafiness, say to us, "No matter how bitter the winter, new life will come again"? Green will rise from the Earth, babies will be conceived and born, and Nature will repeat her endless cycle of renewal.

But is that message the Green Man's only secret? I'm not so sure. Certainly, there's something of the rascal about him, which puts him akin not only to the modern-day Jacks in the Green but also that most beloved of all outlaws—Robin Hood.

Now winter is over, I'm happy to say,
And we're all met again in our ribbons so gay.
And we're all met again on the first day of Spring
To go about dancing with Jack in the Green.
Now Jack in the Green is a very strange man,
Tho' he dies every Autumn,
he is born every Spring.
. . .We will dance through the street,
And in return Jack he will ripen our wheat.

—Martin Graebe

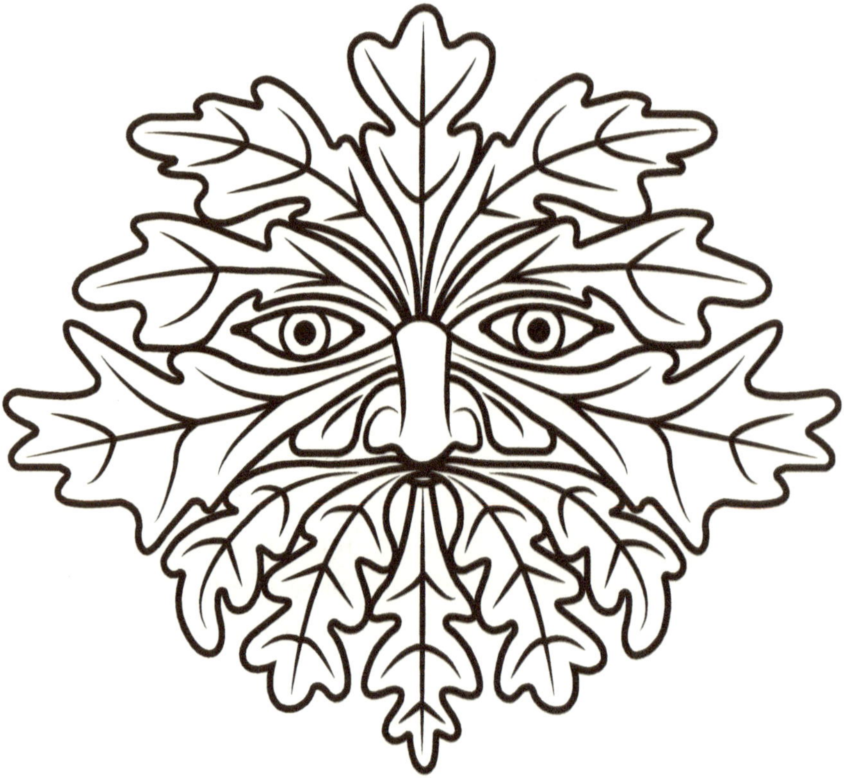

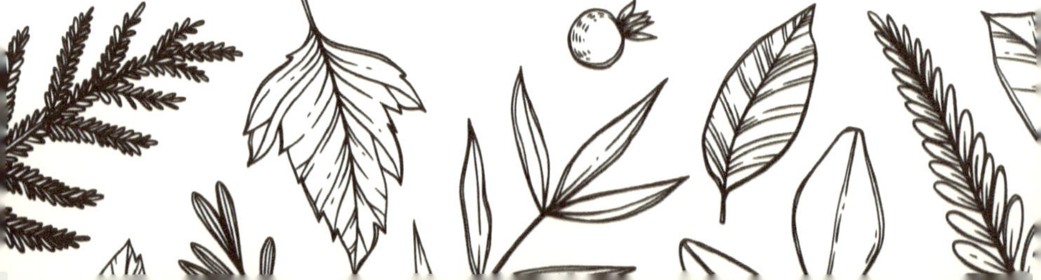

Taken from a modern Green Man on display in Sherwood Forest.

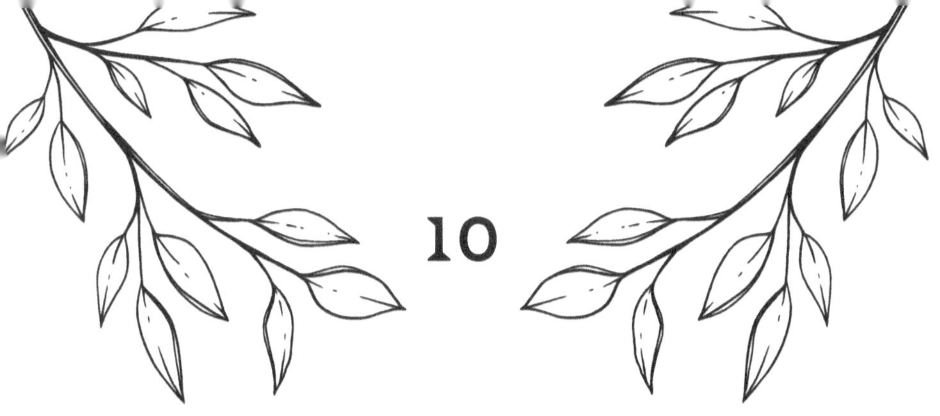

10

The Green Man
and His Merry Men

One afternoon in childhood, I was at my aunt's house watching a black-and-white television set with my cousins, when the 1938 Errol Flynn movie *The Adventures of Robin Hood* happened to be playing. I loved it! How he leapt and swung and tricked the sheriff's men, how he stood up for the little people, all with that look of absolute joy on his face. That night and over the days following, I played Robin Hood with a hastily contrived wooden sword.

Soon after, my parents bought me the Golden Press edition of Howard Pyle's *The Merry Adventures of Robin Hood*. I still enjoy reading that book and looking at the pictures more than fifty years after I first set eyes on it. I've subsequently read histories and novels portraying the great outlaw and seen a myriad screen adaptations. In my opinion, neither Kevin Costner nor Russel Crowe hold a candle to Errol Flynn's Robin, although I did get hooked by Michael Praed's *Robin of Sherwood*.

In 2018, Marsha and I entered the pub at the Dukeries Lodge in Edwin-stowe, where we met a local couple who were Facebook friends (and who proved to be delightful company in real life). They offered to walk us through nearby Sherwood Forest, that same woods that had been the setting for countless imaginary adventures over the course of my life. Thankfully, it was after the visitor center was closed and hordes of tourists had departed. As we stepped into the fern-carpeted forest full of ancient oaks I had one of those rare and wonderful moments when you realizes that a real-world place is just as you imagined it would be. It was easy to envision Robin, Friar Tuck, and Marian crouching behind the foliage.

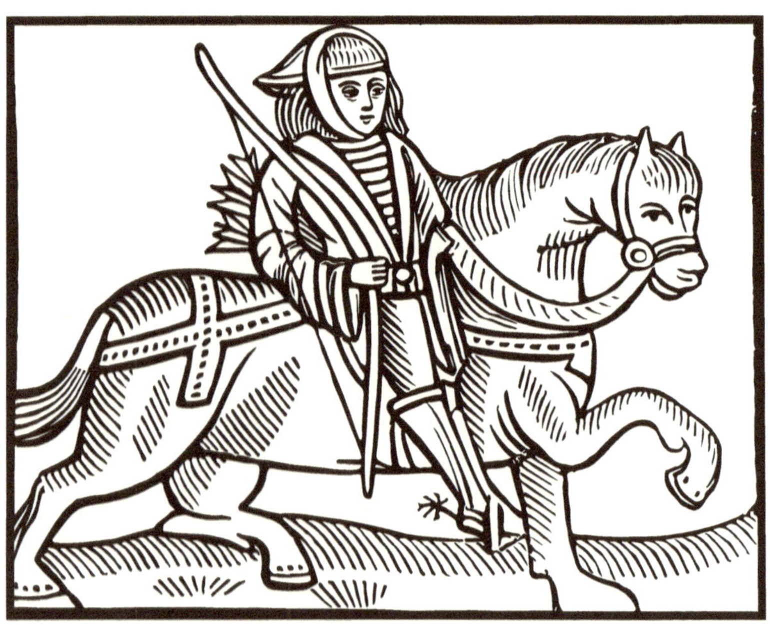

This is a fifteenth-century portrayal of Robin Hood.

Near the Major Oak—believed to the be the site of the Merry Men's forest encampment—who should I meet but my friend the Green Man. There had just been a local event that encouraged artists to adorn the trunks of these venerable trees with the Green Man's visage rendered in impermanent materials.

In fact, the Sherwood Forest National Nature Reserve has embraced the Green Man. A sign outside the visitors' center features a lovely carving of the Green Man and invites visitors to "follow the Green Man" and "discover the Spirit of Sherwood forest." And there you have it—our leafy friend has become the official patron of Robin's woods! In the visitors' center there is the following explanation:

Robin Hood: A Green Man?

Are Robin Hood and the pagan "Green Man" one and the same? Many people think there may be a connection between Robin Hood and this symbol of rebirth and fertility. The Green Man is a very old pagan (non-Christian) symbol, a mysterious spirit of nature often depicted by medieval wood and stone carvers as a face with leaves sprouting from nose, mouth and eyes. Medieval stone masons added these decorative carvings to churches perhaps in reference to their older, pagan beliefs. In many ways Robin Hood is also a symbol of the old ways and the old religion under which life was better, game was plentiful, and taxes less punishing.

In pre-Christian times large old trees like those in Sherwood Forest were regarded as sacred and became the focus of rituals. This is probably how some of our folk traditions like dancing around the May pole started. By the 1500s May Day festivities were commonly called "Robin Hood's Games"—other names for the central figure were "Robin-in-the-Hood," "Robin Goodfellow" and "Jack-in-the-Green." Even today, some May Day games still feature the characters of Robin Hood and Maid Marian.

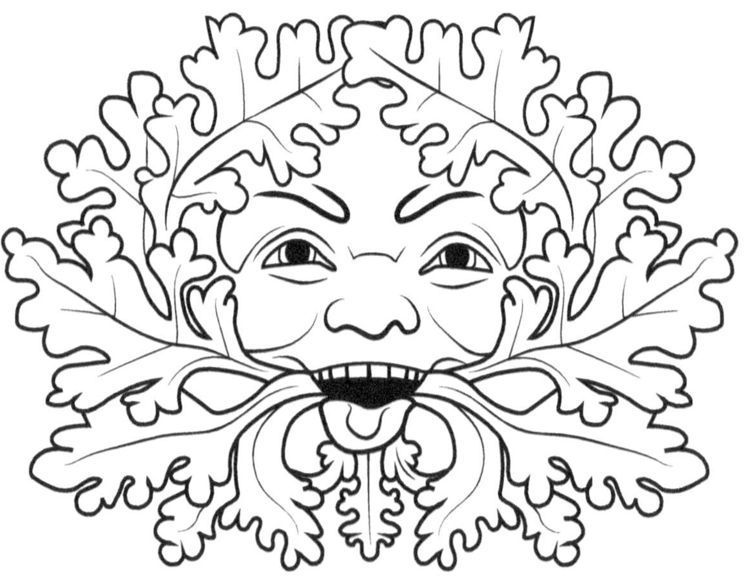

This modern Green Man from a building in Bradwell-on-Sea in England sprouts acanthus leaves like his more ancient brothers. His joyously puckish expression also harkens back to the mischief of Robin Goodfellow.

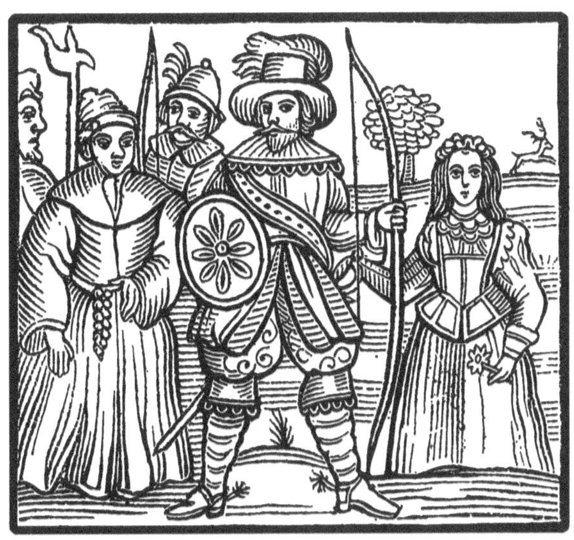

A seventeenth-century drawing of Robin Hood, Maid Marion, Father Tuck, and a couple of other outlaws in their merry band.

Lady Raglan would be delighted to see how—eighty years after her paper on the Green Man—a national institution follows her assertion that the Green Man is a Pagan Nature deity; apparently the curators haven't been reading more recent scholarship. However, the last paragraph in the Sherwood Forest sign—the connection between Robin Hood and the May Day festivities—is correct. There is substantial overlap between Robin Hood and Jack in the Green. (For those interested in learning more about the connections between the Green Man and the outlaw of Sherwood Forest the book *Robin Hood* by John Matthews offers a thorough and detailed explanation.)

Robin Hood's very name connects him with the ancient tales of faeries: Puck, the mischievous character in *A Midsummer Night's Dream*, is also known as Robin Goodfellow. Puck is called Hob as well, and "Hob," "Hod," and "Hood" are interchangeable in old English. Tales were told of Robin Goodfellow and his merry band of wood sprites leading wild dances through the forests, and these tales may have inspired the May Day revelries.

May Day rites focused on the union of the May King and the May Queen. The May King is sometimes

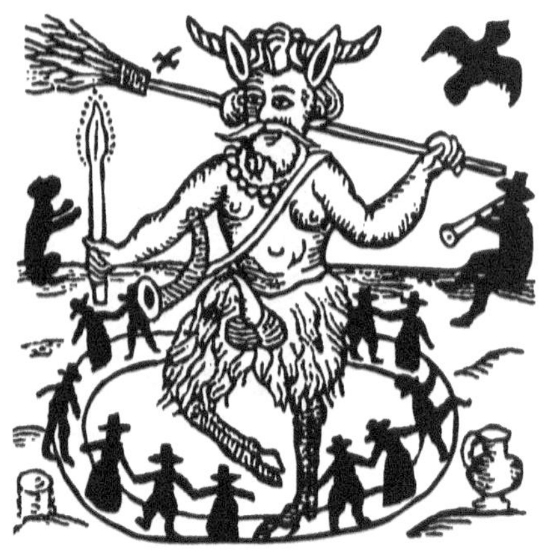

An illustration from Robin Goodfellow: His Mad Pranks and Merry Jests, *published in the early seventeenth century.*

represented by our friend Jack in the Green, but he is also commonly referred to as Robin Hood, and the early tales of the outlaw are woven thoroughly into May Day dances and pageants. The May Queen and May King are married in a ceremonial archway called Robin's Bower.

And consider the heroine of the tale, for in every retelling of Robin Hood, his romance with Maid Marian is paramount. The name Marian—diminutive of Mary—is the most common name imaginable in medieval Europe, where the Mother of God was venerated on level with her Child. Yet there appears to be more going on with Maid Marian's designation. In the very old May Day revelries, the "Maid," "Marian," and the "May Queen" are interchangeable titles for the Flower Bride. So Robin Hood–Maid Marian and Jack in the Green–the May Queen are transposable pairs of symbolic figures in this ritual that heralds the fertility of each new summer.

If you recall in the earlier chapter titled "What About the Green *Women*?" I visited the amazing Chapter House in Southwell Minster, which is adorned with lifelike stone carvings of thick foliage, and in which I found a face that looks like a Green Woman—or an androgynous visage. I wondered if perhaps this face, also known as the Oak King, might not represent a faerie spirit of the forest. The stone carvings in the Chapter House sit above the wooden thrones of the Bishops of the Diocese, each engraved with their title, and one of those reads "Episcopus de Sherwood." I can't help but wonder what connections there might be between the leafy faces in Southwell Minster, Robin Goodfellow, and the legendary outlaw of nearby Sherwood Forest.

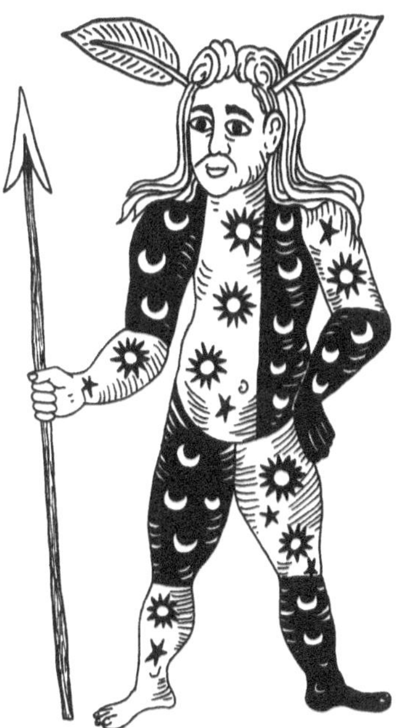

Another seventeenth-century portrayal of Robin Goodfellow. Note the leaves in his hair.

In the centuries between the High Middle Ages and the early twentieth century, there were dozens of pubs and inns named "The Green Man." Lady Raglan and her fellow folklorists used that phrase to describe both the leaf faces and Jack in the Green, forming our popular modern conception of the Green Man. In recent years the institution of the English pub has declined and some of the Green Man pubs have gone out of business. Those that survive have in most cases redone their signs to reflect popular understanding of the Green Man as a foliated face like those found in old carvings. But the Green Man Pub in Prestwood, Buckinghamshire, is more typical of Green Man pub signs of the past, with its portrayal of the Sherwood Forest outlaw bending his longbow. For patrons of public inns and drinking establishment in Victorian England, the Green Man was Robin Hood.

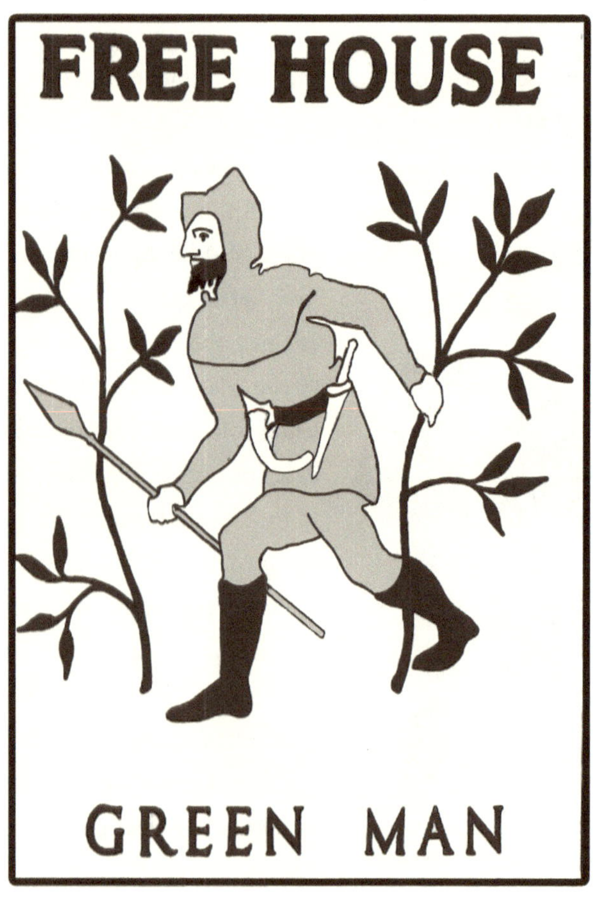

If we were to attempt a chart showing all the connections between Robin Hood and Jack in the Green, it would soon resemble an appropriate tanglewood forest. We may never know which came first—the outlaw champion of the poor, Robin Goodfellow the faerie, or Jack in the Green dancing on May Day—but Robin Hood is definitely a branch on the Green Man's family tree. And that Green Man family tree has kept growing and growing, becoming an enormous forest in our modern age.

And now, let's consider another possible family connection for our green friend. This one comes from much farther afield—the Islamic world of the Middle East.

The trees are our shelter,
and the animals are our companions.
We are all children of the forest.

—Robin Hood (Howard Pyle)

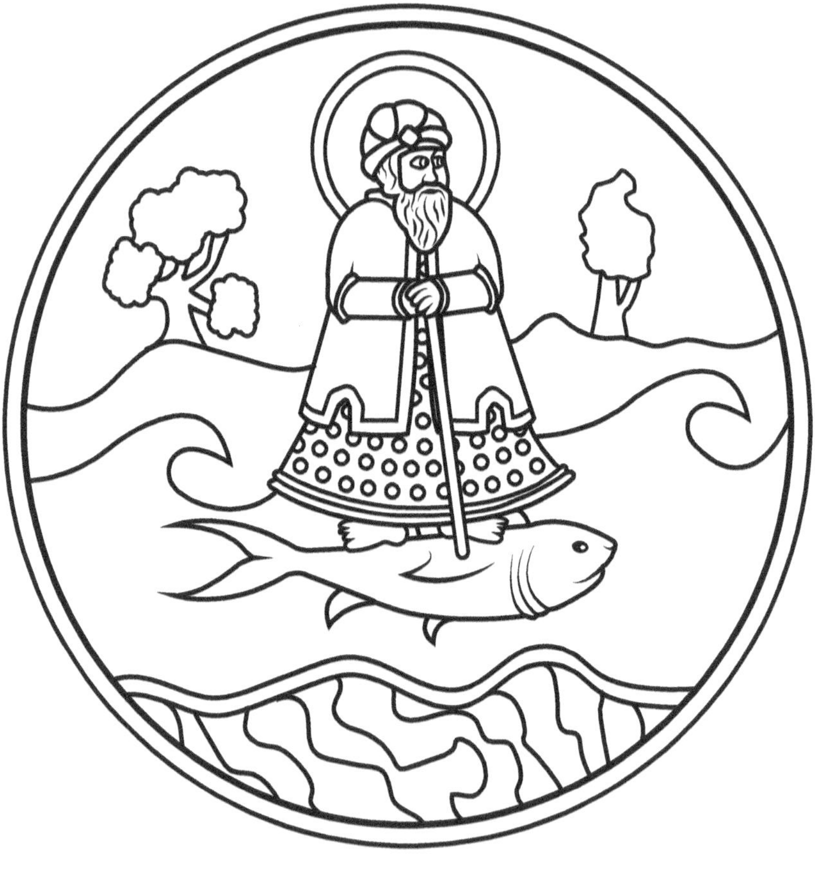

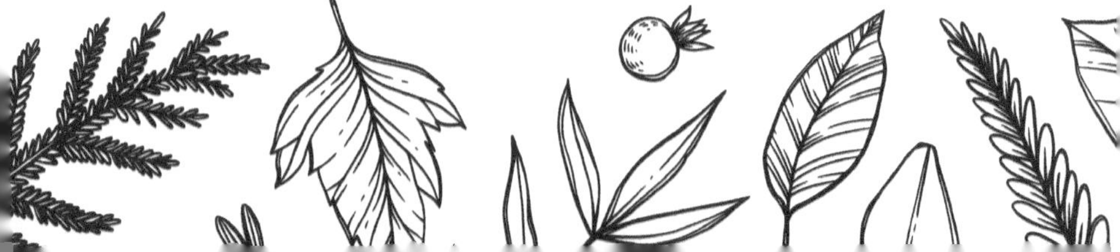

Al-Khidr's green clothing is said to represent freshness of spirit and eternal live-liness, drawn from the Water of Life. According to tradition, Khidr is the guide of all those who seek spiritual growth and life.

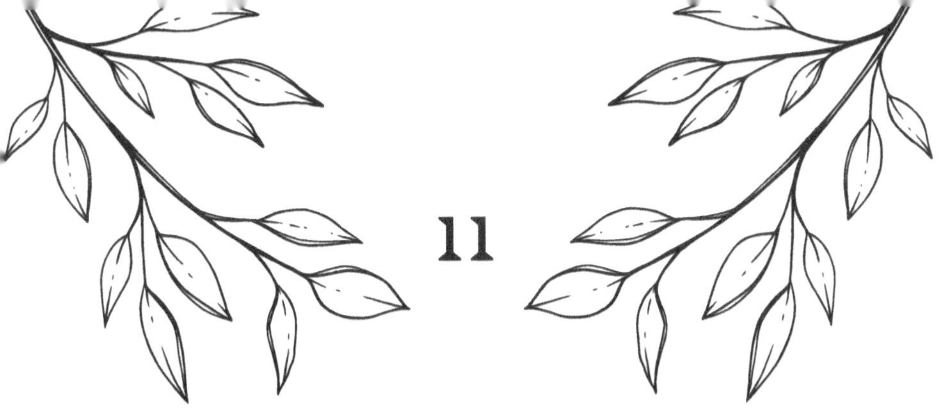

11

A Wise (Green) Man from the East

You never know where you'll gain a fascinating bit of new information (especially if you're willing to be a bit weird).

In July 2016, I spoke about the Green Man at the Flagstaff, Arizona, Celtic Highland Festival, and I dressed appropriately, with oak leaves in my bonnet and green makeup all over my face. Later in the day, I attended a "stand-up" storytelling workshop where the most impressive story came from a man who had only recently learned of Celtic customs passed down in his racially and culturally blended family. A few minutes after that workshop, I found myself next to the storyteller, waiting in line at the beer tent. He asked, "What's up with your outfit?"

I briefly explained the Green Man, and he exclaimed, "Oh, you mean al-Khidr!" When I confessed my unfamiliarity with the name, he explained, "He's the Green Man," and told about this element of his Muslim faith. My subsequent research revealed there is indeed a proposed link between al-Khidr and the Western Green Man.

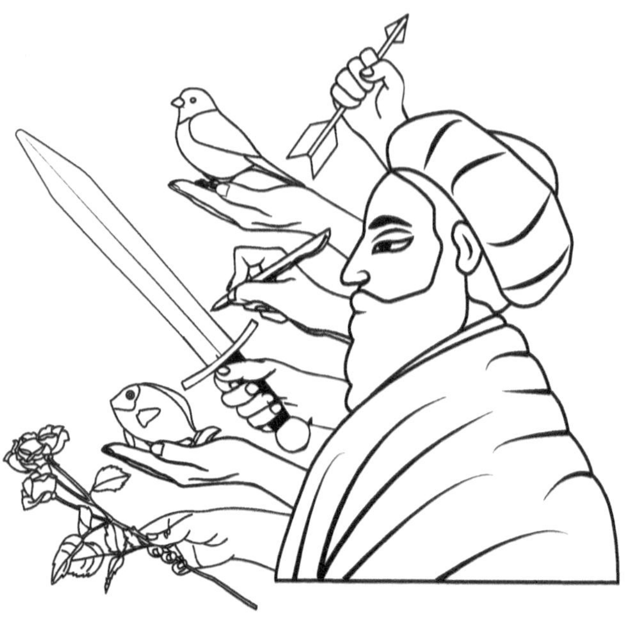

Al-Khidr is said to unite the opposites in life, bringing growth and creative inge-nuity out of destruction. According to Muslim teaching, he is the patron saint of all spiritual seekers who go directly to God without intermediaries, following "the Way of the Private Face."

According to Islamic tradition, Khidr is an angel or an immortal human messenger or prophet who guards the sea, teaches secret knowl-edge, aids those in distress, and guides all of us who are on a spiritual journey. His name literally means the "Green One" or "Verdant One." The word *khadir* means "green leaf, herb," tying Khidr directly to our more familiar Green Man. The verb form means, "becoming green, burgeoning with plant life"; according to one scholar, Khidr is green because the Earth bursts into life at the mere touch of his feet. Some Islamic scholars connect Khidr with the ancient sage, Atra-Hasis, who was basically the Mesopotamian version of the Hebrew scripture's Noah;

his goal was to save not only humankind but also all the Earth's plants and animals. In any case, Khidr is a righteous servant of God who possesses great wisdom and mystic knowledge.

Khidr's ancient origins are debated; he may be a descendant of legends from ancient Canaan or Babylon, or possibly related to other legends from Turkey. You may recall that in the chapter on the Green Man's family tree we looked at the foliated head from Al-Hadr, Iraq, which may also portray an early form of the Khidr tales.

In the Holy Quran, Khidr is not mentioned by name, but he is thought to be the servant of God who meets the Prophet Moses, accompanies him on his travels, does miracles, and teaches Moses that things that appear destructive or unwelcome may—despite first impressions—be blessings. In the Hadith, Mohammad states that the Prophet Elijah meets annually with Khidr in Jerusalem during Ramadan.

Khidr is often portrayed as riding or carrying a fish (or both), because of a story about an encounter he had with Moses. Like the medieval mermen-Green Men found in English churches, Khidr is the spirit of our entire planet, both land and sea. He is intimately connected with the Source of Life, the Life that flows through all reality.

Could the Middle Eastern traditions of al-Khidr have influenced the Green Man we see carved in Britain's churches? Cultural links between Islam and Europe during the Middle Ages render the idea plausible. As an example of cultural exchange between medieval East and West, the pointed arch—a signifier of Gothic era church architecture—may be derived from Islamic architecture brought to Europe via returning Crusaders. Templar churches display Palestinian influence and—we shall see in a subsequent chapter—there are Green Men in Knights Templar chapels. The Franciscan friars, hugely influential throughout Europe in the High Middle Ages, maintained a dialogue with their Sufi counterparts from the time of Saint Francis's meeting with Sultan al-Kamil in 1218. Muslim figures appear in Arthurian tales, and some scholars allege that the Green Knight was inspired by contact with Islam. In fact, the Green Knight and al-Khidr may be closely linked.

The color green has deep cross-cultural meaning. It is the "fingerprint" or "signature" left on our living world by water and light—and Khidr is connected to both, just as all vegetation is. As the Sufi poet Rumi wrote,

The Egyptian god Osiris is also portrayed with a green face, indicating his connection with regeneration, the sprouting of new vegetation after destruction, and the resurrection of the dead. Perhaps he too is an early distant cousin of our Green Man.

The sign is in the face.
You can look at an orchard
and tell if it rained last night.
That freshness is the sign.

Still, the associations between the Green Man of Eastern tradition and the Green Man of European church decoration is unlikely to be very close, due to their artistic distinctions. Khidr is called "the Green One," but he is never portrayed as having vegetation sprouting from his face or mouth. He may be a saint or illuminated master, but he is not a human-vegetative hybrid.

We need to dig deeper for insight into the soul of the Green Man. In doing so, it may prove helpful to consider where in their churches those medieval artists placed the Green Man's image.

Khidr equalizes the seasons,
recrowns the trees with royal green,
unbinds the fleeting streams,
spreads out grass carpets on the meadows,
and hangs his light green mantle
in the evening air.

— *The Thousand Nights and a Night*

My lord Khidr, the green one,
Water our dry plants.

—Palestinian folk prayer

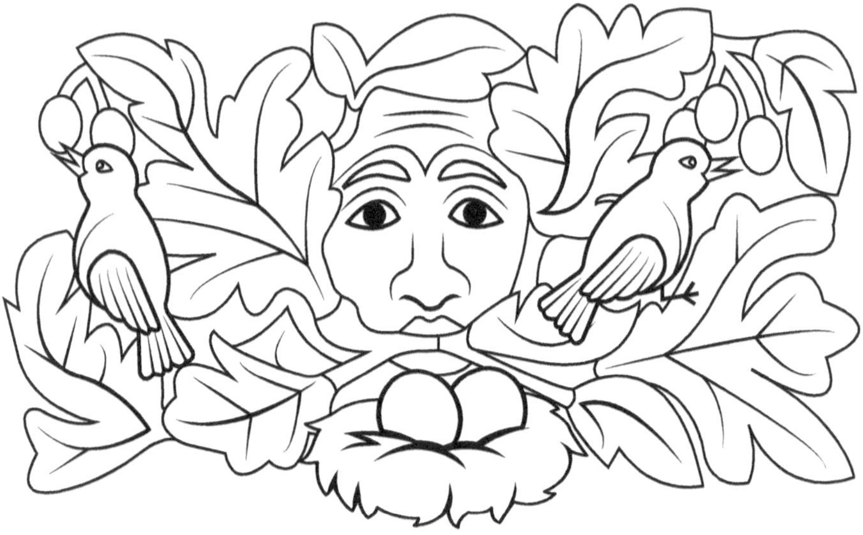

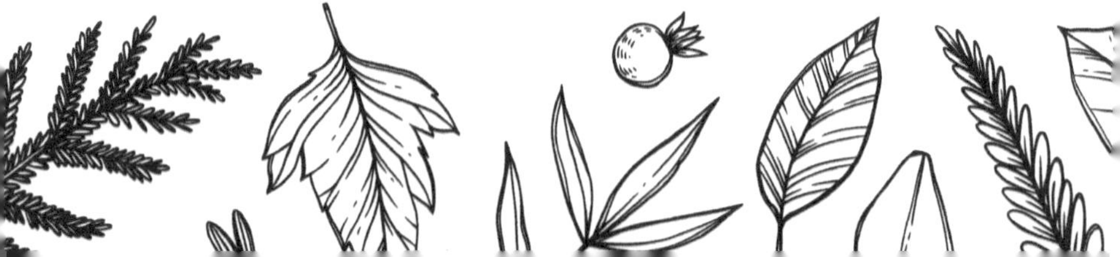

A modern image inspired by the Green Man of Sutton Benger in England, this fellow spews out hawthorn leaves bearing berries. The Celts considered the hawthorn to be a marker between this world and the Other World; the tree often grew beside holy wells. The most famous hawthorn is at Glastonbury; according to legend, Joseph of Arimathea brought it there from the Holy Land. The hawthorn tree's berries—the haws—are beloved by birds, and their inclusion here reminds us of the ways in which all life is interconnected.

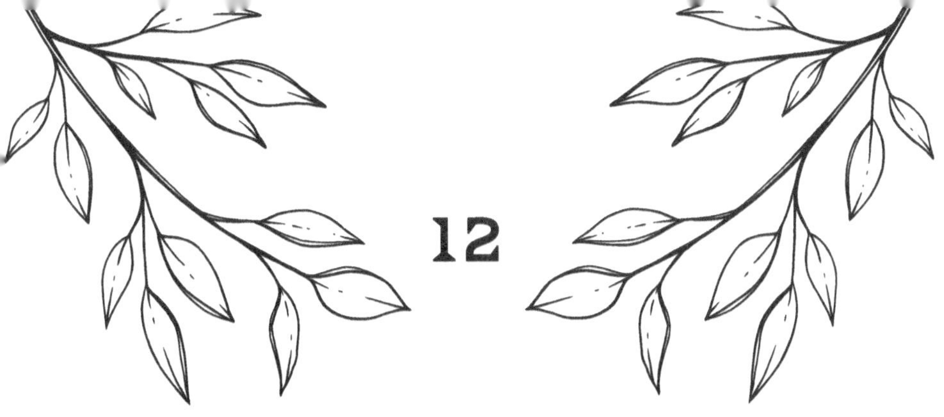

12

The Green Man at
the Sacred Threshold

As I've mentioned, my first meeting with a foliated head was inside St. Canice's Cathedral in Kilkenny, and the tour guide—with all good intentions—introduced the Green Man under false pretenses. Here's basically what she told me: "The masons who carved medieval cathedrals held to the old religion, and to the gods of the old religion, but these beliefs were forbidden by the church. So a mason would labor until an entire church edifice was completed. Then, he would sneak back into the church one night, hammer out the visage of the ancient fertility god in a nook of the church, pack up his tools, and leave town before daybreak. Church authorities were thus left with an undesired pagan symbol carved into the recesses of their sanctuary."

Similar explanations have been retold ad nauseum by church docents, on the Internet, and in guide books. It's basically a variation of Lady Raglan's original thesis, which was based on the work of Jesse Weston and James Frazier. You'll recall that Lady Raglan said, "The fact is that unofficial paganism subsisted side by side with the official religion, and this explains the presence of the Green Man." He is, according to Lady Raglan and countless others who followed her lead, a portrayal of a pre-Christian fertility god, a covert Pagan symbol slyly placed in Christian churches. This has been repeated so often that it's rarely contradicted, even though scholars of art and history are now inclined to reject the idea.

Symbols are multivalent, and there are always shades of meaning. As we've already discussed, it's likely that the Green Man's form is influenced by earlier Classical and Celtic art. It's also possible that Jack in the Green who appears in May Day dances may well be a continuation of ancient fertility rites. But there's little reason to believe that the foliated heads carved in churches are quite the same as Jack in the Green who appears in folk dances.

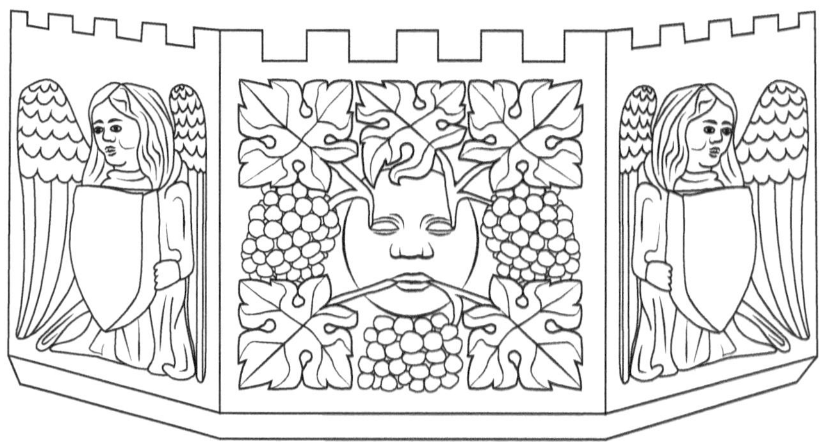

This fifteenth-century baptismal font from St. Andrew's Church in Bulmer, Essex, shows a Green Man with grapes and grape leaves erupting from his eyes and mouth. There is nothing furtive about his placement on this central Christian symbol, and the fact that he is flanked by angels further indicates that his creator felt that he belonged in a Christian setting.

The vegetation-spewing faces in churches are distinctive and indicate a well understood common meaning, agreed upon by artists, clerics, and nobles. I do not believe that the artists who made thousands of Green Men during the Middle Ages intended to convey an "unofficial paganism" with these images, and the places where foliated heads are located in medieval places of worship supports my contention.

Furthermore, medieval Green Man images were not carved in haste. They are usually finely executed, given the same time and attention as surrounding artistic motifs. And they are not usually "hidden." Although sometimes they are up high in the corbels, beams, or roof bosses, they are more often placed in obvious and prominent places, and in some cases—such as the "greeter" faces—they are unmissable. If a master carver could chip one of those images beside the front door of a cathedral and not be noticed by the churchmen supervising the work, that would be the greatest miracle ever heard of. Furthermore, many Green Men are placed within a larger aesthetic whole—in other words, they are part of a larger artistic pattern, again indicating that there is nothing covert or hasty in their design.

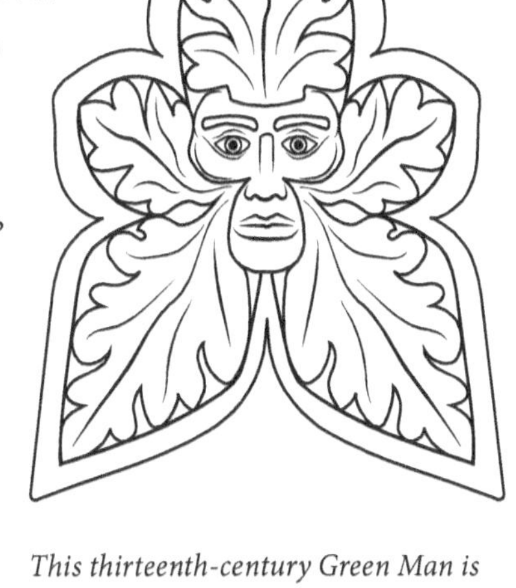

This thirteenth-century Green Man is placed at the very center of the quire screen in Westminster Abbey, indicating that he was considered central to the church's worship.

But could this be an example of physically obvious images with a hidden meaning? Might this be an inside joke, where the peasants knew that the Green Man was the face of their pre-Christian god, while the clerics just thought it was a pretty bit of art? That might be, except that the Green Man frequently appears in places that are central to the patterns of medieval worship. Since the Green Man is commonly positioned in places of utmost sacred symbolism for medieval Christians, he must symbolize values central to their beliefs.

Bernard of Clairvaux, who founded the Cistercian order, a tradition that dominated religious life during the high Middle Ages, opposed fantastical images in church buildings, "which attract the worshipper's gaze and hinder his attention." The Cistercians were known for their deep and simple piety, and if a Cistercian monastic house contained art, that art clearly portrayed Christian beliefs. So, it's worthy of note that there is a cherubic-looking Green Man in the Cloister of Cistercian Dore Abbey, Herefordshire. Bernard's disciples must have seen something edifying in that carved face. Green Men also appear at Melrose Abbey, another Cistercian monastery

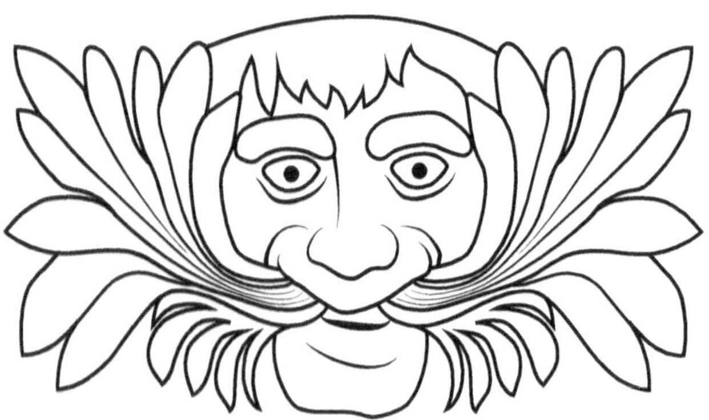

A Green Man in Melrose Abbey.

For another example of the Green Man as a symbol integral to medieval Christianity, consider its appearance on baptismal founts. The baptismal fount at Brecon Cathedral, Wales, which we've already discussed, is almost a thousand years old and has been used to christen untold generations of children into salvation, according to the belief of those who observe this rite. Around the fount

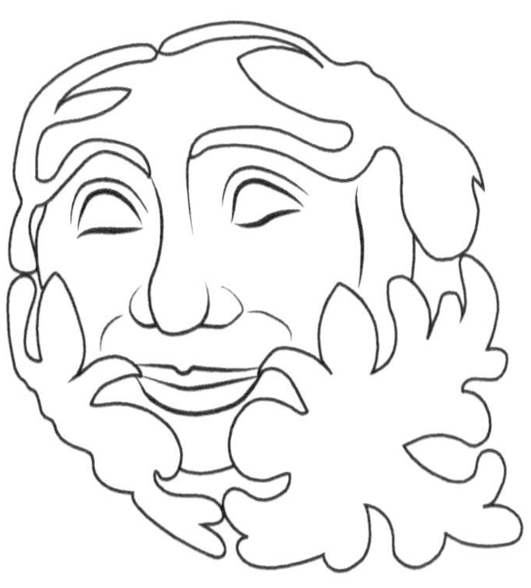

This serene-looking Green Man can be found in Dore Abbey, where his visage must have inspired the Cistercian monks who worshipped there.

are symbols of the four Gospels and—connecting them—prominent faces of four Green Men.

I found further reinforcement for my belief about the Green Man being a Christian symbol at St. Winifred's Church in Branscombe, Devon. Branscombe is a lovely seaside village tucked away on England's southern coast, and the village even includes a working medieval blacksmith shop. Marsha and I have been privileged to stay on several occasions in a sprawling house with parts dating to before the Norman Conquest, and crenellations from the time intended to keep intruders out. The house is also said to be haunted, and the former owner was a famous writer on topics paranormal. Alas, despite best efforts, I've not encountered a ghost in that ancient Branscombe house. But I did find a Green Man at an interesting place in the local parish church.

St. Winifred's Church is a history lesson in stone, with bits dating to Saxon, Viking, Norman, and Tudor eras. As I walked inside, I found myself beside a big medieval baptismal font, ornamented with two protruding Green Men.

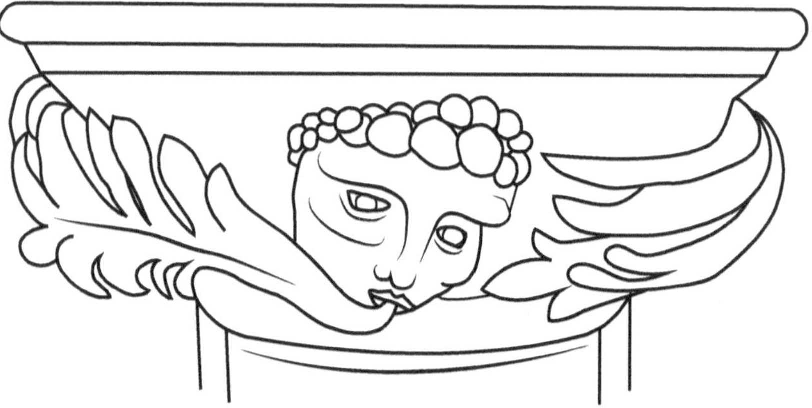

The St. Winifred baptistry is yet another example of a Green Man playing a role in the sacred sacrament of baptism.

Baptism is one of the most important sacraments observed in all Christian denominations; it signifies the entrance of believers into the Church, which makes the baptismal font a portal to the life of faith. For this reason, medieval baptismal fonts are decorated with appropriate images, such as the signs of the four Gospels, the Apostles, grapevines (a symbol of life-in-Christ expressed by Jesus in the Gospels), Christ's resurrection, and so on. Given the Green Man's presence on baptismal fonts, it stands to reason that the Green Man is a symbol that fits beside other symbols of spiritual rebirth and the Christian faith.

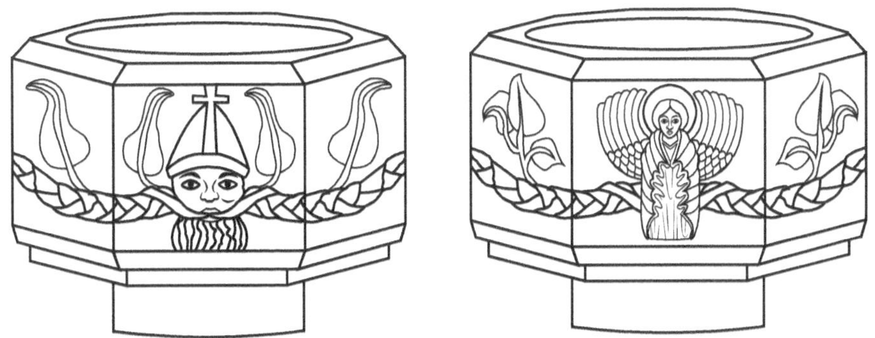

This Green Man drawing, based on a baptismal font in St. John's Church in Coolbanagher, Ireland, is wearing a bishop's mitre, indicating that he is clearly a Christian symbol. The vine the spews out of his mouth encircles the entire font, enclosing within its embrace three angels.

You also see the Green Man on medieval rood screens, the elaborately carved partitions that separate the chancel (used only by priests to celebrate the Mass) from the nave (used by common people). This was a most holy threshold in medieval churches, representing the curtain to the Holy of Holies in the Jerusalem temple, the boundary between what is sacred and what is profane. It would be the last place for an image that didn't represent the Christian faith.

On a brief stop in the Church of St. Michael in Chagford, Devon, I was drawn to the amazing carvings that cover the rood screen, a rare survivor from rot and insects, that dates back to medieval times. The Eucharist, the rite believed to ensure each worshiper's participation in God's salvation, was served at the rood screen. I grinned as I spotted a Green Man. And then I saw another, and another, and . . . Ultimately, I counted eight different Green Men prominently carved on the front of the screen.

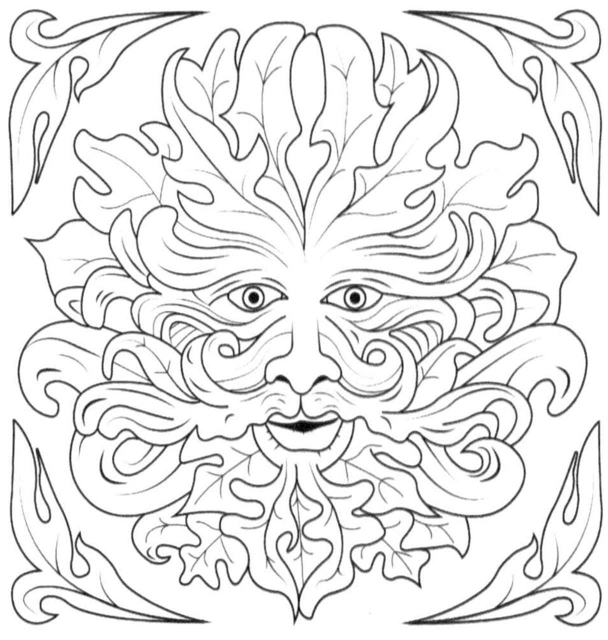

Taken from a Green Man on the sixteenth-century rood screen in the church in Marwood, Devon, England. The custom of screening off the altar—where the rood, or crucifix, was placed—is very ancient. It emphasized the sacred mystery surrounding the place of sacrifice (possibly a survival of Judaism, to which the Celtic Christians felt particularly close). For the Green Man to be placed here indicates the connection between this image and the medieval understanding of Christ.

We've looked at two areas of medieval church architecture—the baptismal font and the rood screen—where the rites central to Christian religion were celebrated, and we have noted that they are decorated with foliated heads. The Green Man was not a representation of unofficial Paganism: rather, he appears at those places that symbolize entrance into the Christian faith (baptism) and then assurance of continuity in that faith (the Eucharist). Both baptism and Eucharist are metaphorical thresholds of faith; they symbolize transition into the Christ-life.

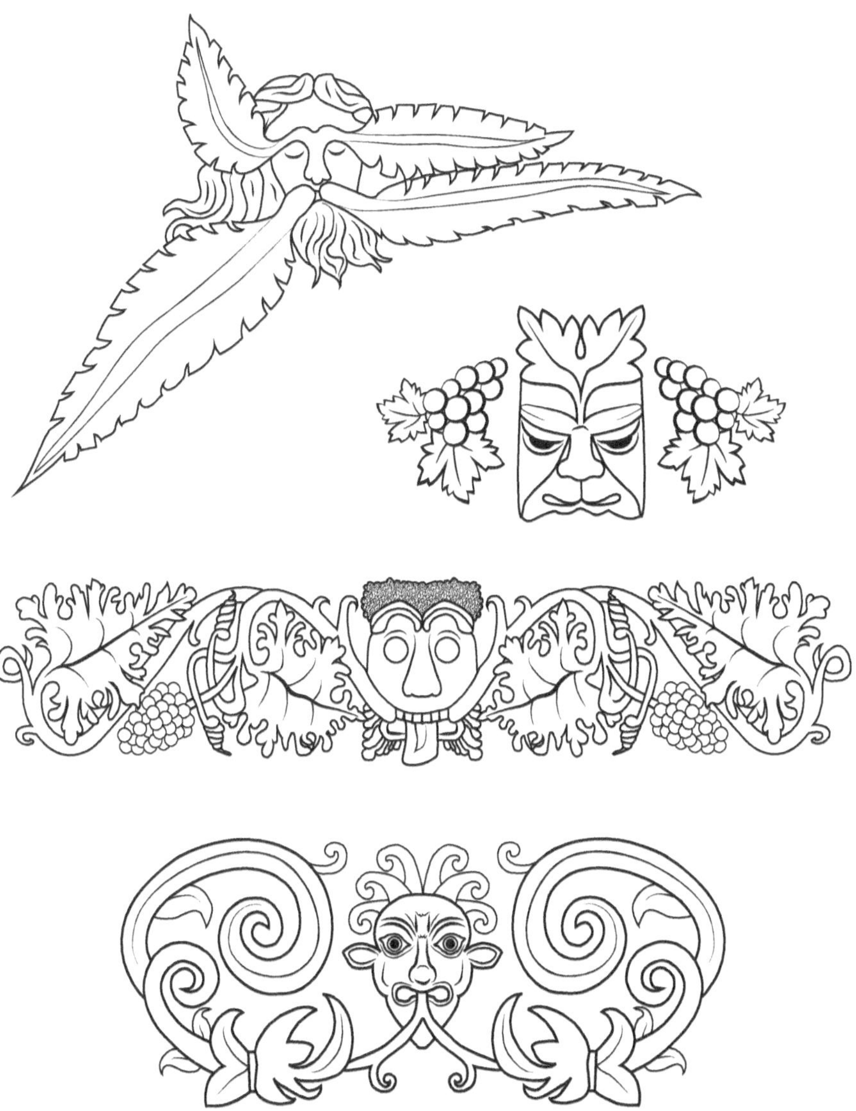

Green Men on rood screens (from top to bottom): the Church of St. Nicholas in Blakeney, Norfolk; the Church of St. Michael in Chagford, Devon; St. Michael's Church in Mere, Wiltshire; and Cartmel Priory, Cumbria.

Are there other examples of the Green Man placed at the portals of religious belief? Yes. In fact, a great many. Remember the "greeter" Green Men at Dornoch Cathedral and at Kilpeck Church? The door into a church was obviously and literally entrance into sacred space. Coming to church (often daily) for celebration of the Mass was a vital part of religious life in the Middle Ages—and here again, we find the Green Man positioned at a sacred portal.

While walking the Camino in 2023, my wife and I trod several kilometers off the path, in hopes of being admitted into the Vilar de Donas. An odd circumstance drove us there: we had stayed at Albergue San Miguel in Hospital de Orbigo, and there we were astonished to see the cover of my book *Water from an Ancient Well* labeling what was literally an ancient well in that very old building. The owner, Arturo Jose Garcia Arana, turned out to be a real Celtophile who was excited to talk about religion and sacred art. He told us we must take a side-route off the Camino to visit the Church of Vilar de Donas, in the Spanish Celtic region of Galicia.

On reaching the church, we discovered that it's only open for viewing twice a month—and the Saturday morning when we happened to be there was one of the

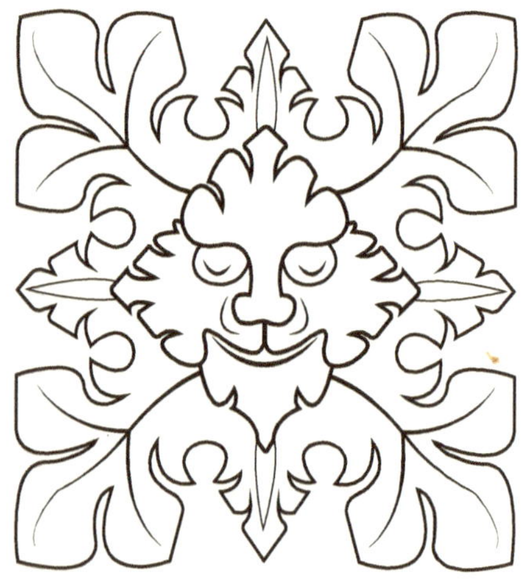

A Green Man from the ceiling of the cloisters of Durham Cathedral.

open days. We were fortunate indeed. Having received Arturo's advice, and then finding it accessible, we felt God's providence was working on our behalf.

Originally a convent, the church became the worship and burial space for the Knights of Saint James, who were warrior-monks dedicated to protecting pilgrims on the Camino pilgrimage, similar to their contemporaries in the order of the Knights Templar. Art historians say the Gothic frescoes inside the church, painted in 1434, are some of "Galicia's greatest works of art."

At the back of the chancel—the focal point of worship in the church—is a gory image of Christ, marked with the wounds of his torture and death, standing within a box-like structure that depicts either the empty tomb or the church altar. On either side of the suffering and risen Christ are pairs of painted Green Men (though they look rather beast-like). They are literally front and center of the Christian symbolism in this fabulously decorated and historically significant medieval church.

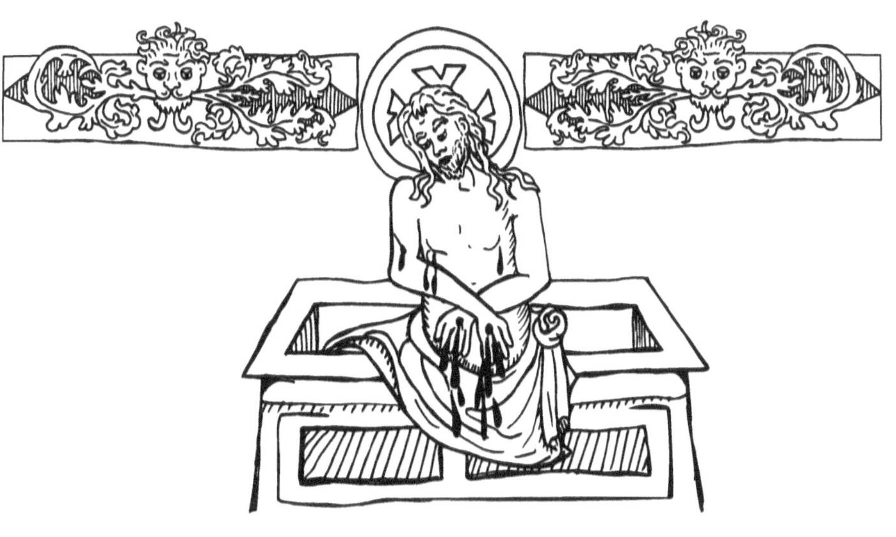

I've been building a case that the foliated faces in worship spaces must represent an idea integral to medieval Christian faith. This is proven by Green Men carved carefully at places of baptism, communion, and entrance to the sanctuary. But what about those Green Men—like the one in Saint Canice's Cathedral—that are put in high places, such as corbels, the tops of pillars, ceiling bosses, or rafters? Were these indeed placed to be hidden—or do they too serve some sort of "threshold" function?

For thousands of years, the abode of God and the angels was thought to be "upward" from the earth. We moderns have more sophisticated notions of the heavenly realm as a "parallel dimension," perhaps more slantwise than upward, but for people in the Middle Ages, upward meant God-ward. The ceiling of a church, along with its supporting apparatus, was a symbolic threshold to the Divine realm.

The Green Man was consistently rendered in places that represent portals of faith—places of rebirth and communion with God—in medieval churches. This is an important clue to his identity. Let's continue to turn over the leaves of history, seeking the Green Man's deeper nature, as we look at Green Men associated with the legend-shrouded order of the Knights Templar.

Death and resurrection
as well as hiding and reappearance
are two different but closely related motifs
in the divine drama.

—Hassan Haddad

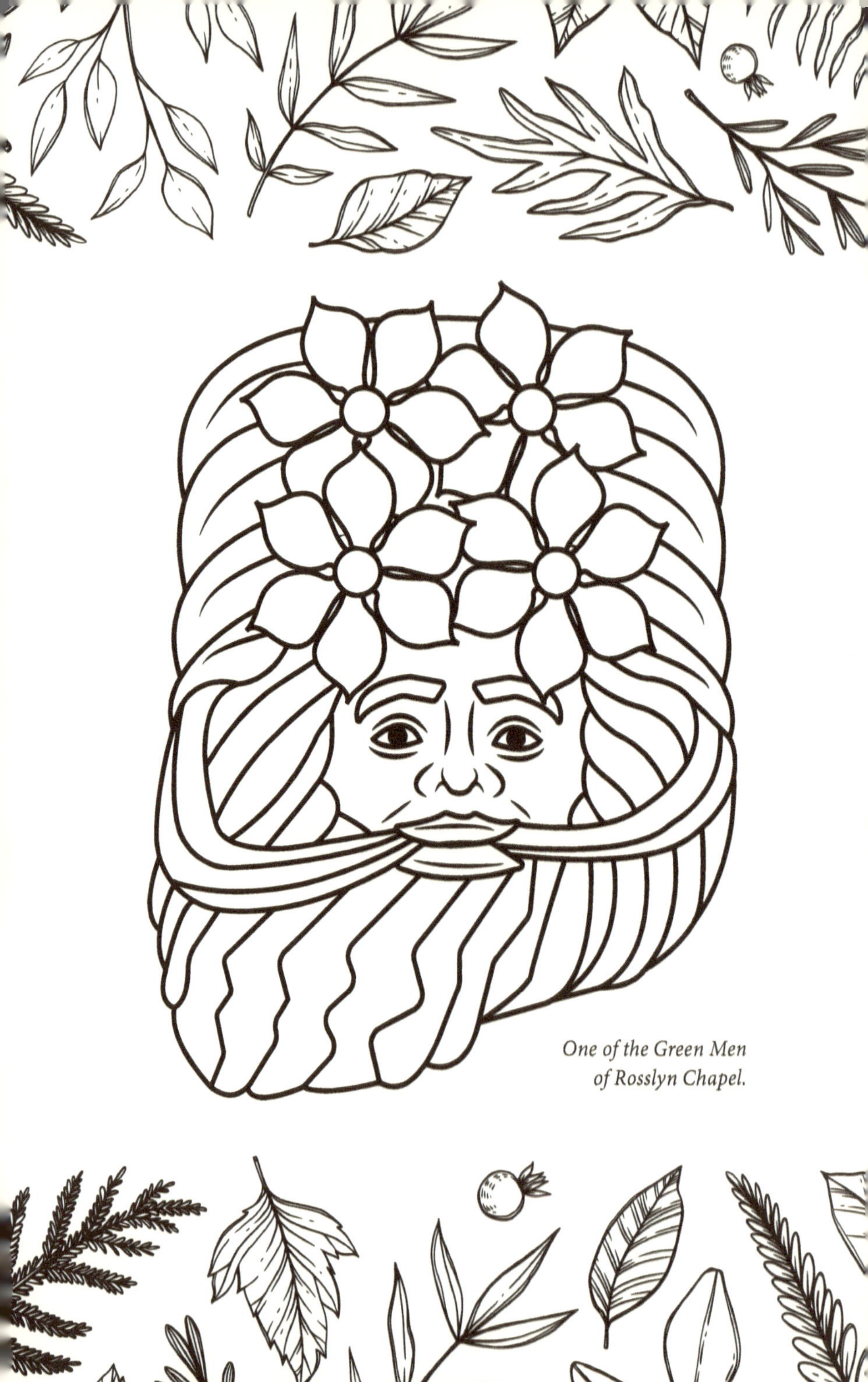

*One of the Green Men
of Rosslyn Chapel.*

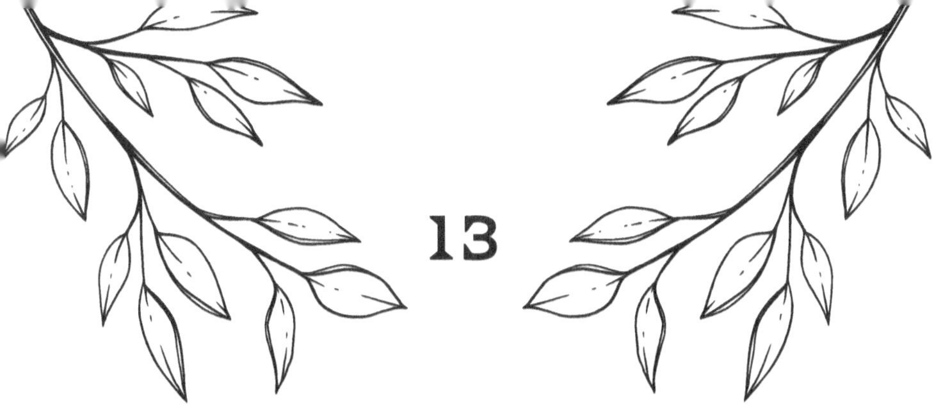

13

In the Temples of
the Warrior Monks

On a lovely May day in rural Herefordshire, Marsha and I stepped out of our rental car, walked past a stately yew, and approached the compact fortress-like structure of St. Michael's Church, Garway, in Herefordshire, a small church with a unique history. I was particularly interested in the mysterious, foreboding Green Man that I'd heard made his home here.

St. Michael's Church in Garway is historically linked with the legendary Order of the Knights Templar. There are only a few bona fide Templar churches still intact in the UK, and Garway is one of those. In recent years, the Templars have entered popular culture in the popular *Da Vinci Code* by Dan Brown, and they are the subject of the onscreen fantasy series *Knightfall*. The Templars have been the subject of centuries of speculations, having to do with the Holy Grail, a lost treasure, the Shroud of Turin, and even an alleged expedition to the New World predating Columbus.

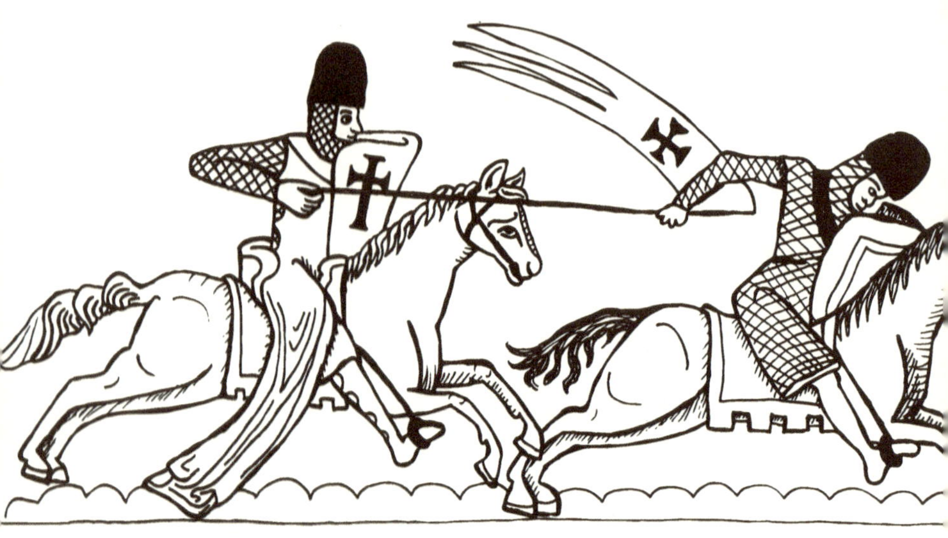

The Templars were founded in 1119 and grew rapidly in membership and power. Templar knights, in their distinctive white mantles with a red cross, were among the most skilled fighting units of the Crusades, but most of the members of the order were actually non-combatants who managed a vast economic infrastructure throughout Christendom, developing innovative financial techniques that were an early form of banking. In effect, they formed the world's first multinational corporation. They were closely tied to the Crusades, and when the Holy Land was lost, support for the order faded. Rumors about the Templars' secret ceremonies created distrust, and King Philip of France, who was deeply in debt to the order, took advantage of this to destroy them and erase his debt. In 1307, he had many of the order's members arrested, tortured into giving false confessions, and burned at the stake. Pope Clement disbanded the order in 1312 under pressure from King Philip.

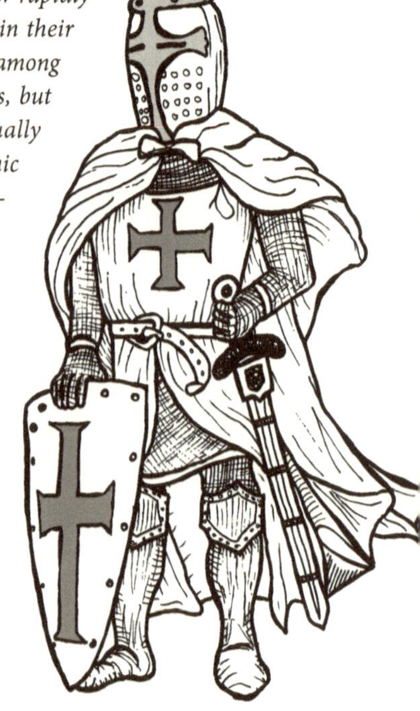

Even in their own time, the Templars inspired tall tales. Despite the pervasive violence of the Middle Ages, people still had some understanding that God does not desire violence; at the end of life, medieval warriors felt the need to be absolved of the killing they'd done. The Templars, who combined the competing values of warfare and religion, inspired the public imagination. They gave more ordinary warriors hope for the salvation of their souls.

The official name of the order was "The Poor Knights of the Temple of Solomon," since they undertook the monastic vow of poverty. Entrusted with banking for Crusaders and pilgrims in the Holy Land, they ironically became incredibly wealthy, which led to the jealousy of monarchs and church leaders—and eventually, to their demise.

Their headquarters was the Temple Mount in Jerusalem, the site of fabled King Solomon and of the Ark of the Covenant, and that added to the Templars' legendary mystique. The Grail Knights of Arthurian legend are much like the Templars, and the Holy Grail was associated with the Templars' Jerusalem center.

The destruction of the Templar order in 1312 also led to a flurry of rumors; under the horrors of torture, Templars confessed to heresy, including the worship of "Baphomet," a heathen idol. Most historians assume that this was a name conveniently planted by torturers, to ensure it came out of the screaming mouths of their victims, but there has been endless speculation over the past seven centuries about what "Baphomet" could be. Some say it was a skull . . . or a three-headed Pagan idol . . . or the devil . . . or—more positively—the Shroud of Turin, or even the Holy Grail.

And "Baphomet" has also been suggested as an explanation for the sinister-looking Green Man situated on the outside of the chancel archway in the Garway Church.

In the twelfth century, 2,000 acres in Garway were given to the Knights Templar. They built the church there and farmed the land to raise funds for their brethren in the Holy Land. The church was built for fortification as well as worship, as these were Norman knights on the contested Welsh Border. Fascinating details of the church connect it with the Templars, including a circular ruined nave that was built to imitate Solomon's Temple. The outside of the church is carved with symbols that include a Jerusalem Cross, a Templar Cross, a dragon, the hand of God, and others. In the floor of the church are Templar gravestones, and a sign in the side chapel says, "In this chapel the Templars were installed into their order."

And there is the so-called Green Man. Before I set foot in Herefordshire, my thoughts about this image

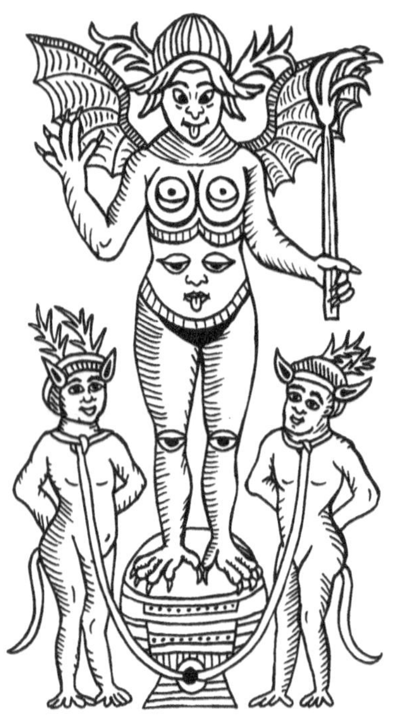

A medieval portrayal of Baphomet. The name appears in trial transcripts from the Inquisition of the Knights Templar starting in 1307.

were influenced by a novel in one of my favorite detective series, the Merrily Watkins mysteries by author Phil Rickman. Merrily is a Church of England priest tasked with ghost-busting for the church. In the novel *The Fabric of Sin*, a Garway Green Man is associated with sinister manifestations (although in the novel, Rickman moved the Green Man outside the church, to a nearby building).

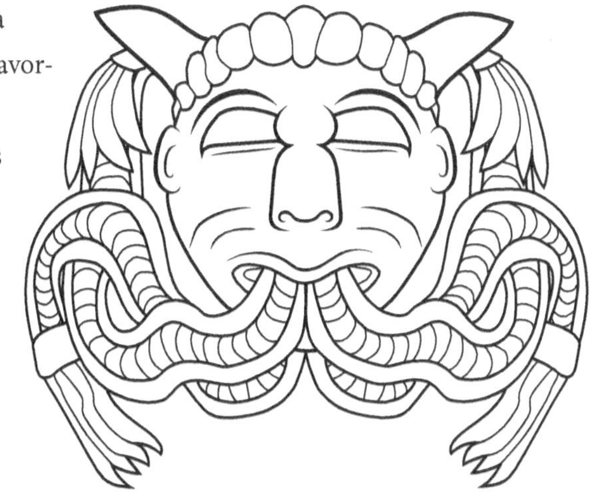

This horned figure, commonly identified as the Garway Green Man, has been used to prove the Pagan roots of the Green Man. Some authors have gone so far as to say that it indicates that the Green Man had diabolic roots as well.

Is there a dark secret hidden in the soul of this Green Man? His gaze made me feel uncomfortable. Most Green Men cheer me up when I'm gazing at them, but this one gave me the shivers.

Signage in the church says this face is "an unusual head with beaded decoration that gives rise to much speculation." And the official church guidebook says it is "a superb head and many explanations are offered as to its identification." Notice that neither official document refers to it as a "Green Man." And, having stared at it a good while, I don't think it is a Green Man.

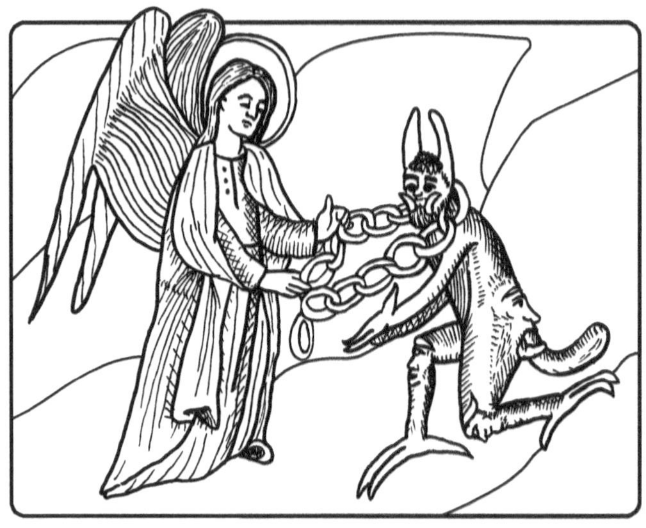

A later medieval portrayal of Michael binding Satan.

Here's my take: the Garway "Green Man" appears on the outside of the entrance to the church's chancel, separating the area around the altar from the more mundane space within the church. As you look at the image on page 147, note that instead of leaves coming out of the mouth, there appears to be a cord—complete with tassels—wrapped around the face. If there's no foliage, it's not a Green Man. The Garway church is dedicated to Saint Michael the Archangel, who in the Book of Revelation binds Satan—and I believe that is what this face portrays: it is an image of Satan who has been bound by the church's patron, the angel Michael, and who is therefore prevented from having influence within the inner sanctum of this sacred space. That would accord well with the symbolism and thinking of the Templars.

There is another church associated with both the Templars and the Green Man, and that is the famous Rosslyn Chapel, officially named the Collegiate Chapel of St. Matthew, which is located about a half hour south of Edinburgh, Scotland.

Like many other readers, I knew of Rosslyn Chapel because of *The Da Vinci Code*; it features prominently in the book, and it was used as a filming location for the movie. I was curious to see this famous site—and it more than lived up to its reputation. Stepping inside the sanctuary took my breath away. The interior is filled, top-to-bottom and side-to-side, with realistic, finely executed carving. Everything you could imagine in the medieval mythic and natural realm appears here.

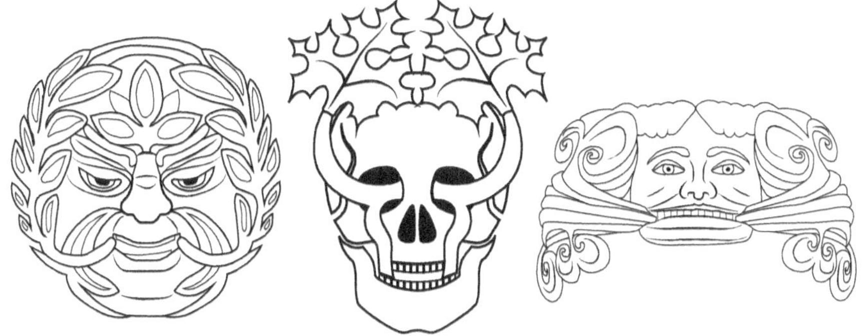

Here are just three of the more than a hundred Green Men that inhabit Rosslyn Chapel. (Note that the center one appears to be a skull with grape vines growing out of the mouth and eyes. This is symbolism we will discuss further in a later chapter.)

Rosslyn Chapel has definite Templar associations, despite being constructed after the dissolution of the Templar order. Ample documentation shows that members of the order found refuge and continued their vocations in Scotland after they were persecuted in England. (For those interested in this topic I recommend *The Knights Templar and Scotland* by Robert Ferguson.) The St. Clair family, who built Rosslyn Chapel, were important in the Templar Order, and there are numerous artistic details in the church that indicate Templar connections.

And it is the forest of the Green Man! In the stone tanglewood of Rosslyn Chapel, there are more than a hundred Green Men; no other church has so many Green Men per square foot. Photography is prohibited in the chapel, so you won't see many of these online or in print, but he appears here in full artistic splendor, each face a distinct individual, some appearing beneficent, others puckish, and a few forbidding. The official guide states, "The Green Man symbolized the capacity for great goodness and the parallel scope for significant evil," which I think is a good summation of the tribe of the Green Man in Rosslyn Chapel.

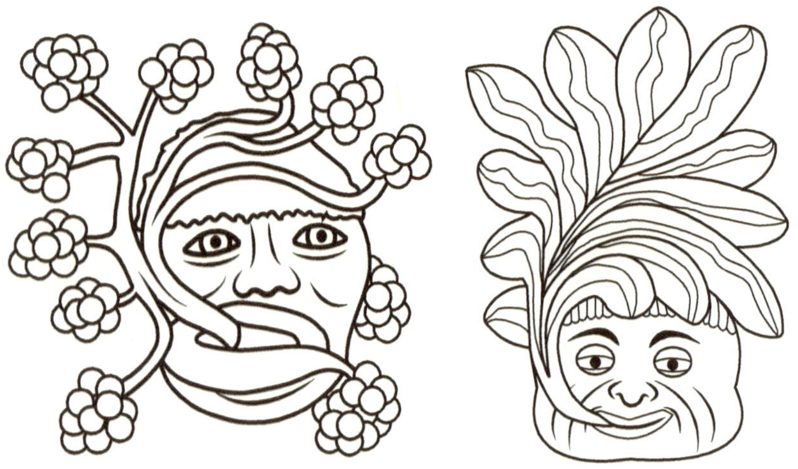

Drawings based on two more of Rosslyn Chapel's Green Men.

Walking the Camino de Santiago Frances pilgrim route in April of 2023, my wife and I took a detour off the main path to visit a truly unique medieval church, Santa Maria de Eunate. In her guidebook to the Camino, scholar and pilgrim Beebe Bahrami says this is "arguably the loveliest and most enigmatic church of the whole Camino."

The church is Romanesque, built late in the twelfth century, but there is no record of who built it? The church's exterior is octagonally shaped, reminiscent of the Jerusalem Temple church. Templars were guardians of pilgrims on the Camino, is this a Templar church? Scholars are unsure.

The church is surrounded by a thirty-three-arched ringed wall. According to custom, if you walk thrice through this outer section, then enter through the church door, you have symbolically passed a hundred thresholds. This gives the church its name "Eunate," which in Basque means "one hundred doors."

On three of the capitals of the outer arches are sculptures with three Green Men on each capital. Inside of the church there are four more foliated faces, arranged two by two on the top of arches that flank the central altar.

These Green Men—curiously, thirteen in total—have bestial, fearsome faces. Are they Green Men or green beasts? It is hard to tell.

The Green Man's ambivalent nature, seen in these temples of the warrior monks, raises a point worth pondering: can we assume that the soul of the Green Man is kindly? Were these foliated heads perhaps harbingers of warning or condemnation? It's a question worthy of our next chapter.

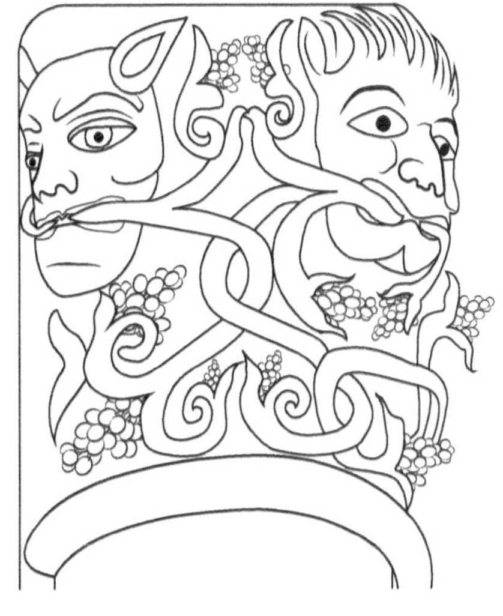

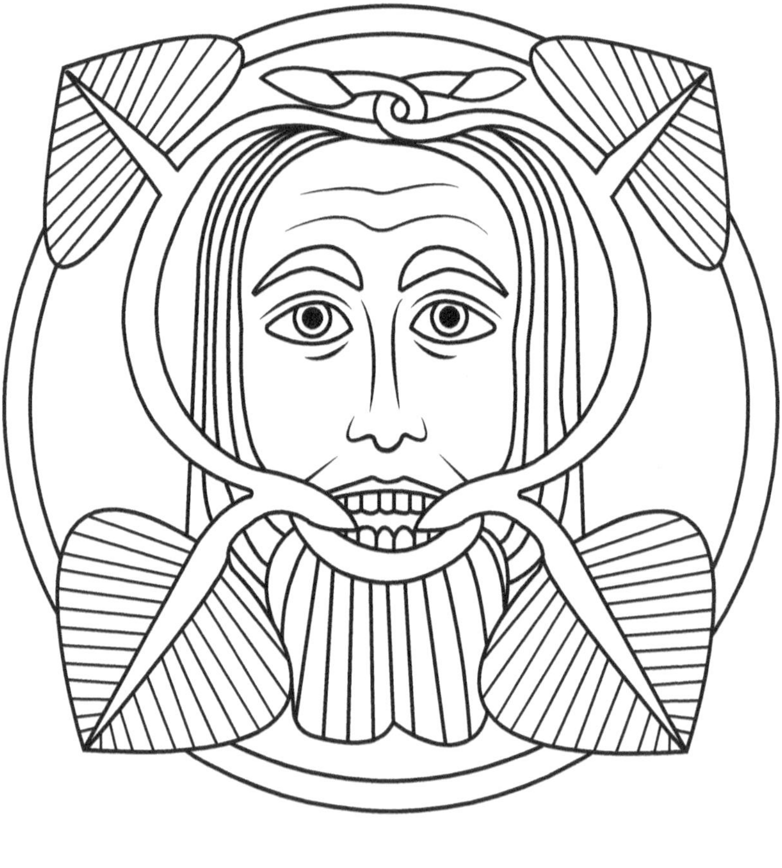

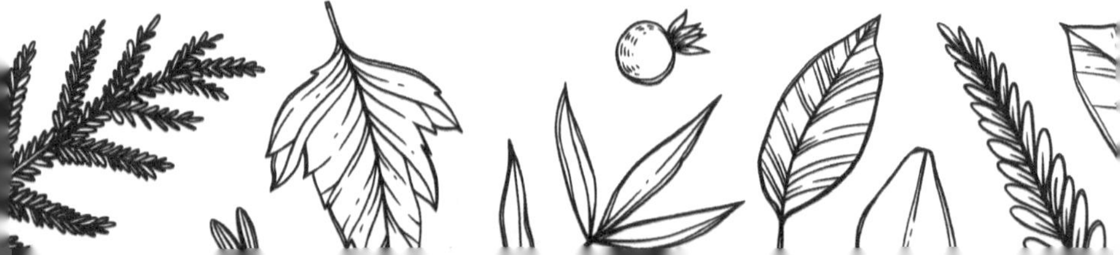

This Green Man is taken from the church of St Andrew, Sampford Courtenay, Devon, where it is a ceiling boss above the altar.

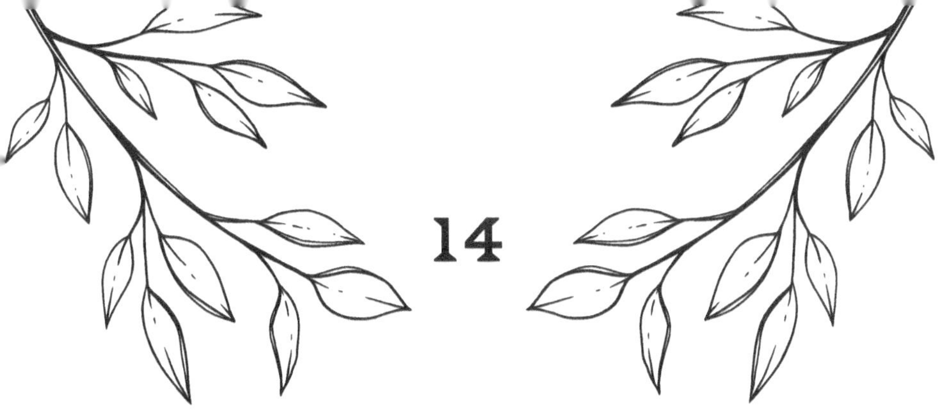

14

All Flesh Is Grass

Before we visited Orkney in 2016, we'd been on multiple trips to the Scottish Highlands and Border region, since Scotland is the land of my family heritage. We had ideas of what to expect from travels in Scotland—but then we discovered that Orkney is different. Orcadians talk about "Scotland" as another country! There are as many Norwegian flags flying there as Scotland's Saltire flag, and the accents are entirely different. All this betrays the fact that Orkney was settled and ruled by the Vikings for much of its history.

St. Magnus Cathedral in Kirkwall offers a rare opportunity—the chance to visit a Viking church, while still in the UK. The cathedral is an enormous edifice of dark reddish stone, dominating the skyline of one of the island's main cities. The entrance is a glorious Romanesque arch of multi-colored hues.

I strolled through the interior of the cathedral, past cyclopean columns, noting a Templar cross carved into the wall. Then I came to a display with illustrations of the life of Saint Magnus, the cathedral's

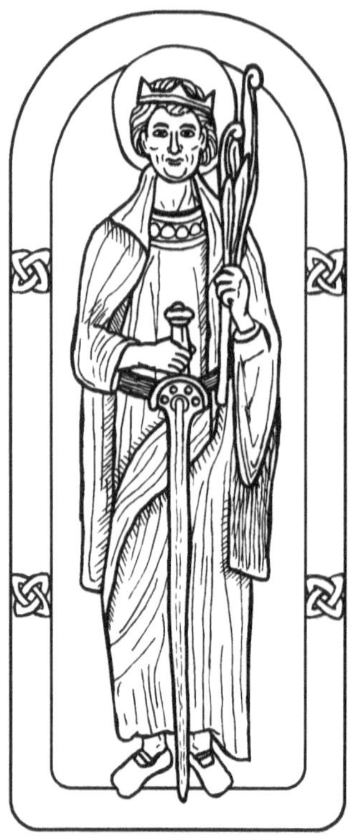

Magnus had a reputation for piety and gentleness, refusing to fight when his kinfolk went raiding. According to tradition, Magnus was killed in a family feud when his cousin's cook hit him over the head with an axe.

patron saint. His story proved to be a real contrast to the warrior monks of the Templar order.

Magnus converted to Christ and got the message that Jesus didn't want him to kill people. He sat through a bloody sea battle reciting psalms from the prow of a longboat, refusing to take life. Later, when confronted by his enemies, he again refused to take up the sword and was martyred. So there I was in Scotland, in a church made by Vikings, celebrating a Viking who was a pacifist.

I had to ask a guide to find a Green Man. There's one on a column near the front of the church, crudely carved, a rather sad-looking fellow, I thought, who appears to be vomiting a string of vegetation out of his mouth. Later, I noticed two other foliated faces photographed in the cathedral guidebook (I'd failed to notice them in the actual building), with this description: "Originally a fertility symbol, it was used to represent corruption of the flesh, the leaves representing sin and decay."

That's certainly a dour take on the Green Man, but others have voiced similar thoughts. Richard Hayman, architectural historian and author of the Shire Library Green Man book, refers to ninth-century theologian Rabanus Maurus who "described leaves as representing lust and sins of the flesh." He also refers to the medieval depictions of vines and leaves as a "tanglewood . . . a metaphor for the human condition," insofar as forest wilderness "trapped men physically" and also "impeded them morally."

Historically, vines, both artistically and linguistically, are more likely to represent life and union with Jesus, but a Bible reference does use vegetation as symbolic of life's ephemeral nature: "All people are like grass, and all their glory is like the flowers of the field; the grass withers and the flowers fall" (1 Peter 1:24 NIV).

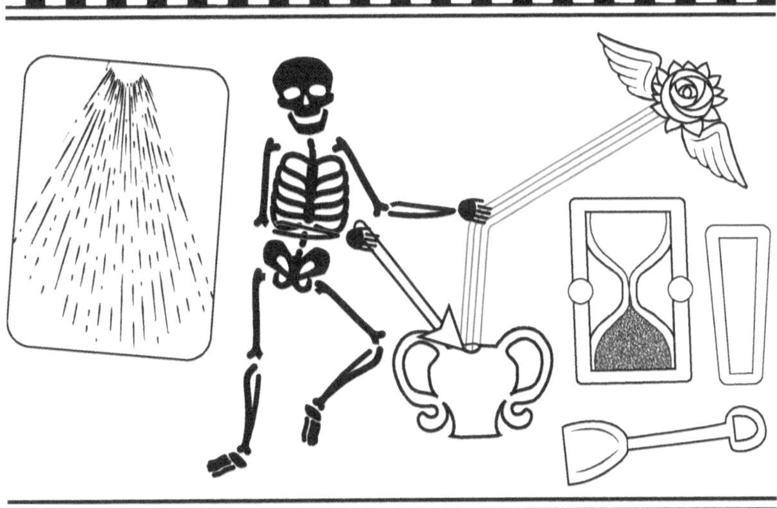

St. Magnus Cathedral contains many graves (besides St. Magnus's). This image, which marks the grave of a man who died in 1673, shows death dancing a jig while it pokes a hole in a burial urn, from which the soul is escaping.

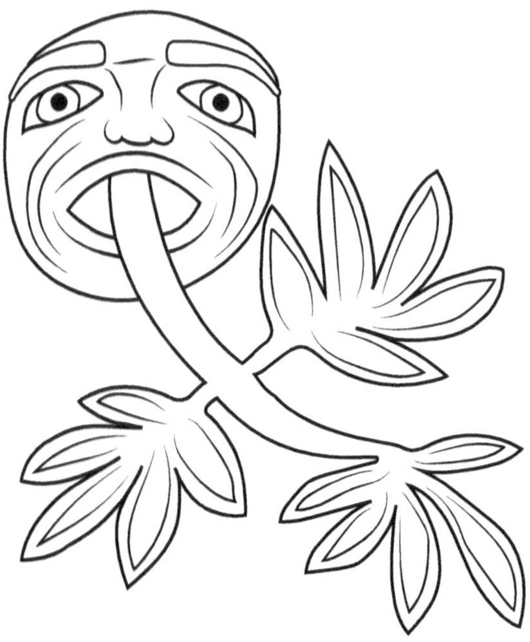

One of the Green Men in St. Magnus Cathedral. These leaves may symbolize sin and decay, but there could also be a far more positive side to this image: the leaves might represent new life taking root out of decay and death (as is true in the natural world). The expression on this Green Man's face indicates the process he's undergoing is not altogether pleasant, a reminder that flesh is mortal—and yet look at that healthy, fully leaved, almost muscular vine springing out of his mouth!

So is the Green Man a reminder of mortality and life's fleeting nature? Maybe. The Green Man's image doesn't only appear in churches; he also populates cemeteries, indicating that the Green Man was associated with death. Often the graveyard Green Man is portrayed as an empty skull exploding with greenery.

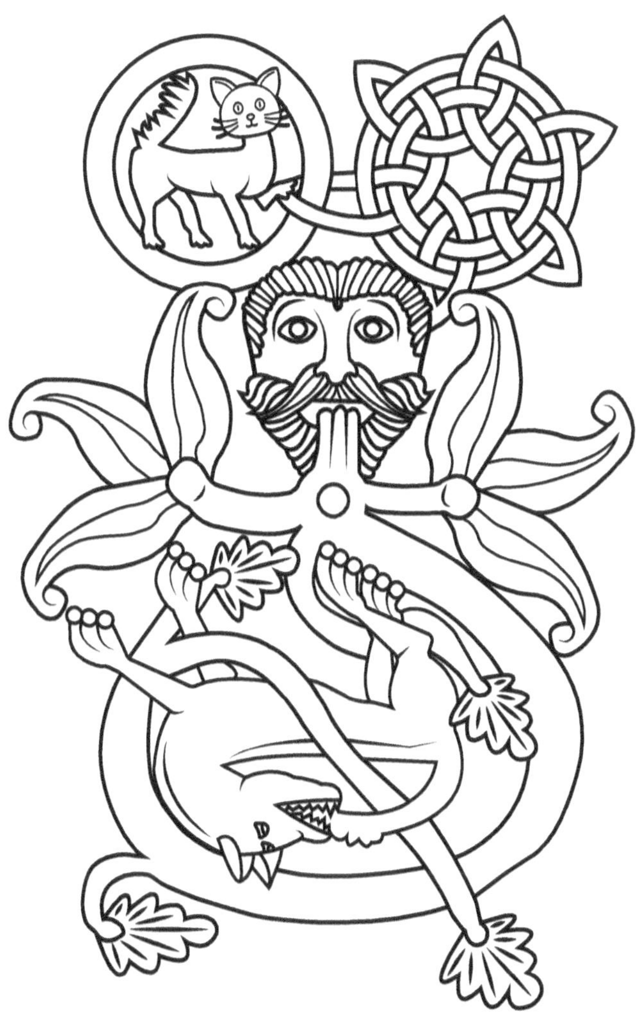

This image is based on on a grave slab that dates back to the tenth or eleventh century. The slab has been attributed to the shrine of Saint Ragenor, an Anglo-Saxon prince who was slain by the Vikings in 870. His grave had been forgotten until the visions of an elderly man drew a priest to the burial site. Many miracles were said to have been wrought at the grave and the king (Edward the Confessor) had a great shrine erected for him. The Green Man's trailing foliage entwines within a number of beasts, including a cat and a dog.

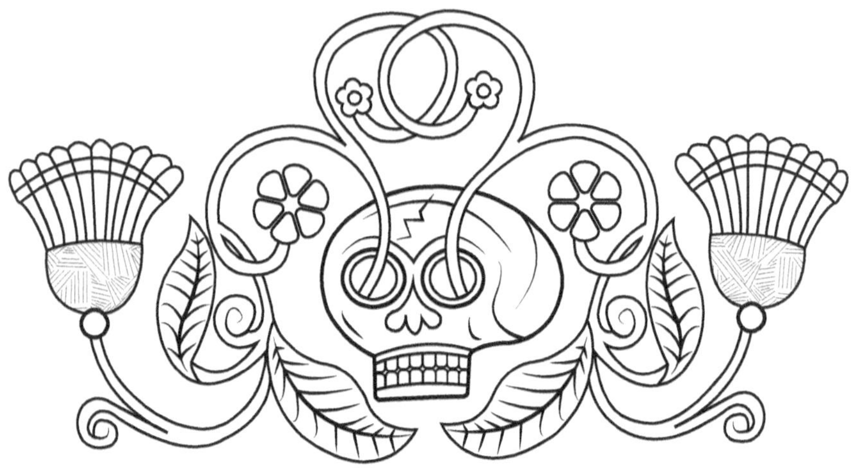

The Green Man's image is often found in cemeteries as well as churches, indicating that he symbolized both death and the promise of new life. This image is taken from a gravestone found in Shebbear, Devon.

In the Middle Ages, people were far more familiar with the concept of death than we are today. Life spans were short, most children died before they reached their fifth birthday, and death was a regular visitor to all families, rich and poor. The great plague that decimated Europe in the middle of the fourteenth century wiped out populations and reduced society to chaos. Medieval artists, reflecting the world in which they lived and its concerns, often portrayed death on the walls of churches. Over the centuries, most of these have faded and been painted over, but a few remain. A common motif is "the dance of death," skeletal reminders of mortality.

Certainly, the soul of the Green Man includes the reality of death. The Green Man is a symbol of transformation, and death is a necessary element in any process of change. As Jesus said in John's Gospel, "Very truly I tell you, unless a kernel of wheat falls to the ground and dies, it remains only a single seed. But if it dies, it produces many seeds" (John 12:24 NIV).

Medieval thought included death as an element contained within all spheres of reality—a more realistic view than modern attempts to sanitize mortality—but the medieval view of Nature was more broadly life affirming. Greenery generally represented not decay but *veriditas*, the power within all living things to replenish, renew, heal, and restore.

As I looked at the Green Man in the immense Norse cathedral in Orkney, I came to a realization: he may be in the process of death and decay—but he's spitting out new life.

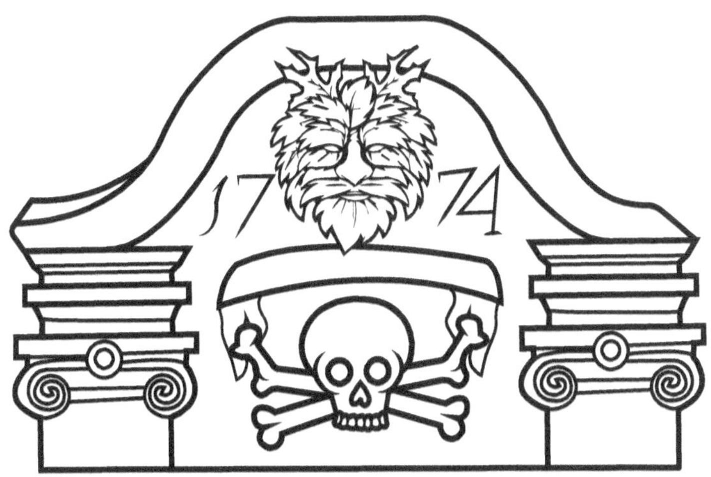

A drawing of an 18th-century gravestone in Edinburgh, Scotland, shows the Green Man's supremacy over the skull-and-crossbones of death.

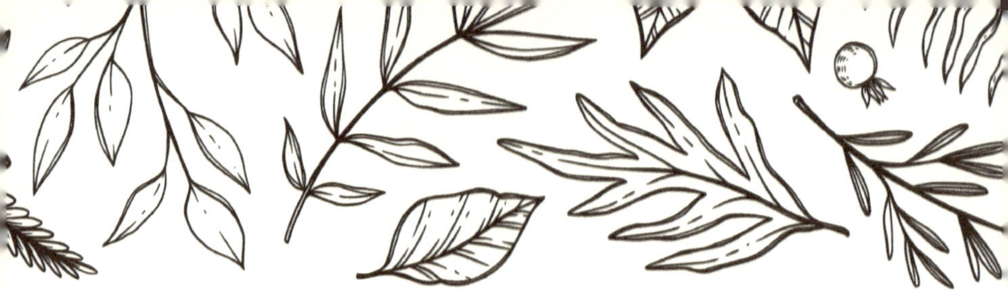

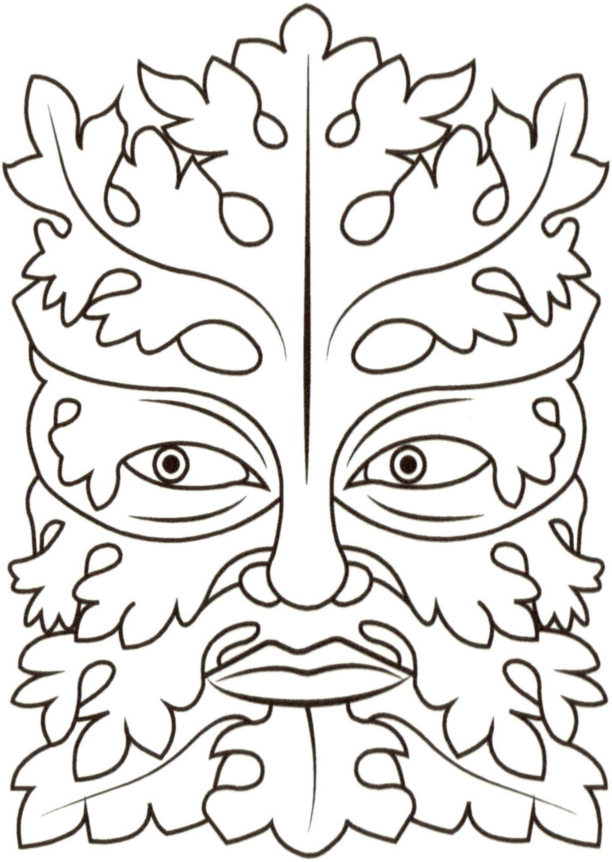

I have a hidden meaning. I was portrayed in a thousand different ways in the past, and I keep sprouting again in the twenty-first century. Don't you want to know who I am? (Thirteenth-century Green Man from Bamberg, Germany, with a face composed entirely of acanthus leaves.)

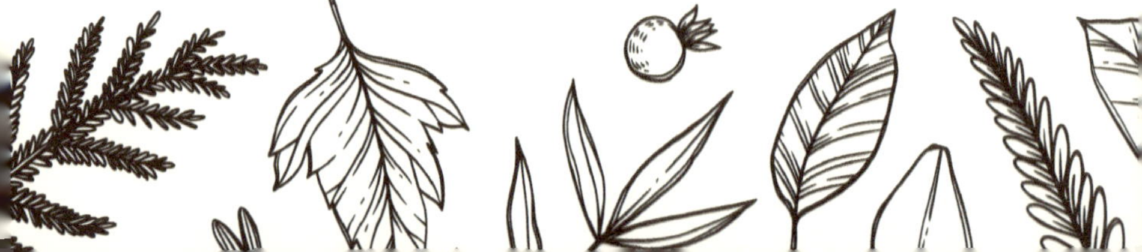

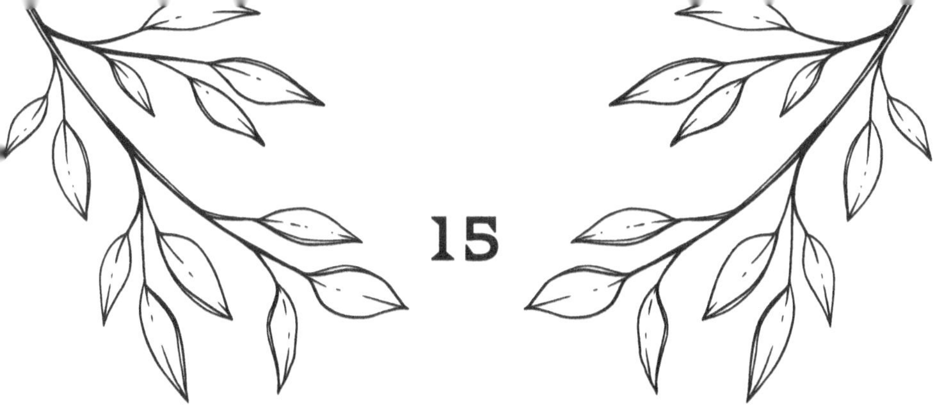

15

The Myth Behind the Face

By now you've armchair-traveled with me through old stone churches, through history from Roman times to the early twentieth century, and through legend from the Islamic Middle East to Arthurian Romance, searching for the secret of the Green Man's soul. I've concluded that the Green Men in medieval churches probably were not intended to specifically portray a Pagan deity, nor Al-Khidr the Muslim sage, nor Gawain's Green Knight. On the side of positive identifications, the Green Man is one inhabitant of the God-infused medieval world, appears in places that symbolized salvation and rebirth, and conveyed something valuable for Christians in the Middle Ages.

So, what *did* these foliated heads found in churches throughout Europe mean to the medieval people who commissioned and carved them? The most convincing explanation that I've found of the Green Man's meaning comes from Oxford writer Tim Healey in an article in the *Glasgow Evening Times,* and also from a more detailed account in *The Green Man Unmasked: A New Interpretation of an Ancient Riddle* by James Coulter.

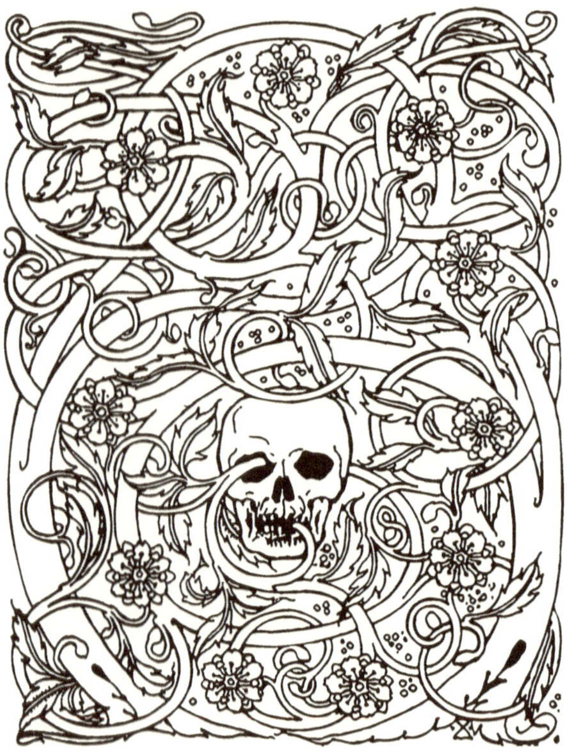

Leaves growing from a skull is an archetypal image still seen today in tattoos and other imagery, hinting at the triumph of life over death.

The foundation of this theory is based on a book titled *The Golden Legend*, a hugely popular collection of Christian tales penned in the thirteenth century (although most of these stories existed in oral tradition before then). *The Golden Legend* was so popular in medieval Europe that a thousand handwritten manuscripts still exist. Contained in this text is the tale of Adam and the Tree of Life. This fable is a sequel to the story contained in Hebrew and Christian Bibles, in Genesis chapter 3. In the Bible's account, God creates Paradise and sets Adam and Eve in the presence of two trees: one is the Tree of the Knowledge of Good and Evil and the other is the Tree of Life. When Adam and Eve are seduced by the serpent to eat of the first tree, God expels them from Paradise. *The Golden Legend* includes a follow-up to the account, a fable based on Jewish writings from the first century, that tells of the end of Adam's life:

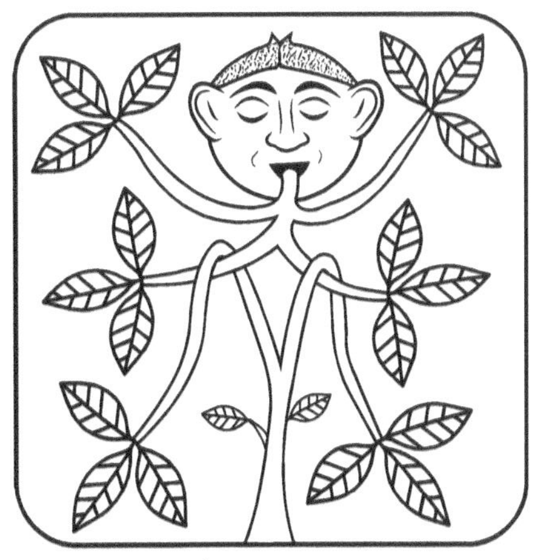

Drawn from a carving from the end of a pew in St. Mary's Church, Bishops Lydeard, Somerset, England. The foliage coming from the Green Man's mouth is the Tree of Life growing from the tongue of Adam. Notice the closed eyes, as if the Green Man is sleeping, symbolic of Adam's death. In the Middle Ages death was most often portrayed in Bible terms as "sleep."

> *And in the end of his life when he should die, it is said, but of none authority, that he sent Seth his son into Paradise for to fetch the oil of mercy, where he received certain grains of the fruit of the tree of mercy by an angel. And when he came again he found his father Adam yet alive and told him what he had done. And then Adam laughed first and then died. And then Seth laid the grains or kernels under his father's tongue and buried him in the vale of Hebron; and out of his mouth grew three trees of the three grains, of which trees the cross that our Lord suffered his passion on was made, by virtue of which he gat very mercy, and was brought out of darkness into very light of heaven.*

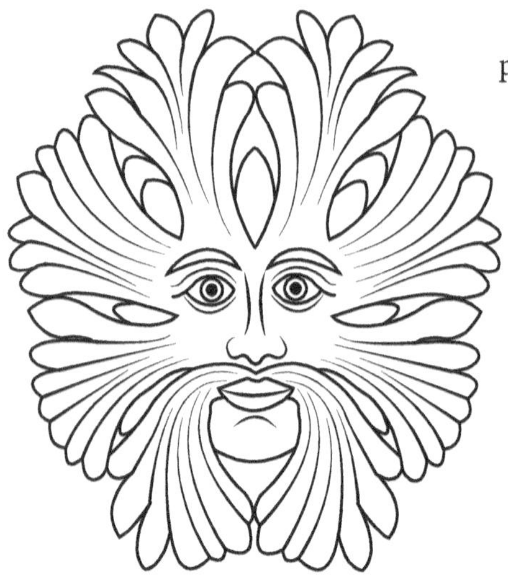

Another acanthus-leaf Green Man, this one from the crypt in Canterbury Cathedral, created in 1350.

Tim Healey, asks, "Is it possible that this specifically Christian story was in the minds of some, at least, of the mediaeval craftsmen as they fashioned their haunting images?"

I think so, and I see confirmation in the Green Men of my acquaintance. One is found in a prominent position of the Lady Chapel in the Church of Saint Mary, Ottery, Devon. The monks used this chapel for more

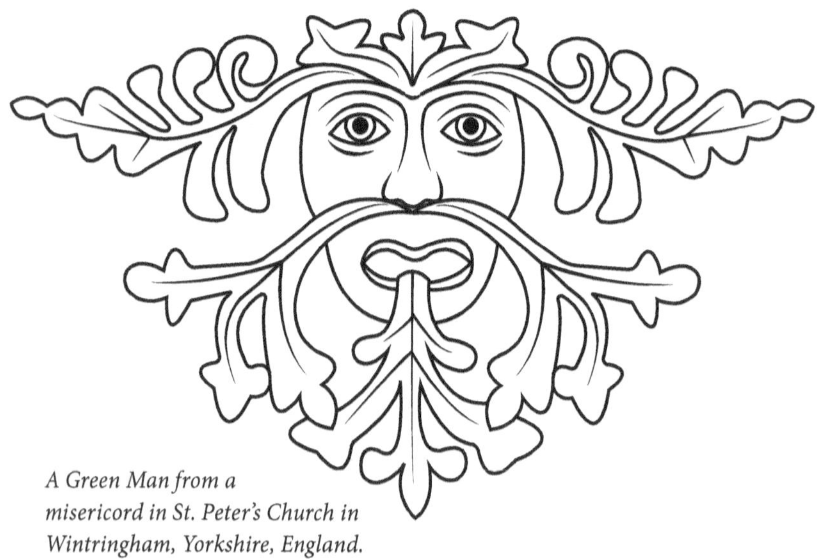

A Green Man from a misericord in St. Peter's Church in Wintringham, Yorkshire, England.

intimate services than those held for laypeople in the larger area of the church. This Green Man appears to be a death mask, with three strands of brightly painted vegetation growing from his pale face. That fits perfectly with the three trees growing from the face of the deceased Adam in *The Golden Legend*. Other medieval Green Men express similar deathly visages.

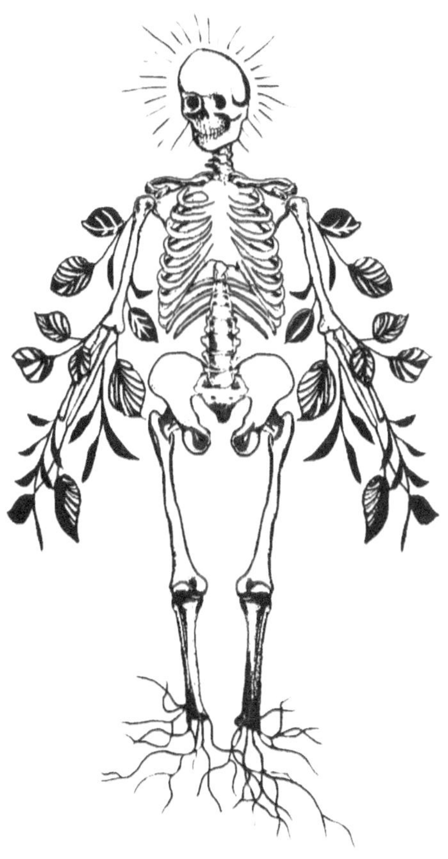

Life grows from death. From this perspective, redemption and renewal not only overcome death but they are also rooted in death. Death becomes the foundation for resurrection.

And then there are the acanthus leaves, which are the most common leaves to surround the Green Man's head. In the ancient world, as we mentioned at the beginning of this books, acanthus symbolized the triumph of life over death. The leaves were often included as architectural features in cemeteries and grave memorials, a comforting visual message indicating immortality. Early Christians appropriated the motif, and for them, acanthus leaves became a potent visual prophecy of transformation, renewal, and resurrection. This confirms that Green Man images were meant to connect the physical and spiritual death that was Adam's legacy to humanity with the eternal life offered by Christ.

In the Middle Ages, people loved the tales in *The Golden Legend* and considered them part of their faith as much as stories from the Bible. The tale of the Tree of Life sprouting from Adam's mouth reverses the negativity of original sin; the first sinner becomes a means of redemption and thus all human failings may grow into betterment, in league with Nature.

If the Green Man is Adam, then he is also all of us. The Hebrew word *adam* used in the Biblical creation stories is not only a proper noun but is also the word for "humanity," as in Genesis 1:27: "So God created humankind in God's image, in the image of God they were created; male and female God created them," where "humankind" translates the Hebrew word *adam*.

Medieval Christians were well familiar with Saint Augustine of Hippo's famous expression *felix culpa* (Latin for "fortunate sin"). This was the concept that Adam's sin was a blessing (fortunate) for humanity. The tale of the Tree of Life sprouting from Adam's mouth reverses the downward path of humanity; the mouth of the first sinner becomes the soil of redemption, and thus all human failings may grow into a renewed future, in accord with the ways of the natural world. The foliated head—portrayal of the tree of life growing from Adam's visage—was a visual portrayal of *felix culpa.*

Given this significance, we can understand why the Green Man appears on the sacred thresholds in so many medieval places of worship. The image of the Tree of Life sprouting from Adam's mouth would be appropriate for rituals of baptism and communion. It also explains why the Green Man found in churches is almost always a *man*, representing the typical medieval understanding of Adam.

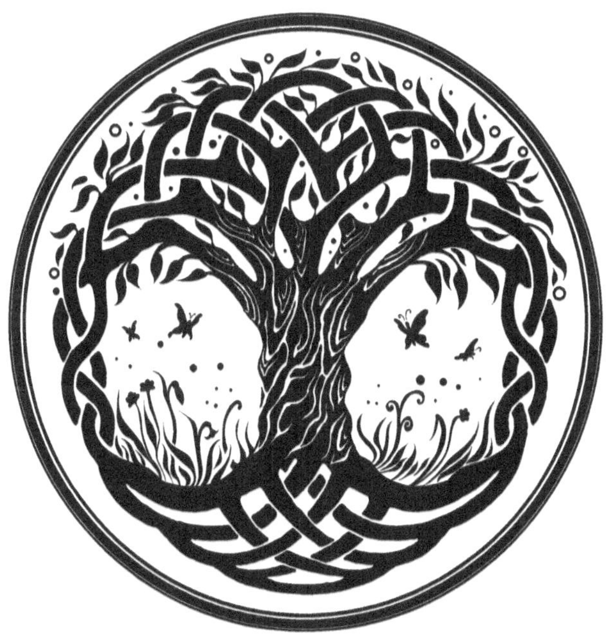

Like the Green Man, the Tree of Life has gained popularity in the twenty-first century. Both images speak of the life-giving relationship between humans and the natural world—and both point to the promise of life eternal that's woven through all green and growing things.

The revision of the story of Adam's apparent "fall" told in *The Golden Legend* suggests that when we bungle things in the worst way, the seeds of an improved future may grow out of those same mistakes. Each of us, in our individual lives, have times when something good emerged from our debacles. And taking this insight into the twenty-first century, we are faced with this new challenge: can we nurture seeds of a healthy life for Planet Earth from the terrible scars we have inflicted on her?

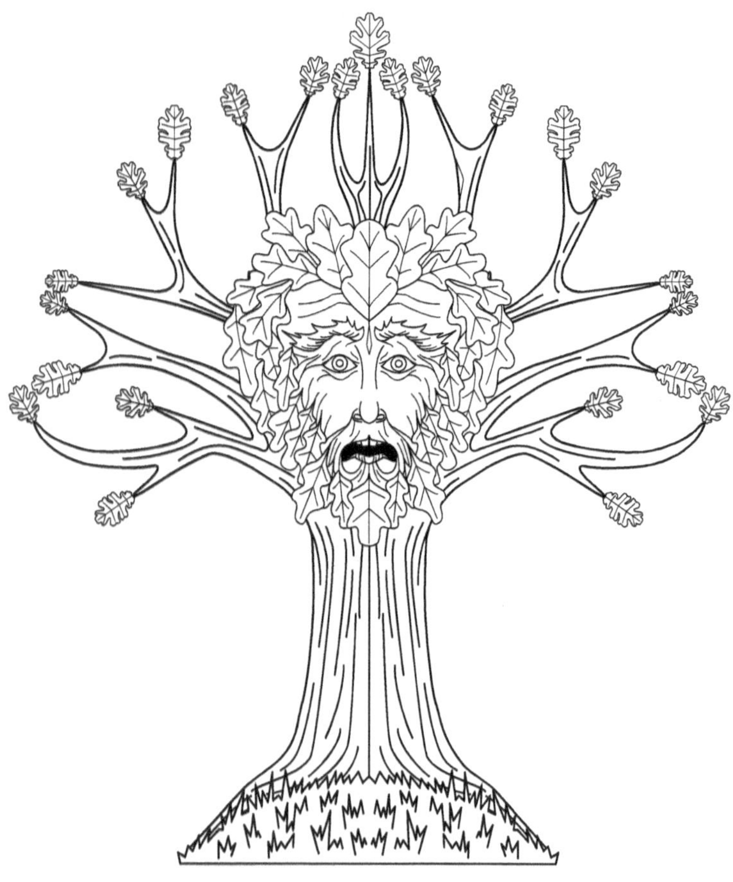

What is the Green Man's secret? *Peer into his eyes and see the soul of Adam, who represents all of humanity. Be comforted and challenged by the glimmer of hope as his death transforms into the greening of a renewed future.* As Carl Jung said, "The colour attributed to the Holy Ghost in the Middle Ages was green, because when the spirt of life is poured over the earth, [it] becomes green."

God works through the love and
freedom of his creatures,
using even our mistakes and the
designs of the Enemy
to bring about our good.

—Stratford Caldecott

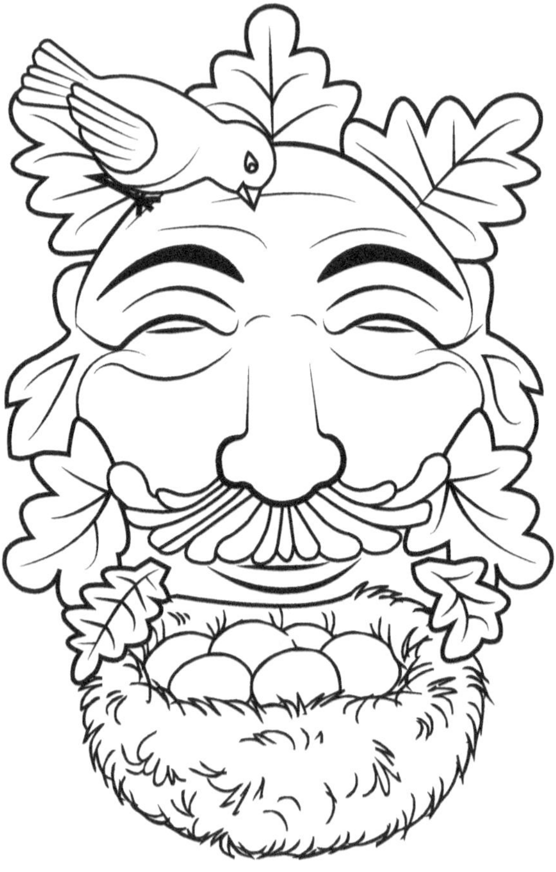

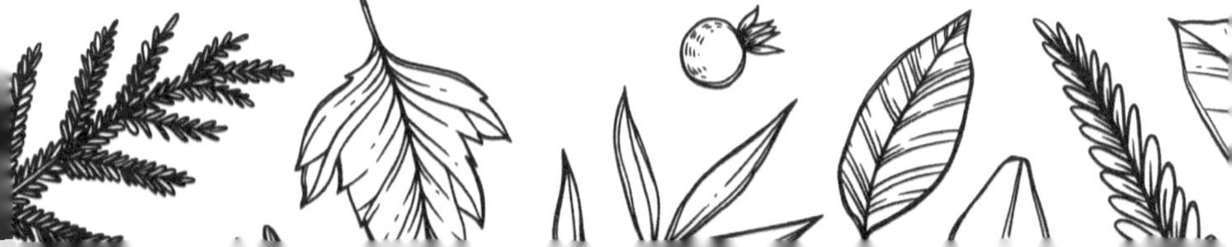

Inspired by a modern-day carving on a garden wall, this Green Man contains multiple meaningful images from Nature: first, acanthus leaves, with their connection to renewal and life's power to endure beyond death; second, a bird, which in many cultures represents the immortal soul; and finally, the eggs, an ancient symbol of resurrection and new life.

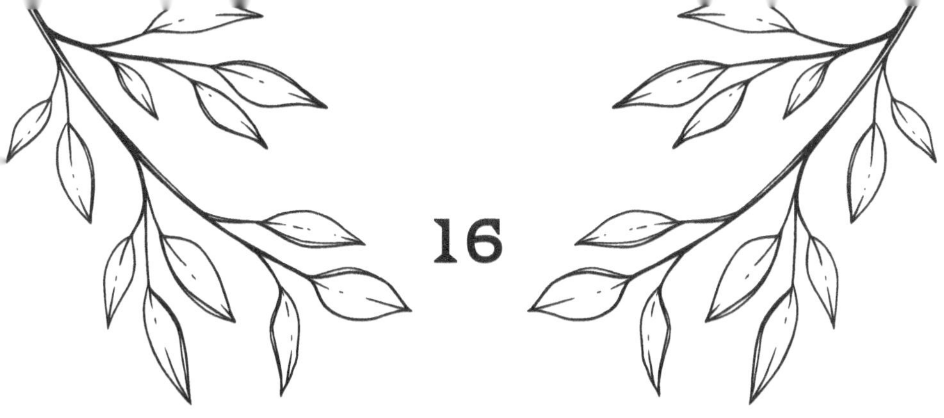

16

The Perennial Green Man

I expect to run into my friend the Green Man when poking about in old churches; it's a surprise, however, to bump into him at a rave-like party with flashing lights and thumping music.

In 2015, Marsha and I attended the Parliament of World Religions in Salt Lake City, Utah, an event that brought ten thousand people from seventy nations together to share in a vast multifaith discussion of the world's pressing issues. At that event, Episcopal Priest Matthew Fox (known for his works on creation spirituality) conducted a "Cosmic Mass" celebrating the struggles and survival of the Earth. At the end of that, amid pulsing lights and the beat of computer-generated electronic music, a figure on stilts appeared wearing an enormous Green Man mask—the Green Man had leapt from the ancient Morris dances into a thoroughly modern celebration. It was another sign that in the twenty-first century, the Green Man has been liberated from the confines of history to bloom anew.

How did the Green Man survive, from the Middle Ages until now? Many elements of medieval church art were banished in the

Reformation era that followed the Middle Ages, but the Green Man continued on. The Protestants who followed the way of Luther and Calvin in the sixteenth and seventeenth centuries could be ruthless in their attempts to eradicate the rival Roman Catholic faith, blowing up abbeys, smashing statues in churches, and killing priests. Christian Europe descended into bloody religious wars. But the leaf-face motif—already centuries old at the time—fared well through this unfortunate phase of religious history.

Martin Luther, the German priest who began the Protestant Reformation, may be one reason the Green Man lasted through this time of spiritual upheaval. The newly invented printing press stamped out thousands of copies of Luther's essays, fanning the sparks of Protestantism into flame, and some of those vital documents included illustrations of the Green Man—big and bold, right on the title page.

Luther wrote and spoke about matters he called *adiaphora*—a word meaning "indifferent things." Adiaphora were things "unessential for salvation" and yet meaningful, such as stories of the saints, church music, or ecclesiastical art.

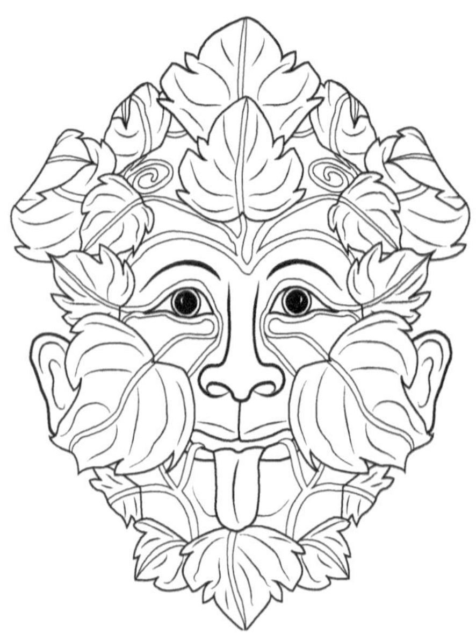

Notice that this thoroughly modern Green Man, who made his appearance at the 2015 Parliament of World Religions, has an out-thrust tongue, like several of the ancient Green Men we've encountered in this book.

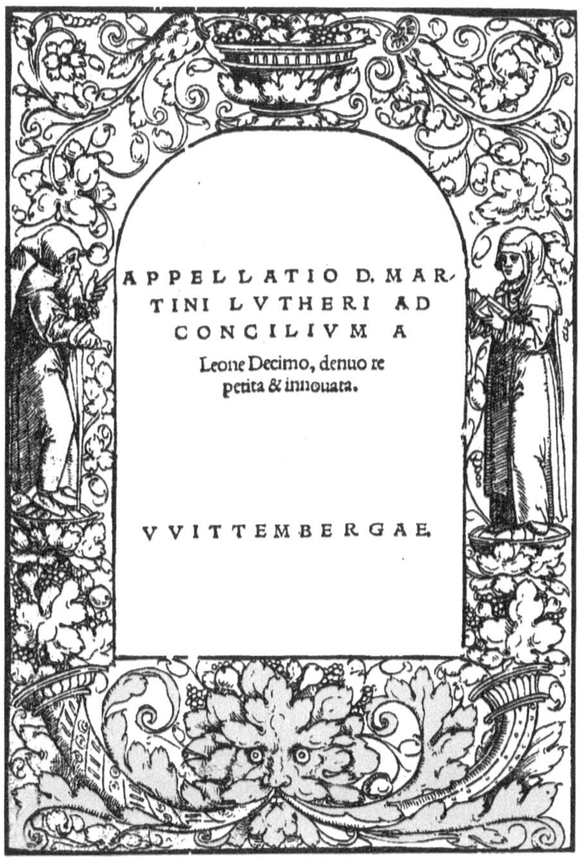

The title page of Luther's Appeal to the General Council, 1520, shows our leafy friend as an integral part of the design.

He compared fellow Reformers to a drunk person who falls off one side of a horse, is righted again, then falls off the other side, symbolizing those who had formerly been addicted to non-biblical traditions, but who now wished to discard such ideas in their entirety. We do not know for certain, but it fits with Luther's understanding that he would not object to the popular tale of the Tree of Life emerging from

Adam's mouth, the legend behind the leaf faces in medieval churches. Luther wrote, "The power of God is present at all places, even in the tiniest tree leaf. Do you think God is sleeping on a pillow in heaven? ... God is wholly present in all creation, in every corner, behind you and before you."

Have you noticed how any item that goes out of popularity—if you hold onto it long enough—will come back again? I count myself fortunate to have bow ties, fountain pens, and vinyl records that were originally prized, then laughably unfashionable, and now have become "hip" again. In a similar manner, the Green Man lived on through the 1600s and 1700s.

Perhaps the Green Man lacked the same vitality as he displayed in the Norman era, but he was still there.

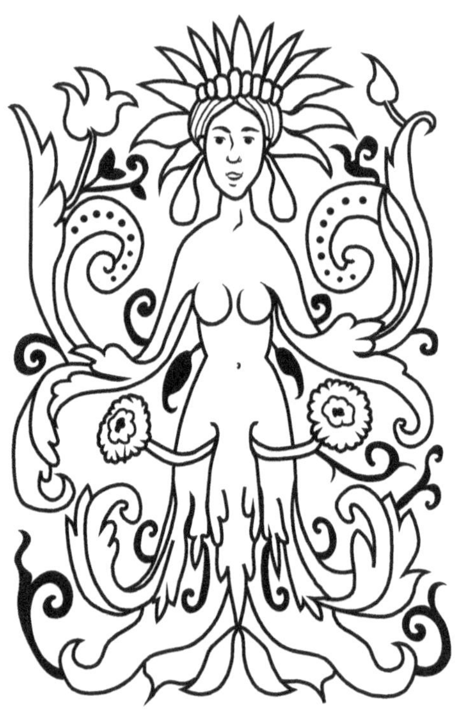

A foliated woman at Traquair House in Scotland, painted on a drawing room ceiling between 1500 and 1600, shows how the leaf face motif branched out into more daring—even erotic—interpretations as it transmuted from sacred to household settings. The ill-fated Mary Queen of Scots stayed at Traquair House her last night in Scotland before entering England and being arrested, and then eventually beheaded. I like to think this leafy image might have given her a little smile on such a sad stay.

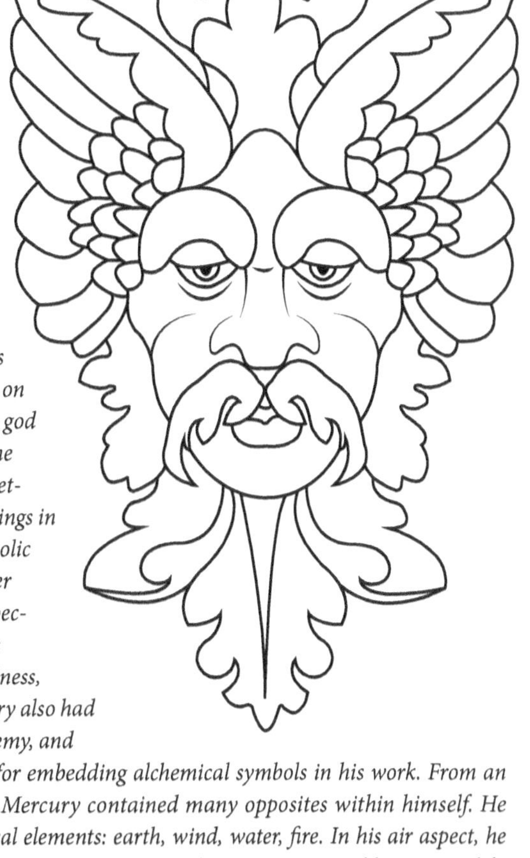

Artists of the European Renaissance sought to revive the arts of Classical antiquity, which included images similar to the Green Man. The original of this image was created in the early sixteenth century by Michelangelo. It shows a Green Man with wings on his head, like those of the god Mercury. Mercury was the god of the market, the fleet-footed messenger god. Wings in general indicated a symbolic connection with the Other World, so from this perspective, this image combines Nature, the world of business, and the heavenly. Mercury also had deep significance in alchemy, and Michelangelo is known for embedding alchemical symbols in his work. From an alchemical perspective, Mercury contained many opposites within himself. He contains the four Classical elements: earth, wind, water, fire. In his air aspect, he is the spirit—the wind—that is present everywhere in Nature and brings it to life. As a hermaphrodite, he unifies the sexes within himself. He is both a helper and a trickster; he is bride and groom; alpha and omega, the beginning and the end. He's depicted as both a young man and an old man (as he appears in this Green Man). His association with the Green Man is appropriate, since the Green Man is also a creature of contradiction. He too is the trickster who turns everything on its head and uses paradox to point us beyond the boundaries we've imposed on our ideas about the world.

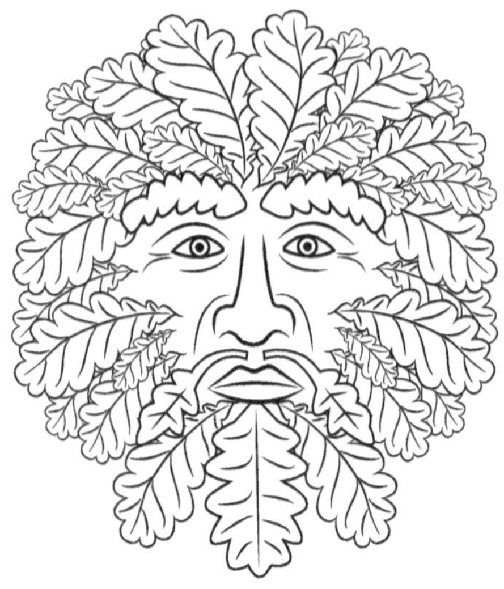

The inspiration for this Green Man comes from a walnut carving on the end of a pew in Northington, England, created in the late nineteenth century as part of the Victorian Gothic revival. The other pews in the church include carvings of the Four Evangelists, while the Twelve Apostles are portrayed in the church's stained glass, so the Green Man is in good company with the central figures of Christianity, just as his medieval ancestors were.

His leaves are still fresh, his message undying.

During the Tudor era in England the Green Man did have to relocate. His favorite places in churches declined in their importance as Protestants changed focus from sacraments (baptism and Eucharist) to the centrality of the spoken word. At the same time, the sorts of ornamentation that were popular in churches during the Middle Ages moved into private homes and civic buildings.

The Green Man survived into the nineteenth century when he flowered again during the Victorian age. Novelists like Sir Walter Scott renewed popular interest in the Middle Ages; dusty old Gothic buildings and rusty suits of armor were suddenly deemed "romantic" and in great demand with collectors. Architects began building homes and churches in "Neo-Gothic" style, a trend that would last more than a century. Scott's Abbotsford House was one of the first examples of this revived medieval fashion, and its interior included several Green Men. At the same time, churches that had been allowed to deteriorate since the Reformation were valued again, and many were restored with Gothic flourishes more opulent than the original fittings. This Victorian restoring of medieval artistic forms enabled the Green Man to return to his ancient abodes on church walls and furnishings.

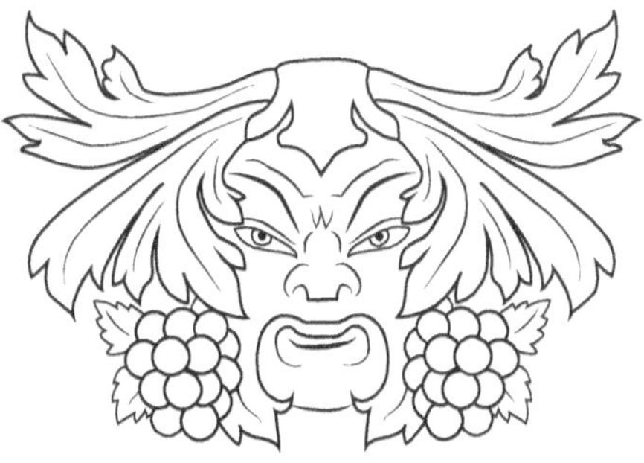

This early twentieth-century leaf face, with both acanthus leaves and grapes, adorns the Crown and Mitre Hotel in Carlisle, England.

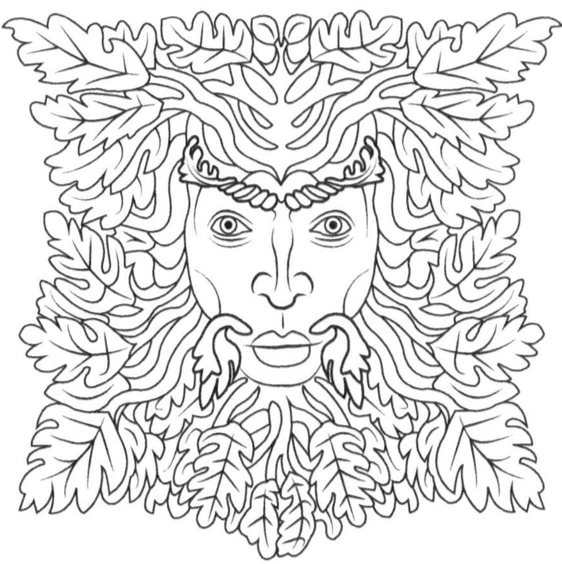

Green Men started out primarily in churches, but eventually, they moved out into the world of everyday life, with their first appearance being on pub signs. This image is inspired by the sign for a pub called the Green Man in Soho, London. "Green Man" became a popular pub name during the seventeenth century, and there are still many pubs with that name in the United Kingdom.

In the late nineteenth century, artists and architects such as William Morris popularized the Arts and Crafts Movement, which emphasized the purity and quality of pre-industrial workmanship, reviving and combining medieval motifs to create new forms of beauty. This movement was influential on both sides of the Atlantic, and it decorated both secular and sacred buildings. At the same time, the Industrial Revolution was coming into full steam with the nascent technologies of electricity and carbon fuels, resulting in the rapid expansion—both outward and upward—of great cities and public works. Ironically, the Green Man benefited from this, flowering both in the abundance and quality of his appearance.

The Green Man struggled through the 1600s and 1700s, bloomed again in the Victorian era, and today, he is sprouting up all over! If numbers are any indication, the twenty-first century is the Green Man's greatest harvest. Just scan Etsy or eBay for Green Man merchandise; you will find pages of plaques, T-shirts, bags, wall coverings, rugs, and other items. Our leafy friend is portrayed on printed and e-reader books, websites, and coloring books. I even have a Green Man bottle opener in the kitchen. While his historical meaning is still a mystery to most people, the Green Man clearly resonates with a great many people in our time.

The Green Man also appears in the most popular contemporary format for storytelling—the screen. Any fan of J.R.R. Tolkien's *Lord of the Rings* will immediately think of Tree Beard and his fellow Ents. *Guardians of the Galaxy* and other Marvel films include Groot, the protective companion of his superhero friends. The *Harry Potter* films feature the screaming and very anthropomorphic Mandrake roots, and the offshoot series *Fantastic Beasts and Where to Find Them* includes the diminutive human-tree hybrids called bowtruckles. The movie *A Wrinkle in Time* makes a significant change from the novel regarding Mrs. Whatsit's non-human form; in the book she becomes a winged horse, but, in the movie, she changes into a winged being with a Classical foliated head.

In recent decades, the Green Man has also taken his place in celebrations of spirituality and environmentalism. Partly this is due to the renewal of pre-Christian Nature religions, including Wicca, Shamanism, Witchcraft, and Druidry. Modern Pagans are well acquainted with Lady Raglan's idea that the Green Man in churches was a portrayal of their pre-Christian deities, and his image can be seen as saying, "See, I never went away, and now I'm out in the open again."

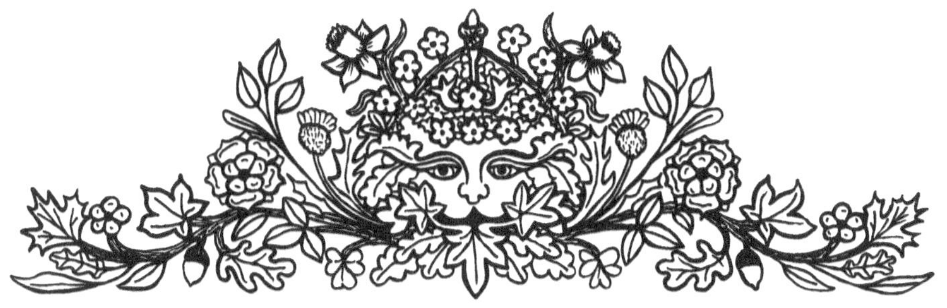

A Green Man had a prominent place on the coronation invitation of King Charles and Queen Camilla, on May 6, 2023. Charles wrote, "It is very strange that we carry on behaving as we do. If we were on a walk in a forest and found ourselves on the wrong path, then the last thing we would do is carry on walking in the wrong direction. We would instead retrace our steps, go back to where we took the wrong turn, and follow the right path. . . . I cannot stress the point enough: we are travelling along a very wrong road." It is time, King Charles implies, for us to form a new relationship with the Green Man.

Yet even without theories as to his historical meaning, the Green Man is a perfect image for Nature-focused spirituality. He cannot be limited to any single religion or philosophy—which makes him a perfect poster boy (poster plant?) for the growing numbers of "spiritual but not religious" believers.

The popular art-and-culture festival called Burning Man, held annually in Nevada, featured the Green Man as its art theme for 2007. The festival site explained:

> *Peering outward from behind a mottled screen of vines and leaves, the Green Man does not speak or sleep; he waits. . . . This year we will appropriate the Green Man and the primeval spell he casts on our imaginations for a modern purpose. Our theme concerns humanity's relationship to nature. Do we, as conscious beings, exist outside of nature's sway, or does its force impel us and inform the central root of who and what we are?*

The Green Man's resurgence in film, art, festivals, and environmental events must be accounted for at a level deeper than words, of things that issue from the greater depths of our subconscious. Carl Jung

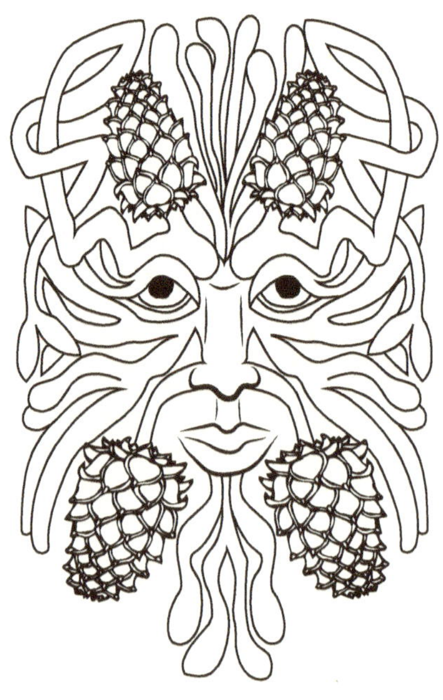

The Green Man has gone international! Twenty-first-century Australian artist Graham Wilson created the statue on which this drawing is based, incorporating Australian native plants in his portrayal of our leafy friend.

proposed that certain symbolic characters—the hero, the dragon, the goddess, for example—are universal archetypes proceeding from humanity's collective unconscious. When we see these figures, we are already familiar with them, even if we have not yet heard their stories, because they are in our ancestral blood. Jung suggests such archetypes rise to the surface of human consciousness when they are especially needed.

The Green Man is certainly needed today. In his postmodern, spiritual, and environmental role, the Green Man is a symbol of hope we can claim both as individuals and as a planetary community. He reminds us of the power and potential of green life to rise and heal the terrible mistakes we have committed.

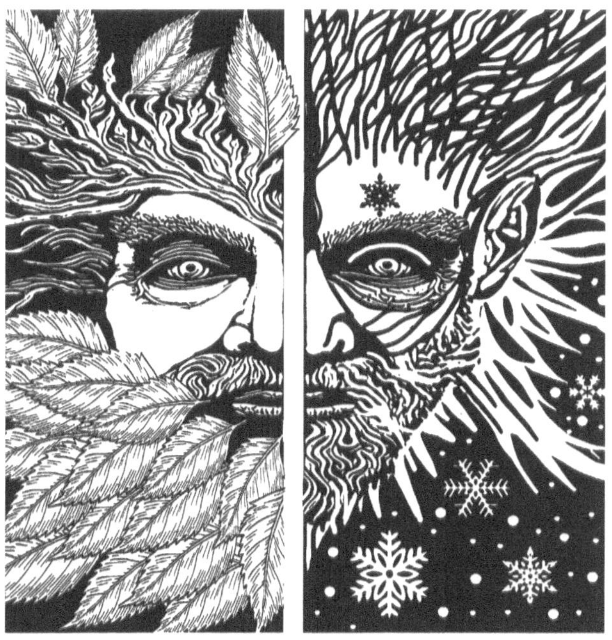

The Yorkshire village of Marsden has a modern-day Imbolc celebration on February 1, in which the Green Man and Jack Frost do battle.

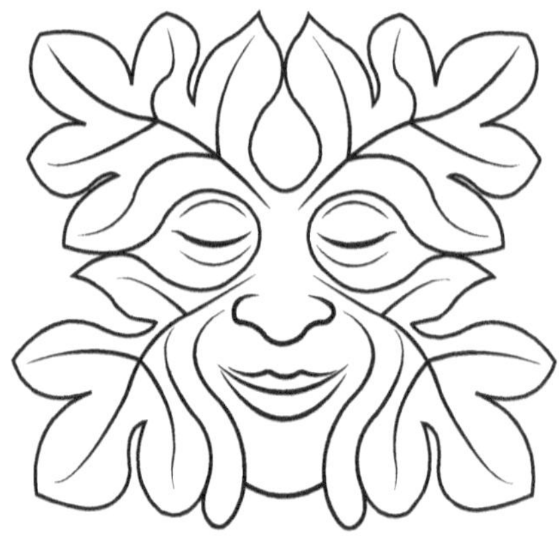

Medieval people, concerned with mortality and the fate of their souls, saw the face of Adam—who symbolizes each one of us—and the Tree of Life growing hope from his tongue. In our time, we cannot escape the brooding fear that our separation from Nature imperils our collective existence. In such a time, we see in the Green Man a symbol of our destinies intertwined with the natural world.

As we contemplate the Green Man as a symbol for our time, allow me to present alongside him another appropriate concept: Pando. Pando is the world's largest single living organism and one of the oldest. A quaking aspen grove in Utah that grows from a single root and shares identical DNA with all its parts, Pando is over 80,000 years old, occupies 106 acres, and is estimated to weigh collectively 6,600 tons. Appearing to be a forest, yet actually a single organism, Pando tells us, "What seems to be many is actually one."

Ilia Delio, scientist and theologian, wrote, "We used to believe that reality was comprised of little separate 'elemental' building blocks, but now we realize that nothing exists in isolation: rather ... everything exists as one interconnected whole." This is not magical or fantastical thinking; in stating this, Delio is wearing her scientist hat. Another scientist-cum-theologian, Teilhard de Chardin, explained how the universe is held together by "Love Energy." This energy has been named many things—the Prime Mover, the Tao, Spirit, veriditas, the Great

Mystery, the Force, and countless others. There is a growing consensus among spiritual masters and scientific theorists that all things are connected by a unitive reality, which works toward awareness, growth, and renewal.

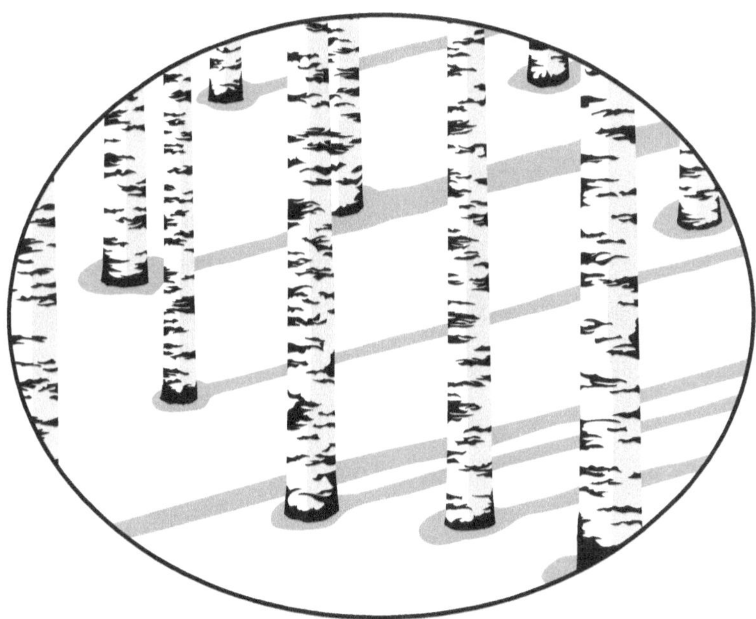

A single genetic male clone, Pando (from the Latin word for "I spread") is the most massive organism on Earth. Sadly, scientists believe that after surviving for thousands upon thousands of years, today he is slowly dying.

Advances in science are also pushing us back toward the Middle Ages' awareness of a living, conscious reality to be found in the world of Nature. Scientists have found that the vegetative world is not "unconscious" as we supposed but alive in ways we did not suspect. Richard Powers, in his book *Overstory*, summarizes some of these findings:

We found that trees could communicate, over the air and through their roots. . . . We found that trees take care of each other . . . seeds remember the seasons of their childhood and set buds accordingly . . . trees sense the presence of other nearby life. That a tree learns to save water. That trees feed their young and synchronize their masts and bank resources and warn kin and send out signals to wasps to come and save them from attacks. . . . A forest knows things. They wire themselves up underground. There are brains down there, ones our own brains aren't shaped to see. Root plasticity, solving problems and making decisions. Fungal synapses. What else do you want to call it? Link enough trees together, and a forest grows aware.

Powers goes on to remind us: "You and the tree in your backyard come from a common ancestor. A billion and a half years ago, the two of you parted ways. But even now, after an immense journey in separate directions, that tree and you still share a quarter of your genes."

In the light of all this, the Green Man speaks to us, communicating both assurance and challenge. His message is for all of us collectively and each of us individually, and it is both ancient and ever-new.

In *Wildwood: A Journey Through Trees*, Roger Deakin writes of the Green Man:

The leaves flow from him like poems or songs. He himself is a kind of folksong. Everyone knows it, but each singer has a different, personal version, a variation on the theme. . . . He is the spirit of the rebirth of nature. He is the chucked pebble that ripples out into every tree ring. He is a green outlaw and he is everywhere.

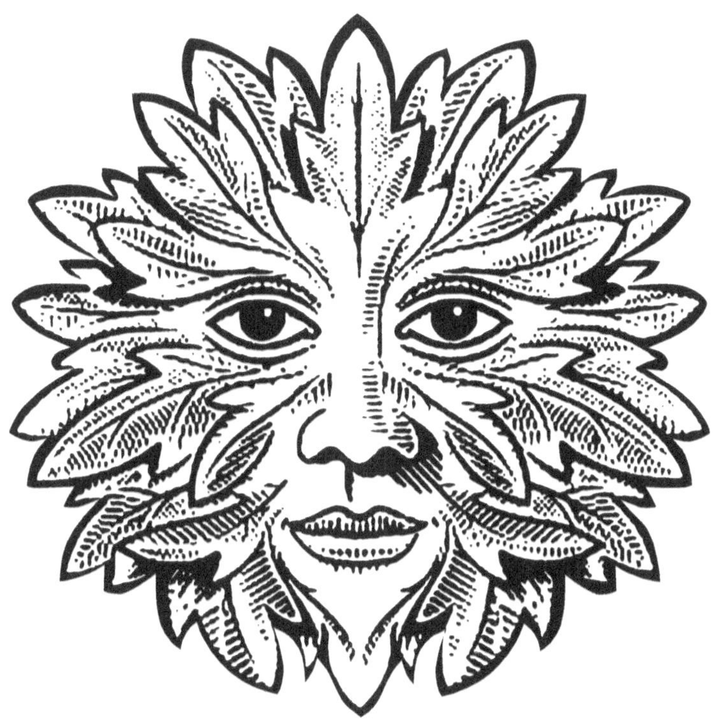

When we gaze into the face of Nature, who gazes back at us? In the depths of these eyes, we see reflections of something totally other than ourselves—and also something intimately akin to ourselves.

What is the secret of the Green Man's soul? Perhaps simply this:

We are united—you, me, the plants, the Earth, the Divine—we are all one.

The knowledge of the heart
is in no book and is not to be found
in the mouth of any teacher,
but grows out of you
like the green seed.

—Carl Jung

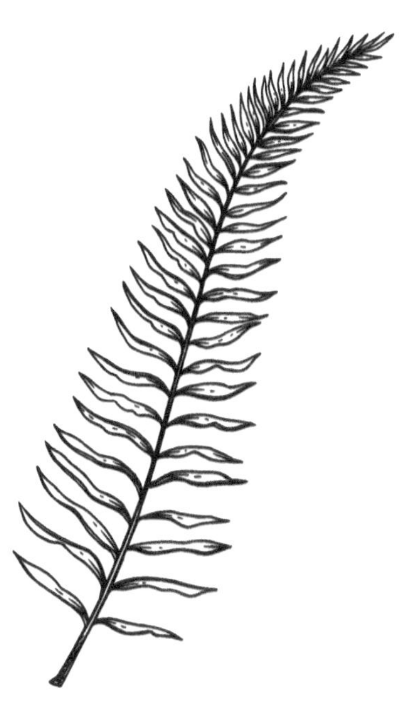

Oak and Lotus

Celtic Christian Spirituality
in the Light of Eastern Wisdom

"Imagine the Celtic saint Brigid and the great bodhisattva Guanyin sitting down together for a cup of tea. I certainly would want to listen in to their conversation! *Oak and Lotus* takes us to a similar place. It's a beautiful, expansive book about the joyful integration of Eastern and Western wisdom, a resource I expect to return to again and again."

> — Carl McColman, author of *The New Big Book of Christian Mysticism* and *Eternal Heart*

"*Oak and Lotus* is a joy to read. Bringing Celtic Christianity into conversation with three major Eastern faith traditions—Hinduism, Buddhism, and Taoism—this book delights the heart again and again with parallels both uncanny and enlightening. Reader-friendly, it draws you in and won't let you go."

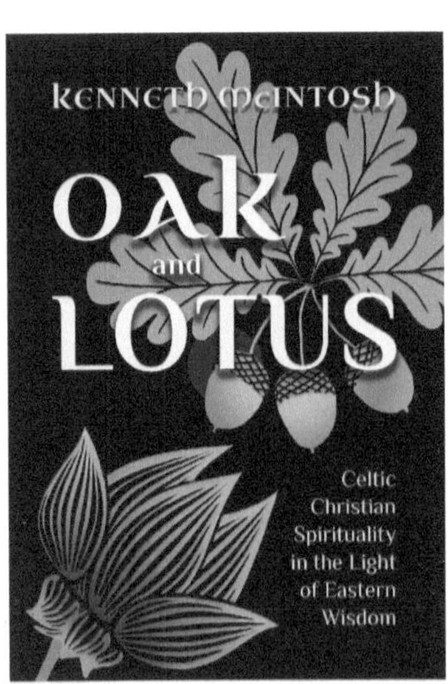

> — Rev. John R. Mabry, PhD, author of *God as Nature Sees God: A Christian Reading of the Tao Te Ching* and *A Christian Walks in the Footsteps of the Buddha*

Forest Church

A Field Guide to a Spiritual Connection with Nature

Brimming with insights and packed with information, this book draws you out, quite literally, into nature to experience a new, well-thought-through pattern of spiritual practice. Bruce Stanley gives you all the resources you'll need, both practical and theoretical, to get going with a group or on your own. Many people can describe transcendent moments in nature where they feel deeply connected to something bigger than themselves, and Forest Church is a way to explore that connection within community, a fresh expression of church drawing on much older traditions when sacred places and practices were outside—but it also draws on contemporary research that highlights the benefits of spending time with nature in wild places. Throughout the ages people have walked this path within the Christ tradition and have found a meaningful expression of their spirituality, finding inspiration and structure through the rhythms

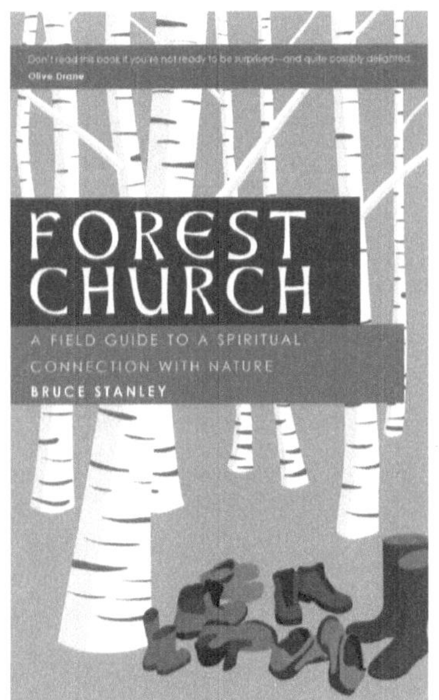

of the seasons, the characteristics of plants and animals, and the sacredness of place—along with the wisdom of the scriptures and the pattern of prayers.

This book will be a resource to anyone facilitating Forest Church, whether as a self-contained group, a retreat, a group holiday, or as an occasional event attached to an existing church. It will also inspire individuals wanting to explore their own sacred nature connections.

Water from an Ancient Well

Celtic Spirituality for Modern Life

Pilgrimage Study Edition

A Fresh Look at Celtic Spirituality

This new version has more than 150 pages of previously unpublished material, including illustrated guides to Celtic pilgrimage sites, study questions, and updated research.

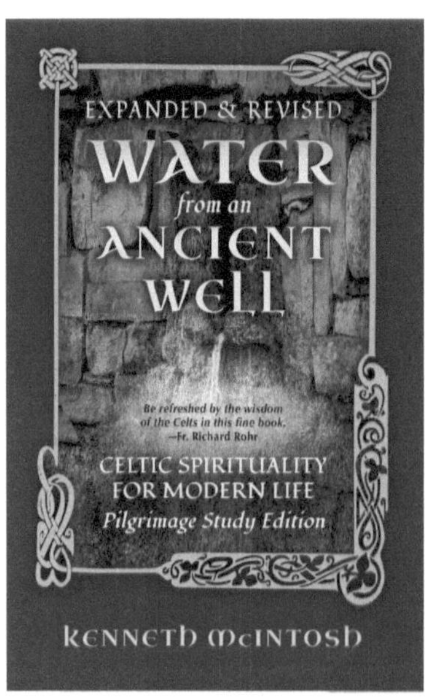

Using story, scripture, reflection, and prayer, Kenneth McIntosh offers us a taste of the living water that refreshed the ancient Celts, allowing them to perceive God as a living Presence in everybody and everything. This Earth-based and inclusive perspective suggests life-giving alternatives to modern faith practices, opening the door to a Christianity big enough to embrace the entire world.

Celtic Nature Prayers
Prayers from an Ancient Well

Find God in Nature Pray for Our Endangered Planet

Long before they had heard about Christianity, the Celts knew that Nature was their portal to a great spiritual reality. Wells, mountain crags, caves, and lochs were "thin places" that allowed access to the realm of spirits. In these temples of Nature, the Celts sought physical and spiritual healing, as well as revelation. The salmon, the eagle, and even the tiny hazelnut, all were allies in helping humanity access the mysterious magic that underlay physical matter.

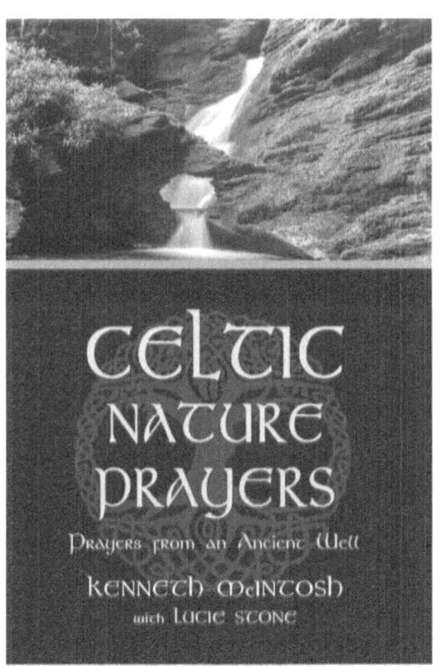

I arise today
Through the strength of heaven:
Light of sun, radiance of moon,
Splendor of fire, . . .
Swiftness of wind,
Depth of sea,
Stability of earth,
Firmness of rock.

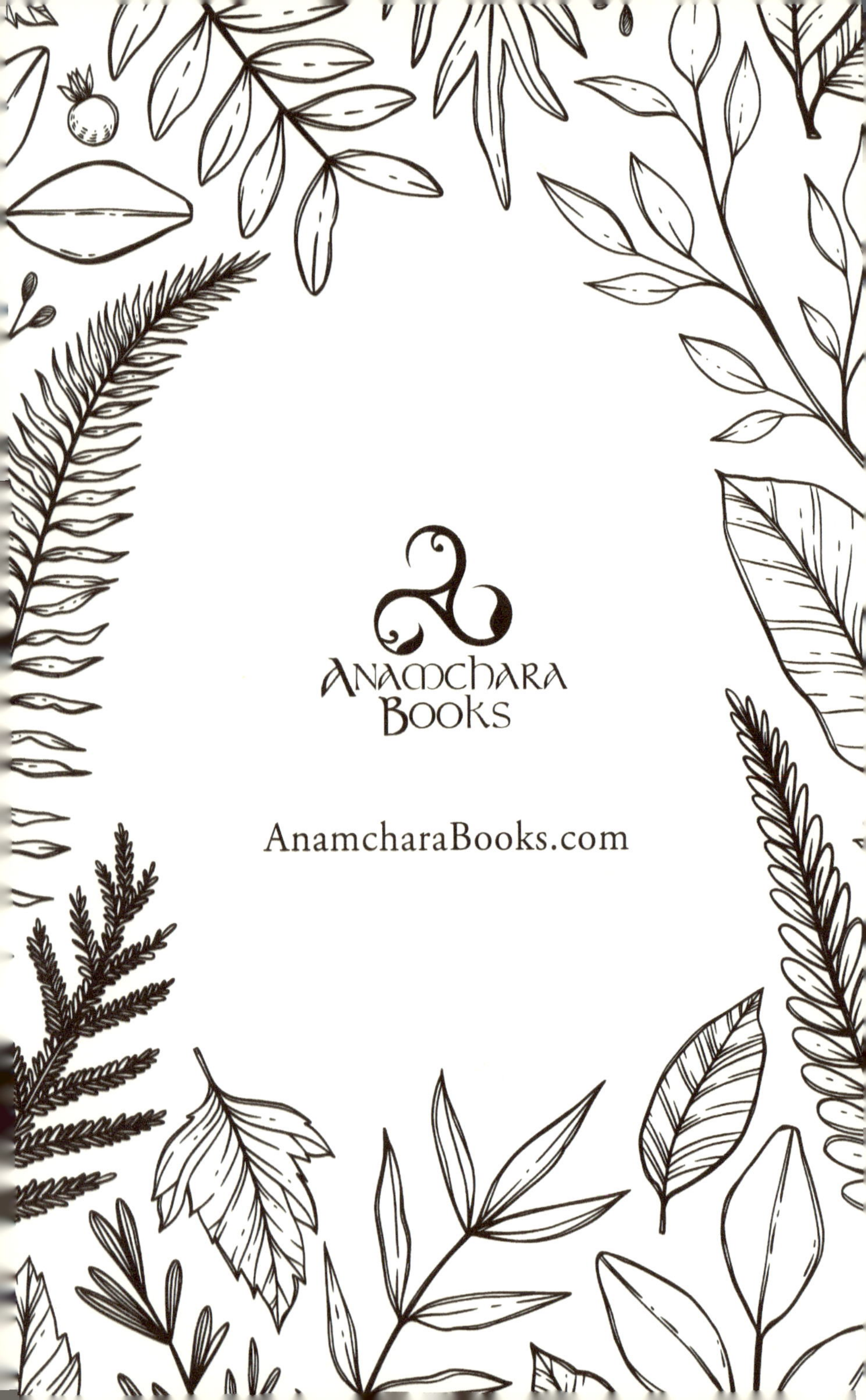

Anamchara
Books
AnamcharaBooks.com